HISTORY
OF MUSIC

About the Author

Hugh M. Miller received his B.A. from the University of Oregon and his M.A. and Ph.D. from Harvard University. Since 1947, he has been Professor of Music at the University of New Mexico, and from 1947 to 1957, Chairman of the Department of Music. During 1957–58, he was Fulbright lecturer at Auckland University, New Zealand, and during the academic year 1965–66 he was exchange professor of music at the University of Hawaii. In addition to having many articles published and belonging to a number of professional organizations, Dr. Miller is a popular lecturer on Music. He is the author also of *Introduction to Music,* a companion College Outline.

College Outline Series

HISTORY
OF MUSIC

THIRD EDITION

Revised and Enlarged

by Hugh Milton Miller, Ph.D.

BARNES & NOBLE, INC., N.Y.

Publishers · Booksellers · Since 1873

Preface

THE acquisition of historical information about music is of little value unless that information is applied directly to the literature of music. In any study of the history of music there is, inevitably, a considerable quantity of factual material that is of purely historical interest. However, in the present outline, nonessentials, such as biographical detail, have been minimized or else eliminated altogether. The present emphasis is upon the organization and presentation of essential historical information that has a direct bearing upon the actual music of any given period, or else upon the development of musical trends. The outline deals primarily with the characteristics of form and style as they apply to music of broad and specific periods, to nationalities or schools, and to the most important composers. This outline, then, is intended to be a substantial guide to the intelligent study of music by the amateur as well as by the advanced student of music. It can be applied equally well to the occupation of listening to records and to detailed analysis of musical scores.

Furthermore, the present work is more than a mere review outline. It is a functional work which can be used as the basic textbook in a college course in the history of music. This does not preclude collateral reading in the many excellent textbooks in general music history which are indeed valuable. But the present outline should be the core of the study.

At the end of each chapter through baroque music, record lists have been provided. These are selected from available recordings including long playing releases, the *Anthologie Sonore,* and 2000 *Years of Music.* As more and more representative works are issued, especially recordings of music prior to 1600, the lists should be supplemented.

Score lists, also, have been provided for representative music up to 1750, music for later periods being much more easily accessible. These lists are primarily based upon three musical anthologies: *Historical Anthology of Music,* 2 volumes, Apel and Davison, 1947, 1949, Harvard University Press; *Geschichte der Musik in Beispielen* ("History of Music in Examples"), Arnold Schering, 1931, Breitkopf & Härtel (reprinted by Broude Bros., 1950); and *Masterpieces of Music before 1750,* Parrish and Ohl, 1951, Norton.

The author here wishes to express his deep gratitude to Dr. Lloyd Hibberd, North Texas State College, Denton, Texas, for reading of the entire manuscript and for numerous invaluable suggestions and criticisms and to Mr. Walter Robert for reading proof.

HUGH M. MILLER

CONTENTS

ILLUSTRATIONS AND CHARTS

TABULATED BIBLIOGRAPHY
OF STANDARD TEXTBOOKS

This *College Outline* is keyed to standard textbooks in two ways.

1. If you are studying one of the following textbooks, consult the cross references here listed to find which pages of the *Outline* summarize the appropriate chapter of your text. (Roman numerals refer to the textbook chapters, Arabic figures to the corresponding *Outline* pages.)

2. If you are using the *Outline* as your basis for study and need a fuller treatment of a topic, consult the pages of any of the standard textbooks as indicated in the Quick Reference Table.

Ferguson, D., *A History of Musical Thought,* 1959, Appleton-Century-Crofts.

II (3–7); III (6, 8–10); IV (8–9); V (21–23); VI (10–17, 24–26); VII (27–29); VIII (60–63); IX (30–35); X (36–47); XI (50–52); XII (52–58); XIII (67–73); XIV (71–72, 74–76); XV (76–79); XVI (89–101); XVII (80–88); XVIII (104–109); XIX (126–128); XX (118–122); XXI (122–125); XXII (138–140); XXIII (151–153); XXIV (152, 155, 159, 163–165); XXIX (136, 147, 153, 161f, 166); XXX (166); XXXI (160f, 172f, 184, 192f); XXXII (173–210); XXXIII (204–208, 223–237).

Ferguson, D., *A Short History of Music,* 1947, Appleton-Century-Crofts.

I (3–6); II (7–19); III (21–26); IV (21); V (27–30); VI (60–63); VII (30–35); VIII (140–153); IX (50–59); X (71–73); XI (74–80); XII (89–103); XIII (80–85); XIV (104–111); XV (127–128); XVI (118–120); XVII (124); XVIII (138–140); XIX (151–153); XX (150–152, 155–156); XXI (156, 159–160); XXII (141–144); XXIII (144–147); XXIV (149–152, 165); XXV (135–136); XXVII (171–178); XXVIII (179–217).

Finney, T., *A History of Music,* 1947, Harcourt, Brace.

I (3f); II (4–7); III (7); IV (8–10, 60); V (21–23); VI (22); VII (10–16); VIII (24–26); IX (27–29); X (30–34); XI (38); XII (38f, 43); XIII (38–42); XIV (50–52); XV (52–58); XVI (67–73); XVII (75); XVIII (74–76); XIX, (76–79, 87f); XX (89–101); XXI (76, 87, 93, 96, 98, 101); XXII (77, 80, 87, 93, 96, 99, 101); XXIII (104–109); XXV (113–121f, 127f); XXVI (116, 122, 124, 128, 131); XXVII (138–140); XXVIII

(141–147) ; XXIX (151f) ; XXX (152, 155, 159, 164) ; XXXI (156, 159f, 165) ; XXXII (145–147) ; XXXIII (149, 152, 156, 160, 163, 165) ; XXXIV (141–144, 147) ; XXXVIII, XXXIX, XL (171–203) ; XLI (167) ; XLII, XLIII (167) ; XLIV (203–217).

Grout, D., *A History of Western Music*, 1960, Norton.
I (3–7) ; II (8–17) ; III (21–26) ; IV (27–29) ; V (30–31) ; VI (31–35) ; VII (43–47, 50–58) ; VIII (38–42, 50–58) ; IX (67–70, 74–76, 80–82, 86–101) ; X (74–83) ; XI (89–101) ; XII (101, 105–108) ; XIII (113–117) ; XIV (118–131) ; XV (138–140) ; XVI (135–137, 148–153) ; XVII (154–163) ; XVIII (141–147) ; XIX (164–167) ; XX (171–237).

Lang, P., *Music in Western Civilization*, 1941, Norton.
I (4–7) ; III (7) ; IV, V (8–10) ; VI (10–16) ; VII (21–26) ; VIII (27–29) ; IX (30–63) ; X, XI (67–109) ; XII, XIII, XIV (113–131) ; XV (138–140) ; XVI (135–137, 141–147) ; XVII, XVIII, XIX (148–167) ; XX (171–183).

Leichtentritt, H., *Music, History, and Ideas*, 1938, Harvard.
I (4–7) ; II (8–10) ; III (21–29) ; IV (30–40, 43–47) ; V (40–42) ; VI (67–101) ; VII (104–109) ; VIII (113–131) ; IX (138–140) ; X (135–137) ; XI (141–167) ; XII (171–183).

McKinney, H. D., and Anderson, W. R., *Music in History,* 3rd ed., 1966, American Book.
II (3–4) ; III (4) ; IV (4–7) ; V (7) ; VI–VII (8–17) ; VIII (10–35) ; IX (36–49) ; X–XII (67–103) ; XIII (104–109) ; XIV (113–141) ; XV (135–140) ; XVI (151–167) ; XVII (141–147) ; XVIII (151–167) ; XIX (135–147, 157–167, 184–217) ; XX–XXI (171–237).

Moore, D., *From Madrigal to Modern Music,* 1942, Norton.
II (30–58) ; III (67–109) ; IV (113–131) ; V (135–167) ; VI (171–237).

Sachs, C., *Our Musical Heritage,* 1955, Prentice-Hall.
I (3–7) ; II (3–7) ; III (3–7) ; IV (8–17) ; V (8–17) ; VI (8–23) ; VII (27–30) ; VIII (30–35) ; IX (30–35) ; X (36–59) ; XI (36–64) ; XII (36–64) ; XIII (71–104) ; XIV (71–104) ; XV (71–104) ; XVI (71–109, 154–156) ; XVII (118–133) ; XVIII (118–133) ; XIX (141–150) ; XX (141–147, 151–153, 157–163) ; XXI (171–183) ; XXII (184–237).

Ulrich, H., and Pisk, P. A., *A History of Music and Musical Style,* 1963, Harcourt, Brace & World, Inc.
I (3–4) ; II (4–7) ; III (8–10, 60–61) ; IV (10–16) ; V (24–26) ; VI (27–29) ; VII (30–31) ; VIII (31–35) ; IX (36–40) ; X (40–42) ; XI (43–47, 50–59) ; XII (67–73) ; XIII (74–80) ; XIV (80–88) ; XV (89–109) ; XVI (113–117) ; XVII (126–129) ; XVIII (130–131) ; XIX (118–125) ; XX (138–140) ; XXI (135–137, 151–153) ; XXII (141–147) ; XXIII (152, 154–156, 159–162) ; XXIV (157–162) ; XXV (161–162) ; XXVI (142, 143–144, 145–147) ; XXVII (160–161, 152, 197) ; XXVIII (173–174, 193, 194, 204–208, 216, 219, 220) ; XXIX (173, 186, 199–201, 208–209, 202–203, 197–198) ; XXX (180–181, 142, 193, 198, 200, 202, 203) ; XXXI (223–237).

QUICK REFERENCE TABLE TO STANDARD TEXTBOOKS

Roman type indicates pages.

Italic type indicates chapters.

CHAPTER	TOPIC	FERGUSON (Musical Thought)	FERGUSON (Short History)	FINNEY	GROUT	LANG	LEICHTEN-TRITT	McKINNEY & ANDERSON	MOORE	SACHS	ULRICH & PISK
I	Antiquity to about 200 A.D.	*2, 3*	1–24	*1, 2, 3*	*1*	*1, 2, 3*	*1*	2–5	—	*1, 2, 3*	*2*
II	The Christian Era	*3, 4*	25–40	*4* 84–86	*2*	*4, 5, 6*	*2*	74–111 140–156	—	*4, 5*	*3, 4*
III	Early Stages of Polyphony	*5*	41–50	*5, 6*	68–80	*7*	*3*	118–124	—	*4, 6*	*5*
IV	The Ars Antiqua	*6*	—	*8*	80–100	*7*	*3*	124–139	—	*6*	*5*
V	The Ars Nova	*7*	65–84	*9*	106–127	*8*	*3*	157–170	—	*7*	*6*
VI	The Netherlands Schools	*9*	102–124	*10, 11*	*5, 6*	*9*	*4*	170–176	—	*8, 9*	*7, 8*
VII	The Sixteenth Century	*10*	125–139	*12, 13*	185–197 206–250	*9*	*4, 5*	189–268	2	*10–12*	*9, 10, 11*
VIII	Instrumental Music to 1600	*11, 12*	140–153	89–92 *14–15*	197–205 250–264	*9*	—	139–140 181–188	33–36	*10–12*	195–205
IX	Musical Notation to 1600	*8*	85–101	43–52 114 120, 163	39 100–103 127–128	—	—	95–98 134–135	—	*9–12*	32–39, 63–64, 75–77, 82–86, 97–100
X	THE BAROQUE PERIOD	*13*	—	219–221 *24*	266–275	*10, 11*	*6*	269–276	37–45	—	*12*
XI	Nuove Musiche	*14*	154–169	*16*	275–297	—	*6*	277–287	—	207–208 *13–16*	*12*
XII	Dramatic Music	*14, 15*	170–182	*16–19, 22* 310–319 341–346	275–297 309–340	—	*6*	288–290 301–349	78–96	*13–16*	*17, 18*
XIII	Church Music	*17*	—	239–261 293 346–348	327–340	—	—	306–307 340–342	—	*13–16*	253–264
XIV	Instrumental Music	*16*	183–204	20, 236 310–328	297–308 *11*	—	*6*	291–300 313–314 346–349	45–78	*13–16*	*15*
XV	Bach and Handel	*18*	215–229	*23*	382–410	—	*7*	350–385	—	*16*	301–311

See pages x–xi for complete list of titles.

Abbreviations

ARC   Archive Production Recordings

EA   Expériences Anonymes (records)

HAM   *Historical Anthology of Music* (scores)

HMS   *History of Music in Sound* (records; Roman numerals refer to volume; Arabic numerals to sides)

MM   *Masterpieces of Music Before 1750* (scores and records)

SB   Schering, *Geschichte der Musik in Beispielen* (scores)

TEM   *A Treasury of Early Music* (scores and records)

WM   Wolf, *Music of Earlier Times* (scores; the American edition of *Sing- und Spielmusik aus älterer Zeit*)

2000YM   *2000 Years of Music* (records)

PART ONE

Monophonic Music to about 1300

CHAPTER I

Antiquity to about 200 A.D.

THE history of music until about 200 A.D. is shrouded in darkness. The limitations of the study are attributable to the fact that there is virtually no extant music because of the absence or inadequacies of early notation systems. Furthermore, except in the rather extensive Greek literature, little about music was written by ancient contemporaries.

Limited Knowledge of Ancient Music

Methods of Studying Musical Antiquity. Some knowledge of antiquity has been gained, however, through certain methods applied by modern scholars. (1) The study of musical systems of old civilizations of today (India, China, etc.) affords some insight into early practices. (2) The study of primitive tribes of today likewise provides some information about music's past. (3) Reconstruction of ancient systems from pictures, drawings, a few actual specimens of instruments, and a few fragments of old musical notation have provided some enlightenment.

Theories about Origins of Music. From the above methods, certain theories about the origin of music have been evolved. (1) Music may have developed from primitive communications: tribal drums, calls, etc. (2) It may have been associated with work rhythms at a very early time. (3) It seems to have been associated almost instinctively with emotional expression.

Ancient Uses of Music. Music probably did not exist as a separate art until the Middle Ages or later. Before then it was undoubtedly used in connection with various functions. Probably the most important of these were religious rituals, mystic ceremonies, festivals, etc.

3

It was probably used with war dances and other ceremonial dances. Work songs were very likely employed.

The Music of Ancient Civilizations

Despite our limitations of knowledge concerning musical antiquity, a few general facts are known about the music. It was not developed as a separate art, and it always existed in primitive simplicity.

Chinese Music. Chinese music made considerable use of a five-tone scale (*pentatonic*). Music was an important part of Oriental mysticism.

Egyptian Music. Egyptian music was very likely quite extensive. It had considerable influence upon later Greek music and musical theory of the 7th century B.C. The Egyptians were largely responsible for the development of the harp and lyre family of instruments.

Early Hebrew Music. Among the Hebrews music was important, judging from numerous Biblical references. It was probably of a ritual nature. The Hebrews employed unison singing, chanting, and considerable melodic embellishment. They also employed *antiphonal singing* (one choir or group of singers answered by another). The historical significance of early Hebrew music lies in the great influence it had upon Christian music, particularly upon plainsong.

Greek Music. The music of the Greeks is the most important in all antiquity for several reasons. (1) Greek theory had a marked influence upon theory in the Middle Ages. Such terms as *perfect consonance* (fourths, fifths, octaves) and *imperfect consonance* (thirds and sixths) come from Greek theory and are still used today. (2) Throughout history there have been recurrences of Greek ideals in music as, for example, the revival of Greek tragedy in the late 16th century which gave rise to opera. (3) The doctrine of *ethos* (see page 6) has been manifest in various ways.

GREEK CULTS. There were two cults that dominated musical concepts in general: (1) The Apollonian cult made use of the *cithara* (a plucked stringed instrument), and was characterized by clarity of form, purity, and objectivity of expression. (2) The Dionysian cult, on the other hand, used the *aulos* (a double-reed wind instru-

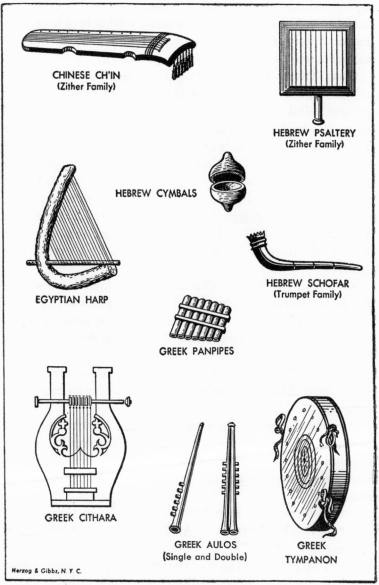

CHINESE CH'IN
(Zither Family)

HEBREW PSALTERY
(Zither Family)

HEBREW CYMBALS

EGYPTIAN HARP

HEBREW SCHOFAR
(Trumpet Family)

GREEK PANPIPES

GREEK CITHARA

GREEK AULOS
(Single and Double)

GREEK
TYMPANON

Herzog & Gibbs, N.Y.C.

SOME INSTRUMENTS OF ANTIQUITY

ment) and was characterized by ecstasy, passion, sensuality, and subjectivity. These two concepts have had varying roles in the subsequent history of Occidental music, the former embodied in classical trends, the latter in romantic trends.

GREEK THEORY. Greek theory was based largely upon the acoustical mathematics of Pythagorean ratios. Various complicated scale patterns, called *modes,* were employed. They, in turn, were based upon *tetrachords* (groups of four adjacent tones) arranged in *conjunct order* (the lowest note of one tetrachord being the same as the top note of the tetrachord immediately below) or *disjunct order* (the lowest note of one tetrachord being adjacent to the top note of the tetrachord immediately below). There were three genera of tetrachords: (1) the *diatonic* (e.g., the tones B C D E), (2) *chromatic* (e.g., the tones B C C♯ E), and (3) *enharmonic* (e.g., the tones B B♯ C E, where B, B♯, and C are theoretically a quarter tone apart).

NOTATION. The ancient Greeks had two kinds of notation: (1) an instrumental notation, the symbols for which were perhaps derived from Phoenician letters, and (2) a vocal notation, where the symbols (Ionic alphabet) were placed above the words of the text.

RHYTHMIC MODES. An important part of Greek theory was the employment of rhythmic modes directly associated with poetry (see page 12).

DOCTRINE OF ETHOS. The doctrine of *ethos* involved the belief that music has a direct effect upon the soul. The doctrine was established by the Peripatetics and Stoics. The determining factors in musical ethos were rhythm, tonality (or mode), and the instrument employed.

EXTANT MUSIC. The most important examples of Greek music are: two Delphic "Hymns to Apollo" (c. 130 B.C.), two short "Hymns to the Muse," a "Hymn to Nemesis," and a quaint little "Epitaph of Seikilos." The few remnants of actual Greek music constitute a wholly inadequate basis upon which to judge Greek music.

WRITERS. Although most of the Greek philosophers dealt in some measure with the subject of music, Aristoxenos is considered the most important Greek writer and theorist.

In general it should be kept in mind that music to the Greeks was not an individual art but was inseparably bound up with poetry and drama.

Roman Music. Very little is known about Roman music. In general, the Romans were imitators of Greek culture. Music did not develop extensively in their hands. It is likely that they were responsible for separation of music and poetry. They developed brass instruments largely for military purposes. Music was also used for enhancing sensual pleasure.

RECORDS
Skolion of Seikilos. HMS I 15b; 2000YM 1.
First Delphic Hymn. HMS I 15a.
Jewish music. HMS I 14; 2000YM 2.

SCORES
Skolion of Seikilos. HAM 7c; SB 1.
First Delphic Hymn. HAM 7a.
Hymn to the Sun. HAM 7b.
Jewish music. HAM 6.

CHAPTER II

The Christian Era

THE Christian Era in music encompasses the development of monophonic music from about 200 A.D. to about 1300. Sacred and secular melody continued to develop long after the advent of polyphony (c. 800 A.D.).

Sacred Melody: Plainsong

Religious melody is referred to variously as *plainsong*, *plain chant*, *Gregorian chant*, and *cantus planus*. These terms may all be used synonymously; Gregorian chant usually implies a special branch of plainsong (see page 10). Catholic plainsong constitutes the greatest body of pure melody known to man, even greater in extent and beauty than folk song of the same period.

General Characteristics of Plainsong. Plainsong (1) is monophonic, (2) is *modal* (i.e., it is based upon the eight church modes), (3) is unaccompanied, (4) is nonmetric, (5) uses a free prose rhythm, following that of the text, (6) has a limited range, (7) uses a Latin text, and (8) makes use of a special neumatic notation (see page 60).

The Eight Church Modes. The church modes are divided into two classes: (1) *authentic modes* which have an approximate melodic range (called *ambitus*) of an octave above the *final* (the plainsong tonic, i.e., the tone on which the melody ends), and which have Greek names, and (2) *plagal* modes which have an approximate melodic range of a fifth above and a fourth below the final, and which use the prefix *hypo-* with the Greek name. The eight church modes are: (1) Dorian, range D to D (scale as on the white keys of a piano), final D; (2) Hypodorian, range A to A, final D; (3) Phrygian, range E to E, final E; (4) Hypophrygian, range B

8

to B, final E; (5) Lydian, range F to F, final F; (6) Hypolydian, range C to C, final F; (7) Mixolydian, range G to G, final G; (8) Hypomixolydian, range D to D, final G. Four additional modes are infrequently used in Catholic church music: the Aeolian and Hypoaeolian modes on A (the same as the natural minor scale), and the Ionian and Hypoionian modes on C (the same as the major scale).

Styles of Text Setting. There are four styles of text setting of plainsong: (1) *syllabic,* where one note of the melody is set to one syllable of the text; typical of hymns and tropes (see page 10), (2) *neumatic,* a few notes to one syllable, the most common style, (3) *psalmodic,* numerous syllables to one note or pitch; used in *reciting tone* psalms and gospel readings, and (4) *melismatic,* numerous notes to one syllable; used in settings of the Alleluia.

Early Chant Cultures. Sacred melody of the pre-Christian eras had an important influence upon later Christian chant. There are four principal pre-Christian chant cultures. (1) Syria, a part of the Roman Empire near the Holy Land, was the scene of much religious activity. The Syrians employed *antiphonal* chant (one choir answered by another) and *responsorial* chant (a solo voice answered by a choir). (2) Byzantine culture contributed hymn writing. It influenced Greek Orthodox Church chant. (3) Armenian chant was developed in connection with an alphabetic notation and later with a system of neumatic notation (see page 60). Armenian chant was in the style of hymns. (4) Hebrew chant was perhaps the most important early chant culture because much early Christian plainsong was taken directly from Hebrew chants.

Branches of Christian Chant. There are five branches of Christian chant: (1) Russian chant is derived from Byzantine chant and is used in the Greek Orthodox Church. (2) Ambrosian chant, named for Ambrose, Bishop of Milan in the 4th century A.D., is characterized by development of hymnody and antiphonal singing. (3) Gallican chant flourished in France until Charlemagne ordered substitution of Roman rites around 800 A.D. A few of these Gallican tunes were carried over into Roman service. (4) Mozarabic chant stems from the Moorish invasion of the Spanish peninsula where Christianity was allowed to continue. The earliest Mozarabic chant manuscripts date from the end of the 9th century. (5) Gregorian chant is the most important branch of plainsong. It begins with the liturgical organization effected by Pope Gregory the Great in the 6th century A.D. He collected and organized liturgical chant.

Catholic Liturgy. Plainsong is used in the Catholic Mass and in all of the smaller services known as Canonical Hours. The Mass includes two types of liturgy: (1) the *Ordinary of the Mass,* including the Kyrie, Gloria, Credo, Sanctus, and Agnus Dei, the texts of which do not vary, and (2) the *Proper of the Mass,* including the Introitus, Graduale, Alleluia, Offertorium, and Communio, the texts of which vary from day to day according to the season or the saint. The Ordinary of the Mass is a later development than the plain-songs of the Proper, which gradually became standardized from about the 7th century.

Tropes and Sequences. From the 9th to the 12th centuries a new development in plainsong took place. This originated with the practice of interpolating plainsong melody and text phrases (syllabic style) between the words of an already existing plainsong, or between the verses of a hymn. These additions were called *tropes.* A special kind of trope, called *sequela* or *sequence,* originated with the practice of adding prose texts syllabically to the *jubilus* (long melismatic passages occurring at the end of the Alleluia). Sequences became detached from the original plainsong. Tuotilo (10th century) is considered the father of the trope. Notker Balbulus (9th century) and Adam of St. Victor (12th century) are important writers of sequences.

Secular Melody

Lacking the organization and systematic dissemination that plainsong received in the hands of the Church, secular music, though doubtless extensive, was not preserved. Little secular music has been recorded earlier than the 10th century. The "Song of the Sibyl" is one of the earliest known secular songs.

General Characteristics of Secular Melody. Secular melody differs from plainsong in various respects: (1) It usually has a metrical basis and is more strongly rhythmic than is plainsong. (2) It often has a wider range. (3) The phrases of secular melody are usually more regular. (4) Secular melody is not strictly modal. (5) It is usually nationalistic in character as opposed to the more universal nature of plainsong. (6) It is now more often harmonized and sung to accompaniment. (7) Secular texts are usually in the vernacular language.

Latin Songs. An exception to characteristic (7) above is a body of songs with Latin texts. From the late 10th to the early 13th centuries vagrant students and men in minor ecclesiastic orders, known as *goliards,* roamed over Europe composing and singing Latin songs on various subjects—love songs, drinking songs, spring songs, ribald songs, and humorous paraphrases of plainsong. *Conductus* is a term loosely applied to all sorts of Latin songs from the 11th to the 13th centuries. These were normally based upon metrical texts and the music was original. However, conductus probably originated as a trope sung during processions in the liturgy.

Jongleurs and Gaukler. In the Middle Ages there was an important class of minstrel entertainers called *jongleurs* in France and *Gaukler* in Germany. They were performers and entertainers rather than poets or composers. They were musically important in that they kept alive a large body of secular melody.

Troubadours and Trouvères. The most important body of secular melody comes from two minstrel groups in France: the *troubadours* and the *trouvères.* Unlike the jongleurs they were persons of rank. The troubadours flourished in Provence in southern France from the end of the 11th century to the end of the 13th. Of this group some 264 melodies are preserved and about 2600 poems. The most important names of this group are Marcabru of Gascony, Bernart de Ventadorn, Guiraut de Bornelh, Guiraut de Riquier, and Bertran de Born. The trouvères, located in northern France, reached a peak of development slightly later than did the troubadours. There are about 1400 extant melodies and roughly 4000 poems of the trouvères. The most important trouvères are Quesnes de Béthune, Blondel de Nesle, Thibaut IV (King of Navarre), and Adam de la Halle, the latter famous for a medieval play with music, *Robin et Marion.*

Characteristics of Style. Troubadour and trouvère songs have virtually the same characteristics. The melodic range is usually within an octave. There is some use of the church modes, but the tendency is toward major and minor. The songs are based upon *rhythmic modes* employing Greek names, and are usually thought to be in some form of triple meter. The basic modes are:

trochaeus ♩♪   dactylus ♩.♪♪   spondeus ♩.♩.

iambus ♪♩   anapaest ♪♪♩.   tribrachys ♪♪♪

Another characteristic of troubadour and trouvère music is the great variety of forms employed. Apparently it was common practice among the minstrels to improvise accompaniments to their songs with the vielle (the most important string instrument of the Middle Ages; four strings, one drone string, bowed) or some form of lyre.

Poetic Types. The main poetic types, according to subject, used by the medieval minstrels were: (1) *canso,* a love song, (2) *sirventes,* a satirical poem sung to a known melody, (3) *planh,* a lament on the death of a great personage, (4) *pastourell,* where a knight woos a shepherdess, (5) *chanson de toile,* a spinning song, (6) *enueg,* a satire, (7) *aube,* the song of a friend watching over lovers until dawn, (8) *tenso* or *jeu-parti,* dialogue between two or three people, and (9) *chanson de geste,* an epic chronicle of the deeds of a hero.

Song Forms. A great wealth of diversified musical forms was employed by the troubadours and trouvères. These forms may be divided into four main classes: those derived from (1) *litany,* (2) *rondel,* (3) *sequence,* and (4) *hymn.*

LITANY TYPES. Musical forms derived from the litany are the *chanson de geste,* the *rotrouenge,* the *strophic laisse,* and the *chanson with refrains.*

a. *Chanson de Geste.* The chanson de geste consists of numerous unequal paragraph-like sections called *laisses,* each of which consists of two short melodic patterns repeated over and over until the end of a thought is reached, at which point a cadential formula is sung or played. The plan of the laisse, then, is: *ab ab ab ab . . . c.*

b. *Rotrouenge.* The rotrouenge form makes use of a refrain, apparently intended for participation by an audience. It consists of a

SATAN PLAYING A VIELLE
(13th Century)

ANGEL PLAYING A REBEC
(13th Century)

JONGLEUR PLAYING
A VIELLE
(15th Century)

A PLAYER ON THE
TROMBA MARINA

Adapted from A History of Music by Emil Naumann   Herzog & Gibbs, N. Y. C.

SOME INSTRUMENTS OF THE MIDDLE AGES

strophe and a closing formula presented by a soloist, and a refrain which is the same melodic pattern as the close of the strophe. It may be represented by the formula: *a a a . . . b B.* (Lower-case letters stand for soloist performance, capitals for chorus refrain.)

c. *Strophic Laisse.* A shorter lyric form growing out of the chanson de geste is the strophic laisse in which a single laisse pattern is used over and over again with each stanza.

d. *Chanson with Refrains.* A fourth litany type is the chanson with refrains. This includes several different refrains borrowed from well-known songs, each being chosen for its appropriateness to the foregoing strophe.

RONDEL TYPES. The rondel types include the *rondeau, virelai,* and *ballade.* These were often dance songs for leader and chorus.

a. *Rondeau.* The rondeau has the musical form: *a A ab AB.* If the text has eight or more lines the complete refrain (*AB*) appears at the beginning as well as at the end. The rondeau continued to be a popular form for several centuries.

b. *Virelai.* When a two-part refrain (*AB*) is used at the beginning and at the end, but different material is used by the soloist, the form is called a virelai and is represented by the formula: *AB cc ab AB.*

c. *Ballade.* Three principal ballade forms are represented by the following formulas: (1) *AB cd cd ef AB,* (2) *AB cd cd e ab AB.* and (3) *ab ab cd E* (which drops the introductory refrain).

SEQUENCE TYPES. The various forms derived from the plainsong sequence are various forms of the *lai* and the *estampie.* They are characterized by melodic phrases immediately repeated to new words.

a. *Lai.* The lai may be represented in general by the formula: *aa bb cc dd ee,* etc., or by *aa₁ bb₁ cc₁ dd₁,* etc., in which the repetition is a slight variation of the preceding phrase.

b. *Reinforced Lai.* A group of phrase pairs repeated together is called reinforced lai. For example it might be represented by the formula: *aa bb   cc dd ee ff   cc dd ee ff   gg hh.*

c. *Strophic Lai.* A shortened version of the lai plan includes fewer phrase units (single phrases or phrase pairs), and it may be represented by the typical pattern: *a bb cc d.* The pattern might be further reduced to the formula: *aa b a,* which is the familiar plan of later song form and the da capo aria. Other shortened versions of the lai form are called *lai segments.*

d. *Estampie.* A dance form, known as the estampie (see page 52), employs the general sequence construction, but is characterized by grouping of the pairs (called *puncta*) as follows: ab_1 ab_2 cb_1 cb_2 db_1 db_2 eb_1 eb_2. (This would be an estampie with four puncta.)

HYMN TYPES. Forms derived from plainsong hymns are the *vers, chanson* (without refrain), and *rounded chanson.*

a. *Vers.* Each strophe or stanza of the vers, as with the plainsong hymn, consists of different musical phrases (*a b c d e f g*).

b. *Chanson.* The chanson without refrain is represented by a repeated section and an unrepeated one: *ab ab cd,* in which the unrepeated section (*cd*) is longer than the repeated section.

c. *Rounded Chanson.* The rounded chanson resembles the chanson but with the addition of the second phrase of the opening section heard again at the end: *ab ab cdb.*

Minnesingers. The *Minnesingers* (singers of chivalrous love) flourished in Germany in the 12th and 13th centuries, largely as an outgrowth of the troubadour movement in France. Their songs closely resemble the style of the troubadour and trouvère music. They used duple as well as triple meter and employed the Ionian (major) mode as well as the older church modes.

NAMES. The most important names of this class are Walther von der Vogelweide, Neithart von Reuenthal, Heinrich von Meissen (called "Frauenlob"), and Heinrich von Müglin (14th century).

FORMS. The principal types employed by the Minnesingers are: the *Lied,* the *Tagelied* (similar to the French aube), the *Leich* (similar to the French lai), and the *Spruch,* a proverb.

Meistersingers. The *Meistersingers* of the 14th to 16th centuries, unlike the aristocratic Minnesingers of an earlier period, were of the burgher class, and were resident members of the typical guild organizations of the Renaissance. Characteristic of the Meistersinger music are the numerous pedantic rules governing musical creation, the recurrent use of standard melodies, and a certain amount of crudity and lack of inspiration. The principal Meistersingers were Conrad

Nachtigall, Sebastian Wilde, Adam Puschmann, and Hans Sachs (immortalized, along with the whole Meistersinger movement, in Richard Wagner's *Die Meistersinger von Nürnberg*).

English Secular Melody. The extant music of the British Isles prior to the 15th century is not extensive, but it indicates a high degree of artistic development. In the Anglo-Saxon period two classes of minstrels existed: *scops,* who were resident minstrels, and *gleemen,* traveling minstrels. Both classes seem to have practiced the recitation of long poems to harp accompaniment. One name is associated with early English melody: St. Godric (12th century), a half-legendary hermit of northern England from whom numerous songs are supposed to have come.

RECORDS
   Plainsong
   Byzantine Chant. HMS II 1, 2.
   Mozarabic Chant. HMS II 3a, 3c; TEM 3.
   Ambrosian Chant. HMS II 2b, 3b; TEM 1.
   Gallican Chant. TEM 2.
   Gregorian Chant. Solesmes Choir, 5 12″ London A 4501; ARC
      3001, 3050, 3088–90, 3031, 3102; HMS II 3–8; TEM 4; MM 1, 2, 3;
      2000YM 3.
   Lauda. TEM 8.

   Secular Melody
   ARC 3002, 3051; EA 0012, 0023; HMS II 9–12; MM 4, 5; TEM 6,
      7, 22; 2000YM 5, 6.

SCORES
   Plainsong
   Byzantine Chant. HAM 8.
   Mozarabic Chant. TEM 3.
   Ambrosian Chant. HAM 9; TEM 1.
   Gallican Chant. TEM 2.
   Gregorian Chant. HAM 11, 12, 13, 14; MM 1, 2, 3; SB 2; TEM 4.
   Tropes. HAM 15; SB 3.
   Sequences. HAM 16; MM 3; SB 4, 5, 6.
   Lauda. TEM 8.

Secular Melody

Troubadour and trouvère songs. HAM 18, 19; MM 4; SB 11, 13, 14; TEM 6.

Minnesingers. HAM 20; MM 5; SB 12, 21.

Meistersingers. HAM 24; TEM 22.

Latin songs (conductus). HAM 17.

Latin songs (religious laude). HAM 21; TEM 8.

English song. HAM 23.

Spanish songs. HAM 22; TEM 7.

PART TWO

The Polyphonic Period (800–1600)

CHAPTER III

Early Stages of Polyphonic Music

THE most significant innovation in the entire history of music is the advent of polyphony in the 9th century. The polyphonic concept —more than one single melodic line at a time—dominates the artistic development of all Occidental music. The early stages of its development (800–1200) take place in the late Carolingian period and the early Middle Ages.

Organum. The term *organum* is applied to various types of early polyphony. The terms *organum, discant,* and *diaphony* were used interchangeably at first. Organum began about the 9th century with the practice of singing plainsong melody in two parts simultaneously a fourth or fifth apart. In other words, the organum moved in parallel motion without melodic or rhythmic independence of the parts.

Theories concerning the Origin of Parallel Organum. (1) Belaiev, a Russian musicologist, holds that the practice of singing in parallel fourths and fifths appears in secular music before it does in sacred. (2) One explanation of parallel organum is based upon the physical series of overtones: octave, fifth, fourth, third, etc. Beginning with the much earlier practice of singing melodies in octaves (called *magadizing*), this is also the order in which these intervals appear chronologically in parallel organum. (3) Another theory relates early organum to the fact that the natural pitch ranges of the human voice lie approximately a fifth apart, hence it would be natural for tenors and bases to sing the same melody a fifth apart. (4) It is believed that two-part music was played on an organ at an early time, leading to the practice of doubling the voice part at the interval of a fourth or fifth, and in general experimenting with parallel polyphony. (5) Finally, parallel organum may have originated from the practice of repeating a sequence phrase a fifth higher by a second chorus, which was only a step from both choruses singing the same phrase simultaneously.

Types of Organum. The following types of organum are presented in approximate chronological order, although no dates can be affixed to the beginning or end of any one practice. There are two factors in the development of polyphony: (1) melodic independence, departure from strict parallel motion of two or more voice parts, and (2) rhythmic independence, where two or more notes in one voice part are sung to one note in the other parts.

STRICT SIMPLE ORGANUM. The most primitive stage of polyphony is called *strict simple organum*. It consists of two voice parts moving in parallel motion a fourth or a fifth apart. It is based upon a plain-song melody, called *vox principalis*. The added part, the same melody sung simultaneously a fourth or a fifth below the principalis, is called *vox organalis*.

COMPOSITE ORGANUM. For polyphony of more than two parts the vox principalis was doubled an octave below and/or the vox organalis doubled an octave above. This is called *composite organum,* which is simply a manner of adding parts without departing from strict parallel motion.

FREE ORGANUM. Melodic independence began with the practice of beginning two-part organum in unison (both parts on the same note); then while the vox organalis remains stationary the vox prin- cipalis moves until the interval of a fourth is reached. Both voices then move in parallel motion until the close of the melody (called *occursus*) where they again move to unison. This form was preferred by Guido d'Arezzo (11th century). Strict organum was probably still used in the 11th century, although the interval of a fifth was no longer permitted in parallel motion.

SUSTAINED-TONE STYLE, ORGANUM PURUM. Free organum gave melodic independence to polyphony. The next step was toward rhythmic independence, gained in the *sustained-tone style,* some- times called *organum purum*. Here each tone of the plainsong melody was sustained, or held out (hence the term *tenor*), while added counterpoint moved in free melismatic style. The tenor part may have been played by an instrument.

GYMEL. The practice of singing a given melody in thirds was called *gymel* or *cantus gemellus* (i.e., "twin song"). This practice seems to have had no connection with ecclesiastical developments in organum and it may have existed prior to organum. It was probably of Welsh or English origin.

Writers and Documents Pertaining to Organum. The first distinct reference to part singing was by Bishop Aldhelm (c. 640–709). The first detailed description of organum is in an anonymous work entitled *Musica Enchiriadis* of the 9th century or earlier. An early mention of organum is found in the treatise *De Harmonica Institutione* by Hucbald. The *Winchester Troper* is an important 11th-century manuscript collection of tropes with organum. John Cotton, an English theorist in the early 12th century, prescribed the use of fourths, fifths, and octaves in parallel and contrary motion, the crossing of voices, and two or three notes of the organalis against one note of the plainsong cantus firmus. These writings of Cotton show that polyphony had achieved some degree of melodic and rhythmic independence by the early 12th century.

RECORDS
    ARC 3051; HMS II 13; MM 6, 7, 8; TEM 9; 2000YM 4.

SCORES
    HAM 25, 26, 27; MM 6, 7, 8; SB 9; TEM 9.

CHAPTER IV

The Ars Antiqua

THE music of the 12th and 13th centuries (the Middle Ages or the Gothic period) is referred to as the *ars antiqua*.

General Characteristics of the Period. In the Middle Ages Paris became the cultural center of the world. This was the time of the troubadours and trouvères, the late crusades, and the building of the great Gothic cathedrals of Europe. Important developments in polyphonic music took place at St. Martial in Limoges and at Chartres in the 12th century, and at Notre Dame in Paris in the late 12th and 13th centuries.

General Characteristics of the Music. (1) Complete melodic and rhythmic independence was established. (2) All intervals were employed in various combinations. Octaves, unisons, fifths predominated as perfect consonances. Thirds and sixths were more frequently used than before. Seconds, sevenths, ninths, and fourths were treated as dissonances. (3) Frequent sharp, dissonant clashes of the voice parts characterize the harmony of the period. (4) Triple time (*tempus perfectum*) was used almost exclusively. (5) Adherence to the rhythmic modes often resulted in rhythmic monotony. (6) Three-voice polyphony prevailed. Two-part polyphony continued to be used and four-part polyphony began. (7) A device known as *hocket* or *hoquetus* was used. It consists of frequent arbitrary interruptions in the melodic line of one part alternating with similar interruptions in another part.

Forms. Various styles of free organum were employed, particularly the sustained-tone style. In addition to these, new forms were created.

CLAUSULA. At the beginning of the 13th century there arose a new polyphonic form called *clausula*. As opposed to organum, which used an entire plainsong as the cantus firmus basis, the clausula used a short melisma from a plainsong for the cantus firmus tenor. To this were added two contrapuntal parts in faster-moving note values. All the parts were sung without text or possibly played by instruments. In the manuscripts only a word or two or sometimes just a syllable were used to indicate the plainsong from which the tenor was borrowed.

POLYPHONIC CONDUCTUS. Another important form of the period is the *polyphonic conductus*. Here a freely composed tenor is used, rather than a plainsong. All the parts move in more or less uniform rhythm and use the same text throughout in all parts.

PARIS MOTET. The most important form of the period is the *motet*. This is usually called the *Paris motet* or the *13th-century motet* to distinguish it from the very different style of the later Renaissance motet. The lowest part, the tenor, is a plainsong broken up into one of the rhythmic modes, usually the slower-moving spondeus. Two upper-voice parts with different rhythms usually move in faster values than the tenor. The upper voices were set to different religious texts in Latin. Late in the 13th century secular texts in French were used for the two upper voices, and eventually for all three parts. The tenor part has a Latin text, but it was probably often performed instrumentally. Harmonic clashes of the voice parts are particularly characteristic of the motet.

RONDEL. A less important form of the *ars antiqua* is the *rondel* or *rondellus*. It is a polyphonic form that makes use of the principle of *exchange*, which means that different melodic motives or phrases are exchanged between two or more voices. For example, the lowest of three voices might sing the melodic phrases *a, b,* and *c,* while a second voice at the same time would sing the same phrases in the order *c, a,* and *b,* and the top voice would sing the same phrases in the order *b, c,* and *a.* This practice is important because it opened the way to the contrapuntal devices of imitation and canon.

Important Names and Manuscripts. Perhaps the first important composer in music history is Léonin, connected with the Notre

Dame school in the middle 12th century. His successor was Pérotin in the late 12th and early 13th centuries. An important writer and composer of the late 13th century is Franco of Cologne. Pierre de la Croix (or Petrus de Cruce) in the late 13th and early 14th centuries represents a transition from the 13th- to the 14th-century styles. The largest manuscript collection of 13th-century motets is the *Montpellier Codex*. The famous *rota* or round, "Sumer Is Icumen In," was formerly thought to belong to the 13th century, but recent evidence established by Dr. Manfred Bukofzer shows it to be a product of the early 14th century.

RECORDS
  ARC 3051; HMS II 14, 15, 18, 19, III 1; MM 8–11; TEM 9, 10, 12; EA 0021, 0024, 0035.

SCORES
  Organum. HAM 29, 31; MM 8, 9; TEM 9.
  Motets. HAM 32–35; MM 10; SB 18–20; TEM 10, 12; WM 3.
  Clausulae. HAM 30; SB 15.
  Conductus. HAM 38, 39; MM 11; SB 16.

CHAPTER V

The Ars Nova

T HE music of the 14th century was referred to as the *ars nova* ("the new art") by contemporaries to distinguish it from the older practices of the 13th century which they referred to as ars antiqua.

General Characteristics of the Period. In general, the 14th century is marked by great literary activity with such names as Petrarch, Dante, Boccaccio, and Chaucer. The most important painter of the period is the Florentine Giotto. It was also a period of trouble in the Church, resulting in a dual papacy (Avignon and Rome) between 1378 and 1418. Two additional historical events belong to the 14th century: the "Hundred Years' War" between France and England (1337–1453) and the Great Plague of the black death (1349). Italy shares musical leadership with France in the ars nova.

General Characteristics of the Music. (1) Predominance of secular music in the ars nova is attributable to trouble in the Church. (2) New polyphonic forms were added to the old ones. (3) Imitation and canon were employed rather extensively for the first time. (4) An important characteristic of the ars nova was the development of a new rhythmic freedom. *Tempus imperfectum* (duple time) now predominated over tempus perfectum (triple time). Strict adherence to the rhythmic modes disappeared, along with the monotonous, short, recurrent patterns characteristic of the ars antiqua music. (5) There was a predominance of two-part writing (especially in Italy). Three- and four-part polyphony was used mainly in France and England. (6) Melodic style was generally more florid. This was especially true in Italy. (7) Harmonic style was characterized by a more extensive use of thirds and by a bold treatment of dissonance. There was little parallelism.

27

Important Names. Philippe de Vitry (c. 1290–1361), a French theorist and composer, is noted primarily for a treatise entitled *Ars Nova* which deals with expansion of systems of notation. The first prohibition of parallel fifths appears in this work. De Vitry was probably a great composer as well, but not much of his music has been preserved. Guillaume de Machaut (c. 1300–1377) is the foremost French composer of the 14th century. Francesco Landini (c. 1325–1397), a blind organist, is the greatest Italian composer of the 14th century.

French Ars Nova Forms. Most of the forms used by French composers in the 14th century are a continuation of earlier forms of the Middle Ages.

ISORHYTHMIC MOTET. The most important 14th-century liturgical form is the *isorhythmic motet,* developed from the Paris motet of the 13th century. It is a polyphonic composition of three or four parts, based upon a liturgical cantus firmus in the tenor. Instead of the short modal patterns of the Paris motet tenor, however, longer patterns are employed. These are called *talea* (i.e., "cutting" where a rhythmic pattern begins again). There is also repetition of melodic units, called *color,* which do not coincide with talea. This isorhythmic plan was applied less strictly to the upper parts of the motet, than to the tenor.

BALLADE. In the secular field perhaps the most important form was the *ballade,* a polyphonic form derived from the troubadour type of the same name.

OTHER FORMS. Other forms employed in the French ars nova music are the *lai, chanson balladé* or *virelai,* and the *rondeau.* Credit for the first complete polyphonic setting of the Mass by one composer goes to Machaut.

Italian Ars Nova Forms. In Italy new forms were developed. These were largely secular forms. Little sacred music was produced in Italy in this period.

MADRIGAL. An important form of the early 14th century is the Italian *madrigal.* The origin of the term has been explained variously as being derived from *mandriali* (a pastoral poem), *matricale* (a rustic song in the mother tongue), and *madriale* (a hymn to the

Virgin). The ars nova madrigal was usually a two-part composition, the upper part characteristically florid and the lower part in slower-moving values, often played on an instrument. The formal plan of the madrigal consists of two or three strophes of three lines each and a final strophe of two lines called *ritornello*. The musical setting was usually the same for the strophes but different for the ritornello. Frequent use of imitation and a free rhythmic style are typical of the madrigal.

CACCIA. A second important form of the period is the *caccia*, a hunting song. It was most often a three-part composition with two parts in strict canon, while the lowest part (tenor) did not imitate the melody of the other voices but was free and was probably performed instrumentally. The caccia was a lengthy composition.

BALLATA. The third most important form of the Italian ars nova is the *ballata*. It corresponds to the French virelai and not to ballade. The poetic form consists of several six-line stanzas, each preceded and followed by a refrain. Landini made two- and three-voice settings of ballatas.

RECORDS

    French Ars Nova. ARC 3032; HMS II 19, III 2, 3; MM 13; TEM 13, 14, 17.

    Italian Ars Nova. ARC 3003; HMS III 4, 5; MM 14; TEM 16.

    14th-century English music. HMS II 19, 20, III 6; EA 0029, 0031.

SCORES

    French Ars Nova. HAM 44–48; MM 13; SB 26, 27; TEM 13, 14, 17; WM 5.

    Italian Ars Nova. HAM 49–54, 56, 57; MM 14; SB 22–24; TEM 16; WM 7.

CHAPTER VI

The Netherlands Schools

IN the 15th century leadership in polyphonic development shifted from France and Italy to the Netherlands area. This includes the activities of two schools: the Burgundian in the first part of the 15th century, and the Flemish in the second half. The techniques of the latter dominated the 16th century, and spread over all of continental Europe.

General Historical Background. The 15th century represents the transition from the Middle Ages to the Renaissance. There is a general breakdown of feudalism, and in its place the rise of the bourgeois class, particularly in the new commercial cities. France and England rise as national powers. Of particular significance to the history of music is the important cultural influence of Burgundian courts under Philip the Good (1419–1467) and Charles the Bold (1467–1477). Their patronage of music, both sacred and secular, gave great impetus to the art. In painting, this is the period of Leonardo da Vinci, Van Eyck, and Raphael. The invention of movable type (1454) does not directly affect music until the 16th century.

The Burgundian School

There is a marked difference of style between the music of the first half of the 15th century represented by the Burgundian school and that of the later 15th century referred to as the Flemish school.

Characteristics of the Music. The following characteristics distinguish the music of the Burgundian school from that of the Flemish school. (1) Three-voice polyphony prevails. (2) Melodic and rhythmic interest centers on the upper voice. (3) The melodic interval of a third becomes the chief characteristic of melodic style in general. (4) Harmony is characterized by many incomplete triads (without thirds), but open fifths and octaves are not used in parallel motion. (5) Parallelism does occur in sections of polyphonic compositions in the form of devices known as *fauxbourdon* and *English discant*. This consists of progressions of first inversion triads (triads arranged so that the third of the chord is the lowest-sounding member; e.g., the chord C–E–G with E in the bass). (6) Contrapuntal imitation is infrequent. (7) The *7–6–1 cadence* (sometimes mistakenly called the "Landini cadence") is commonly employed. This cadential formula, employed at ends of phrases and in final cadences, consists of the melodic progression of the scale degrees 7, 6, and 1 (e.g., the tones B, A, and C in the key of C). (8) Polytextuality disappears. (9) The use of a cantus firmus, or "borrowed tenor," is less frequently employed than before or after the first half of the 15th century.

Principal Composers. In the early 15th century there is an important group of English composers. They are Roy Henry (Henry V, King of England), Cooke, Pycard, Damett, Lionel Power, and, the most important, John Dunstable (c. 1370–1453). Power and Dunstable were well known on the Continent and are directly connected with the Burgundian school proper. The two most important names of the Burgundian group are Guillaume Dufay (c. 1400–1474) and Gilles Binchois (c. 1400–1460).

The Flemish School

The Flemish School is perhaps the more important because the techniques of polyphony established by its composers were the basis of style and form for the entire 16th century in sacred vocal polyphony.

Characteristics of the Music. A comparison between the corresponding elements of style of the two schools will show the marked differences in the respective music. (1) Four-voice polyphony predominates. (2) There is more equality of parts. (3) A bass part is added, giving a lower register to the music. (4) There are more complete triads, and more sonority. (5) Sections using *chordal style* (sometimes called *familiar style*) alternate with sections more rhythmically independent. The latter are often *fugal* (i.e., employing imitative counterpoint). (6) There is a technical mastery of counterpoint revealed in this period. This does not mean that technical facility in counterpoint was featured at the expense of real artistry. The following contrapuntal devices were established: canon, imitation, *augmentation* (increasing the time value of each note of a melody or theme), *inversion* (turning the theme upside down), and *retrogradation* (theme or melody read backwards). A composition consistently using the latter device is called a *cancrizans,* or "crab canon." (7) Duet style is frequently found in the late 15th century, particularly in the motets of Josquin. This consists of passages during which only two voice parts at a time are performing. (8) Fauxbourdon and the 7-6-1 cadence disappear. The latter is replaced by *authentic* (V I), *plagal* (IV I), and *modal cadences* of various kinds. (9) In general, expressive beauty is achieved by the Flemish composers. This quality was later referred to as *musica reservata.*

Principal Composers. The composers of this school did not for the most part remain in the Low Countries but established themselves in courts all over Europe, thus broadly disseminating their art. The principal composers of this group in the late 15th century are Jean Ockeghem (d. 1495), Jacob Obrecht (d. 1505), Josquin Desprez (d. 1521), Pierre de la Rue (c. 1460–1518), Jean Mouton (d. 1522), and Heinrich Isaac (c. 1450–1517).

15th-Century Forms, Manuscripts

Throughout the 15th century the same forms of musical composition were employed. Sacred polyphony was more important in the period than secular polyphony. The latter developed more prominently in the second half of the century.

Religious Forms. The forms which dominated the religious music of the 15th century are liturgical, i.e., composed for definite functions in the Catholic service. There are two principal forms: the Mass and the motet.

POLYPHONIC SETTINGS OF THE MASS. From the time of Machaut polyphonic settings of the Ordinary of the Mass became more prevalent until they constituted a major part of polyphonic literature of the 15th and 16th centuries. Settings of the Mass naturally conform to the five main sections of the Ordinary (Kyrie, Gloria, Credo, Sanctus, and Agnus Dei). The cantus firmus for each part of the Mass was borrowed either from plainsong or, strangely enough, from secular song. One of the most popular of these was a French tune, "L'Homme armé," used as a cantus firmus by all the principal composers through Palestrina. The cantus firmus was almost always in the tenor part and in longer note values than those of the other voices. The text was invariably in Latin.

MOTET. The *motet* of the 15th and 16th centuries may be defined as a sacred polyphonic composition composed to Latin text (usually Biblical). It is a shorter composition than the complete Mass setting, and it is used in the Proper of the service or at certain canonic offices, principally Vespers. It differs further from the Mass in that it makes more use of imitation, less use of cantus firmus. In all other respects its musical style is identical with that of the Mass. In other words, an excerpt from a motet would sound exactly the same as an excerpt from a Mass, except, of course, for the text which is standardized for the Mass.

Secular Forms. Developments in secular form lagged somewhat behind those in religious music. Secular forms, on the whole, were less conventionalized than religious forms. Also, they were less sophisticated and less scholarly. Much of the secular music of the 15th century was still monodic. Some 14th-century forms were still employed in the 15th century (ballades, rondeaus, virelais, etc.). However, some forms that became highly sophisticated in the 16th century found their inception in the 15th century.

FRENCH CHANSON. The French *chanson,* either polyphonic or homophonic, is characterized principally by its lively dance rhythm. The Flemish masters contributed considerably to this type of secular music.

ITALIAN SECULAR FORMS. In Italy an important body of secular music was created. Here again, it is mostly of an unpretentious folk-like nature. The *villota, canzonetta,* and *balletto* are secular forms mostly derived from dances. In the late 15th and early 16th centuries *carnival songs* were developed in the Medici court in Florence. These are simple, chordal part songs. Heinrich Isaac composed a number of these.

POLYPHONIC LIED. In Germany the *polyphonic lied* had its origin in the late 15th century. Folk songs were given polyphonic settings. Isaac was one of the most important composers of polyphonic lieder in the 15th century.

Important Collections. The *Old Hall MS.* is a collection of Mass compositions and hymns written by English composers of the 15th century. The most important manuscript collection of 15th-century music is contained in the seven volumes of the *Trent Codices.* About 75 composers are represented in this collection. The *Odhecaton* is historically significant as the earliest publication of polyphonic music (printed in 1501 by Petrucci). It is a collection of late 15th-century compositions, mostly secular. The first complete cycle of motets for the entire church year is the *Choralis Constantinus* by Heinrich Isaac. Important collections of secular music, including monophonic as well as polyphonic songs, are the *Lochamer,* the *Münchner,* and the *Glogauer Liederbücher.*

RECORDS
    ARC 3003, 3033, 3052 (*Glogau Songbook*); HMS III 7–19; MM 15–19; TEM 18; 2000YM 7, 8; Esoteric 546 (*Choralis Constantinus*).

SCORES
Religious Music
Mass. HAM 63, 66, 73, 77, 89, 92; SB 29, 39, 55, 59, 65; MM 15, 17.
Motets. HAM 62, 64, 65, 76, 90; SB 30, 31, 34, 37, 38, 43, 52, 54, 60, 66, 76; TEM 18; WM 9, 11–13, 15; MM 18, 19.

Secular Music
Accompanied song. HAM 61.
"L'Homme armé." HAM 66a.
Ballade. HAM 67.
Rondeau. HAM 68, 69, 71, 72, 79; SB 42.
Chanson. HAM 70, 91; SB 35, 40, 41; WM 14; MM 16.

Virelai. HAM 74, 75.
From *Lochamer Liederbuch*. HAM 81a.
Lieder. HAM 87, 93; SB 44–47, 85, 87, 88; WM 16.
Canto carnascialesco. HAM 96; WM 18.
English part songs. HAM 85, 86; SB 32.
Canon. HAM 89; SB 61.
Frottola. SB 69–72; WM 20–23.
Ballata. MM 14.

CHAPTER VII

The Sixteenth Century

THE 16th century witnesses the full flower of the Renaissance. In music it sees the culmination of a vocal polyphony that has never been surpassed. For this reason the period is sometimes referred to as "The Golden Age of Polyphony."

General Considerations

General Historical Background. In the 16th century European politics were dominated by Charles V and Philip II of the Holy Roman Empire. The predominant philosophy of the period was humanism, a philosophy away from medieval theology and toward man's interests on earth. The Renaissance spirit is most clearly manifest in the arts and in literature. In painting some of the greatest artists belong to the 16th century: da Vinci (d. 1519), Michelangelo, Titian, Dürer, Holbein. Literature claims the following great names: Machiavelli in Italy, Rabelais, Montaigne, and Ronsard in France, Cervantes in Spain, and Shakespeare, Spenser, Bacon, and Ben Jonson in England. Copernicus and Galileo lead the field of science. 16th-century religion is dominated by the name of Luther, the Protestant Reformation, and the Catholic Counter Reformation. The Protestant Reformation perhaps had more direct influence upon music—certainly upon religious music—than any other historical event of the period.

General Characteristics of the Music. The broad characteristics of 16th-century music may be stated as follows: (1) Vocal polyphonic style, developing almost continuously from the 9th century, reaches an ultimate degree of perfection in the 16th century. (2) Secular music greatly increases in importance. (3) Religious music is fostered by the Catholic Church; secular music is primarily fostered by nobility. (4) An independent instrumental style emerges in the late 16th century. (5) Modality still prevails in both sacred and secular music; but definite signs of its breakdown appear in the second half of the 16th century. (6) Music printing contributes greatly to the dissemination of musical literature throughout Europe. The first printing of music was accomplished by Ottaviano Petrucci in a collection of 15th-century vocal polyphony entitled *Odhecaton* (1501). (7) Italy takes musical leadership from the Flemish school. France and England also become important musical powers.

Sacred Polyphony of the Catholic Church

General Characteristics of Style. Among all schools of sacred polyphony in the 16th century there is a high degree of uniformity of style. This is because of the widespread influence of the Flemish school, the masters of which established their technique everywhere on the Continent. This does not apply to Reformation music, to which a separate section will be devoted (see page 40). (1) There is complete mastery of counterpoint: melodic and rhythmic freedom of voice parts, and at the same time a beautiful, euphonious texture of the whole. (2) Tranquillity of mood prevails in the liturgical music of the Renaissance. Because of the sacred atmosphere of the music, which does not attract attention to itself, 16th-century sacred polyphony is the perfect religious vehicle for worship. (3) The number of voice parts ranges from four to eight or more parts, five-part polyphony being the most usual. (4) Fugal style and chordal style are often employed in the same composition. (5) The complete triad becomes the basis of the harmony. No unprepared seventh chords are employed until the 17th century. (6) Universally strict treatment of dissonance is characteristic of sacred polyphony of the 16th century. The non-chordal dissonances employed are: passing tones, neighboring tones, suspensions (particularly prominent in polyphonic texture), and changing-note groups. (7) Diatonic modality still prevails, but there are marked tendencies toward a feeling for major and minor. In a treatise entitled *Dodecachordon* (1547) the theorist Glareanus established modes on A and C. (8) The beginning of chromaticism (the extensive use of altered tones, e.g., C, C♯, D, E♭), which eventually undermined modality, is to be found in the late 16th century in the works of Lasso and the late Roman school. (9) Archaic effects such as parallelism, open fifths, etc., completely disappear. (10) Liturgical music of the Renaissance was probably composed *a cappella* (for voices alone without instrumental accompaniment). At least there was no separate instrumental accompaniment, although it is likely that instruments were employed to double voice parts or occasionally to carry voice parts by themselves. Instruments undoubtedly played a more important part in the secular music of the Renaissance.

Forms. The two liturgical forms, the Mass and the motet, constitute the main body of Catholic Church music of the Renaissance. A body of nonliturgical music called *laudi spirituali* (religious songs of praise) were used outside the auspices of the Catholic Church. Such pieces were employed mainly in Italy. They were written in a simple chordal and rhythmic style, often resembling secular music, and they used Italian rather than Latin texts. Nonliturgical music in other countries was less significant.

Schools and Composers. Despite the general universality of style in religious music of the Renaissance there were several different schools of development that in varying degrees and extent have special characteristics.

FLEMISH SCHOOL. Flemish composers held important musical posts all over Europe, continuing the traditions and styles established in the 15th century by such composers as Josquin. The most important Flemish composer of the 16th century is Orlando di Lasso (or Orlandus Lassus) (c. 1532–1594), who ranks with Palestrina in his contributions to Catholic Church music. Other important Flemish composers of the period are Philippe de Monte (c. 1521–1603) and Clemens non Papa (c. 1510–c. 1558).

ROMAN SCHOOL. It was natural that the composers working in Rome directly with the mother church would constitute the most significant school of sacred polyphony. This school continued the traditions of *a cappella* style through later periods when other composers had turned to operatic styles and forms. At the head of the Roman school stands Giovanni Pierluigi da Palestrina (c. 1525–1594), whose complete mastery of his art has made his name synonymous with the perfection of sacred vocal polyphony. Other composers of this school are Ingegneri (c. 1545–1592), Nanino (c. 1545–1607), and F. Anerio (c. 1560–1614), all of whose styles show increased use of chromaticism in the late Renaissance.

SPANISH SCHOOL. The contributions of two Spaniards, Cristobal Morales (c. 1500–1553) and Tomas Ludovico da Victoria (c. 1540–1611), are sufficient to establish a Spanish school. Their styles are essentially those of the Roman school, with the possible addition of a certain starkness of expression reminding one of the later canvases of El Greco.

VENETIAN SCHOOL. Perhaps the most outstanding style in sacred polyphony of the 16th century is that developed by the Venetians. There are two contributions of this school that differentiate its style from that of other schools. (1) The Venetians made extensive use of *polychoric music* (music written for two or more complete choirs of voices), and antiphonal effects created by various choirs situated in different parts of the church. (2) Magnificence characterizes the music of the Venetians. This is partly because of the polychoric technique developed and also because of bold harmonies and rich textures. The most important composers of this school are Adrian Willaert (a Flemish composer, d. 1562), Andrea Gabrieli (c. 1510–1586), and his nephew, Giovanni Gabrieli (1557–1612).

ENGLISH SCHOOL. A great and extensive literature of Catholic Church music was created in England in the 16th century, despite religious conflicts and the rise of Anglicanism. Many fine Masses and motets were written by English composers. The Anglican Church retained most of the practices of the Catholic Church. In its music it used motets and a modified motet style of polyphony but with English texts. These motets were called *cathedral anthems* or *full anthems*. Late in the 16th century a new form and style came into being. This was the *verse anthem* which makes use of soloists and instrumental accompaniment as well as chorus. Soloist and choir alternate by sections. The principal composers of English church music are: Thomas Tallis (c. 1505–1585), who wrote both Catholic and Anglican Church music; William Byrd (1543–1623), the greatest English composer of the 16th century, who also wrote Catholic and Anglican Church music, although he remained a staunch Catholic throughout his life; and Orlando Gibbons (1583–1625), who wrote only for the Anglican services.

GERMAN SCHOOL. Catholic Church music did not flourish in Germany in the 16th century because of the Lutheran Reformation. Hence there is really no German school of sacred polyphony. Jacobus Gallus (Handl) (1550–1591) is the only German name of real significance in this field. Ludwig Senfl (c. 1492–c. 1555), a Swiss, wrote fine Catholic and Protestant church music.

Reformation Music

Perhaps the most cataclysmic event in the history of Christian religion is the Reformation of the 16th century. The rise of Protestantism had great effects upon music, which effects were manifest principally in Germany, to a lesser extent in France and England, and not at all in Italy. However, not until after the 16th century did Protestant music rival the great art of Catholic Church music of the Renaissance.

Martin Luther and Protestantism. The principal figure of the Protestant Reformation is Martin Luther (1483–1546), whose *Ninety-five Theses* (1517) and political and theological attack on the Church (1520) brought open conflict on matters of long standing pertaining to Church authority and to certain Church abuses. The Protestant revolt spread to Switzerland under the leadership of Zwingli and Calvin, who, however, were not favorably disposed toward music in religion. In France, the Huguenots (part of the Calvinist movement) developed an important Protestant music. Protestantism in England under Henry VIII, involving a somewhat different situation, gave rise to the Anglican Church, also fostering some important musical developments (see pages 39 and 42).

Luther's Influence upon Music. Luther had strong convictions about the importance of music in religion. He retained some of the music of the Catholic service (Mass and motet) but modified it to meet the needs of the German Reformation. There was a general tendency to substitute the German language for Latin, even before Luther's time. He encouraged congregational participation in the Protestant service, a practice abandoned by the Catholic Church with Gregorian reforms at the end of the 6th century. Congregational participation brought about the birth of a great body of religious song, called *chorale,* comparable in importance to Catholic plainsong. Johann Walter (1496–1570) was Luther's principal collaborator in this musical development. Chorales were sung in unison by the congregation, sung in parts by the choir, and at a later time they were played on the organ.

Protestant Chorale Melody. Chorale melody is of great importance to church music of the late Renaissance and Baroque periods.

CHARACTERISTICS OF CHORALE MELODY. The style of chorale melody differs considerably from that of Catholic plainsong. (1) It is definitely metric. (2) The rhythm is characterized by a slow, even, plodding pulse. (3) The phraseology of the chorale melody is clearer and more regular than that of plainsong. (4) Chorale melody is more major or minor than modal. (5) Because of its limited range, evenness of rhythm, and melodic progression, it is easily singable. (6) Chorale melody is more often harmonized than is plainsong. The chorale harmonizations by Bach in the 18th century are the most famous. (7) Chorale melodies are sung in the vernacular language (German) as opposed to the Latin of plainsong.

SOURCES OF CHORALE MELODY. There are three main sources of chorale melody: (1) Plainsong was modified and set to German texts. (2) Secular melody was also employed with religious texts. For example, Isaac's "Innsbruck, ich muss dich lassen" ("Innsbruck, I must leave thee") becomes "O Welt, ich muss dich lassen" ("O World, I must leave thee"). The famous "Passion" chorale, "O Sacred Head now wounded," that Bach uses in the *St. Matthew Passion,* comes from an old German love song, the first line of which runs, "Mein G'muth ist mir verwirret, das macht ein Jungfrau zart" ("Confused are all my feelings; a tender maid's the cause"). (3) Finally, original chorale melodies were composed by Protestant musicians. Perhaps the most famous of these is Luther's "Ein' feste Burg" ("A Mighty Fortress").

USES OF THE CHORALE. The significance of the chorale can be seen in the fact that it soon became the very backbone of the Lutheran musical service. Not only did it constitute a superb body of melody for congregational singing and use in the home, but it was extensively employed as cantus firmus in various polyphonic forms: (1) in the organ chorale prelude, (2) in vocal polyphonic settings, and (3) in sacred cantata choruses and instrumental parts of the cantata (see page 82).

French Reformation Music. In France the Huguenot movement gave rise to a comparatively modest body of religious music. Clément Marot and Théodore de Bèze versified Psalms. These were set to music by Claude Goudimel (c. 1505–1572), Claude Lejeune (1528–c. 1600), and Jacques Mauduit (1557–1627). The French Huguenot Psalter was completed in 1561. These Psalms were probably intended for use in the home rather than for congregational singing.

CHARACTERISTICS OF HUGUENOT PSALTER MUSIC. The Psalm settings resemble the German chorale harmonizations. In general they have the following characteristics: (1) They have a simplicity of style. (2) Although they are usually set in a simple, chordal style, a free polyphonic style is not entirely excluded. (3) The principal melody is in the soprano voice, the uppermost part in a four-voice setting. (4) The Psalms employ a straightforward rhythm, somewhat more varied and animated than the German chorale. Rhythm and meter follow the accentuation of the text.

Anglican Church Music. The most important aspects of English Reformation music have been discussed in connection with the English school of sacred polyphony (see page 39). One additional feature of English church music is _Anglican chant_. It is a method of singing psalms, canticles, etc., differing from that of the Catholic Church in that: (1) it is sung in English, (2) it is harmonized in simple, four-part chordal style, and (3) it is more strictly metrical. 16th-century composers who made settings of Anglican chant are Tallis, Byrd, Morley, and Gibbons.

Secular Polyphony

In the 16th century great developments in secular vocal polyphony took place, and for the first time the secular art rivaled that of religious polyphony.

General Characteristics of Style. Secular polyphony differs from sacred polyphony in the following ways: (1) It has a tendency toward a stronger and more lively rhythm than is usually employed in sacred polyphonic music. (2) It has a tendency toward major tonality and has less modal flavor. (3) It consistently employs secular texts in the vernacular tongue. (4) It is usually limited to four or five voices. (5) Cantus firmus is less often and less strictly employed as the basis of secular polyphony.

Italian Secular Music. The Italian Renaissance not only produced great literature, painting, and sacred music, but it also contributed a great wealth of secular music in various forms.

FROTTOLA. One of the first important secular forms to develop in the 16th century is the *frottola*. It originated in northern Italy in the early 16th century from a dance form. It is definitely secular and popular in style. The melody is in the soprano voice. Usually four voice parts in chordal style are employed. The lower voices probably were played on instruments. The principal composers of this form are Marco Cara and Bartolommeo Tromboncino.

VILLANELLA. A form related to the frottola is the *villanella* or *canzona villanesca*. It comes from southern Italy and flourishes about the middle of the century. It is similar in style to the frottola, but its texts are generally more refined and the music somewhat more sophisticated. It may also be parodistic. The principal composers of this form are Adrian Willaert, Baldassare Donati, Giovanni Gastoldi, and Luca Marenzio, all of whom are also important madrigal composers.

MADRIGAL. The *madrigal* of the Italian Renaissance is not to be confused with that of the ars nova, where the term first appears. The 16th-century Italian madrigal is a more highly developed form and a more sophisticated style than either the 14th-century madrigal or the 16th-century frottola and villanella. The madrigal as a form continues its development well into the 17th century. There are three broad periods of its development.

a. *The Early Period.* The first period (roughly from 1525 to 1560) is characterized by homophonic style, the melody in the uppermost of three or four voices, and a general quiet sentiment somewhat resembling sacred polyphony. Composers in this period are Adrian Willaert, Jacques Arcadelt (c. 1514–c. 1570), Philippe Verdelot (d. before 1567), and Costanzo Festa (d. 1545).

b. *The Middle Period.* The madrigal of the second period (roughly 1560 to 1590) usually employs five parts and is more polyphonic in style. It is further characterized by breaking of the text by rests for emotional expression and by considerable naïve tone painting (i.e., expressing simple pictorial ideas of the text in the music). The composers of madrigals in this period are Lasso, Palestrina, Andrea Gabrieli, Cyprian de Rore (1516–1565), and Philippe de Monte.

c. *The Late Period.* The third period of development (1590–1640) reveals a transition from polyphonic to homophonic treatment with more use of solo voices. It is further characterized by a new dramatic expression and a certain amount of *virtuosity* (display of technical facility). There is also an extensive use of chromaticism. The principal composers of late Italian madrigals are Luca Marenzio, Baldassare Donati, Orazio Vecchi (c. 1550–1605), Don Carlo Gesualdo (c. 1560–1614), Giovanni Gastoldi, and Claudio Monteverdi (1567–1643).

MADRIGAL COMEDY. An interesting forerunner of early 17th-century opera is the *madrigal comedy*. These were quasi-dramatic forms consisting of a chain of madrigals in dialogue centered around pastoral themes. An example of a madrigal comedy is *L'Amfiparnasso* (1594) by Vecchi.

MADRIGALE SPIRITUALE. A madrigal of religious and moral content was called a *madrigale spirituale* ("spiritual madrigal"). These madrigal-style religious pieces are related to the laudi spirituali, and do not belong to the category of secular music.

English Secular Music. The flowering of English secular music in the Renaissance is coeval with the Elizabethan period and its great achievements in drama and verse. It reaches a peak of development somewhat later than the Italian madrigal.

ENGLISH MADRIGAL. The *English madrigal* was influenced by secular developments in Italy. However, it was definitely developed along individual lines and bears unmistakable qualities of English treatment of melancholy and merriment. The English madrigal is characterized by these factors: (1) The excellence of English verse contributed no little to its artistic value. (2) It was undoubtedly intended for solo voices singing in small groups. (3) From four to six voice parts were used. (4) On the whole, English madrigals are more chordal and more rhythmic than the Italian madrigals. (5) They are characteristically diatonic, in contrast to Italian chromaticism. (6) Use of the *fa-la-la chorus* is fairly common. Nonsense syllables (such as "fa-la-la") were employed in a recurrent chorus or refrain, a practice probably borrowed from the Italian balletto or villanella. (7) It is not uncommon to find changes of meter in the madrigal (i.e., the use of three-four and four-four time in the same composition). The principal composers are William Byrd, Thomas Morley (c. 1557–1603), John Wilbye (c. 1574–1638), Thomas Weelkes (c. 1575–1623), John Ward (d. c. 1640), John Bennet (fl. 1600–1620), Thomas Bateson (c. 1570–1630), Orlando Gibbons (1583–1625), John Farmer (fl. 1591–1601), and Francis Pilkington (d. 1638). The most important collection of English madrigals is the *Triumphs of Oriana* (1603), composed by the leading madrigalists of the time and dedicated to Queen Elizabeth. Each madrigal ends with the line, "Long live fair Oriana." The idea imitates a similar collection of Italian madrigals entitled *Il trionfo di Dori* (1592).

CANZONET. The *canzonet* is similar to the madrigal in general style. It is written for only two or three voice parts and has characteristically lively rhythms and merry texts, usually of a pastoral nature. Thomas Morley was the principal writer of canzonets.

AYRE. A form developing somewhat later than the madrigal, the *ayre,* is a strophic song in homophonic style. The melody is supported by other voices or by instruments, sometimes by both. The lute was a favorite accompanying instrument for English ayres. The principal composers of this form are John Dowland (1563–1626), Thomas Campion (1567–1620), Francis Pilkington (d. 1638), Philip Rosseter (c. 1575–1623), and Robert Jones (fl. c. 1597–1617).

The French Polyphonic Chanson. The most important French contribution to Renaissance music lies in the field of the *polyphonic chanson.* As in the case of the English madrigal, much of the excellence of the French chanson is attributable to the high quality of verse of such poets as Ronsard. The characteristics of the French chanson are: (1) They were usually written for four voices, the upper most prominent. (2) A lively rhythm characterizes most of the chansons. (3) Two metric styles were employed. The first, called *chanson rimée,* employed regular meters. The second, *chanson mesurée* (or *vers mesuré*), was a later 16th-century development. In this type strongly accented syllables were given twice the note value ($\downarrow$) of the unaccented syllables ($\downarrow$), resulting in irregular metric effects. (4) There is frequent use of repeated-note motives at the beginning of the chansons. (5) The French polyphonic chansons were freely composed (i.e., not based upon a cantus firmus). (6) There are three general styles of chanson. The first is the fugal style which makes use of imitation among the voices. The second is a chordal style in which there is vertical alignment of text syllables for all voices. The third is the solo chanson usually with a polyphonic instrumental accompaniment.

Composers. The composers of French chansons are numerous. The principal ones are: Pierre de la Rue (c. 1460–1518), Clément Jannequin (c. 1485–1560), who is particularly noted for the "portraiture chanson" which makes use of naïve, realistic effects; Lasso, Jacques Mauduit (1557–1627), William Costeley (1531–1606), Claude de Sermisy (c. 1490–1562), Nicolas Gombert, Jacques Arcadelt, Claude Lejeune (1528–1600), Claude Goudimel (c. 1505–1572), Bertrand, and Jacob Regnard (c. 1540–1599). Bertrand and Regnard are especially noted for chanson settings of Ronsard poems.

The German Polyphonic Lied. German polyphonic secular music was invariably based upon an already extant folk song melody. Some of these melodies were given simple chordal settings. But a fine polyphonic literature developed in the form of the *polyphonic* *lied.* Between about 1450 and 1550 the polyphonic lieder utilized imitation of the principal motives of the secular melody in all voices, of which there were usually four. There were numerous organ arrangements of these vocal compositions. In the second half of the 16th century the style of the secular polyphonic music in Germany is definitely derived from Italian models.

COMPOSERS. The composers of the first period are Adam von Fulda (c. 1440–1506), Heinrich Finck (1445–1527), Heinrich Isaac, Paul Hofhaimer (1459–1537), and Ludwig Senfl (c. 1492–c. 1555). In the second half of the 16th century the principal composers are Hans Leo Hassler (1564–1612), Lasso, and Johannes Eccard (1553–1611). Ludwig Senfl was particularly noted for compositions called *quodlibets,* which are humorous pieces incongruously and simultaneously combining different folk songs. Quodlibets were popular in the 15th and 16th centuries.

The Spanish Villancico. The principal form of secular polyphony in renaissance Spain is known as the *villancico.* Usually in three or four parts and predominantly in chordal style, it was the counterpart of the Italian frottola and villanella. The form A B B A consists of an introductory refrain called *estribillo* (A), followed by a stanza (*copla*) of two couplets sung to the same music (B), and a return to the refrain sung to different words (*vuelta*). In the 16th century, villancicos were also composed as solo songs with lute accompaniments. Juan del Encina (1469–1529) was the principal composer. *Cancionero del Palacio* was the principal collection of villancicos.

RECORDS

Sacred Polyphony (Catholic)

ARC 3074, 3077; HMS III 20, 21, IV 6–12, 15, 16; MM 23–25; TEM 23, 28; 2000YM 11, 12, 17; EA 0027. Anthology of (sacred) Renaissance Music (Des Prés, Lassus, Morley, Victoria, Palestrina, Mouton, and others): Period SPL 597. Palestrina, Magnificat and motets: Period SPL 513. Isaac, Motets from *Choralis Constantinus:* Esoteric 546. Byrd, Mass for 4 Voices, Mass for 5 Voices: EMS 234. Victoria, motets: Lyricord 46. Victoria, *Messa da Requiem:* Angel 35668. Victoria, Selected works (Vatican

Choir): Period 706. Motets by Victoria, Lassus, Palestrina, Anchieta (Sistine Chapel Choir): Period SPL 706.

Reformation Music
ARC 3053, 3072; HMS IV 13, 14; TEM 24–27; 2000YM 9, 10.

Italian Secular Music
ARC 3034, 3073, 3076; HMS IV 1, 2; MM 27; TEM 20, 33; 2000YM 13. Marenzio, madrigals: Westminster 18712.

English Secular Music
ARC 3004, 3053; HMS IV 3, 4, 18; MM 28; TEM 34; EA 0034. Elizabethan and Jacobean Ayres, Madrigals and Dances: Decca 9406. Elizabethan madrigals: Esoteric 520, Westminster 18764.

French Secular Music
ARC 3034, 3076; HMS IV 5, 17; MM 20; TEM 31. French Renaissance Vocal Music: Decca 9629.

German Secular Music
ARC 3075; TEM 32; 2000YM 14.

Spanish Secular Music
ARC 3078; HMS IV 17; TEM 19.

SCORES
Sacred Polyphony
HAM 109, 112–114, 125, 127, 128, 139–141, 143, 144, 146b, 149, 150, 156, 157, 164, 166; MM 23–25; SB 53, 97, 102, 104, 107, 120 (lauda), 121, 122, 126–131, 163; TEM 23, 28; WM 30, 37 (lauda), 41.

Reformation Music
HAM 108, 110, 111, 126, 132, 151, 167a, 169, 171, 172; SB 77, 80, 84, 108, 109, 110, 123, 142, 143, 159–162, 285; TEM 24–27; WM 35, 36.

Italian Secular Music
HAM 95, 129–131, 142, 146a, 155, 158, 160, 161, 186, 188; MM 27; SB 69–72, 98–101, 106, 132, 140, 164–167; TEM 20, 33; WM 20–23, 33, 38, 45–48, 56.

English Secular Music
HAM 159, 162, 163, 170; MM 28; SB 145, 146; TEM 34; WM 50, 51, 66.

French Secular Music
HAM 91, 107, 138, 145a, 147; MM 20; SB 116–118, 133, 144; TEM 31; WM 27.

German Secular Music
HAM 87, 93, 165, 168; SB 85, 87, 88, 111, 124, 125, 141, 152; TEM 32; WM 16, 25, 28, 31, 42, 62, 63, 64.

Spanish Secular Music
HAM 97, 98, 114; SB 96, 114; TEM 19; WM 44.

CHAPTER VIII

Instrumental Music to 1600

U NTIL about 1600 the principal developments in music took place almost entirely in vocal music. But the Renaissance saw an awakening of interest in instrumental music that continued to grow until in the 18th century its importance surpassed that of vocal music.

General Considerations

Characteristics of Instrumental Style. A growing awareness of the fact that musical instruments have certain special properties eventually led to an independent instrumental style. The presence of any one, or a combination, of the following properties implies the use of instrumental idiom as opposed to vocal idiom: (1) angularity of melodic line, the use of skips, (2) wide range of melodic line, (3) long sustained notes, long phrases, (4) sharp rhythm, strong accents, syncopation, (5) a freer treatment of dissonance than practiced in vocal music, (6) rapid, repeated notes and figures, (7) rapid scales, (8) freely added parts and chords filled in (called *Freistimmigkeit*), particularly in lute and keyboard music, (9) melodic ornamentation, including *figuration* (repeated figures or patterns on each note of the basic melody), *embellishment* (mordents, turns, trills, etc.), and *coloration* (free melismatic material added to the basic notes of the melody). The latter is not exclusively instrumental.

Instruments and Instrumental Music before 1600. In general, it should be kept in mind that a completely instrumental style was not evolved until the 17th century, although lute and keyboard music of the 16th century shows unmistakable signs of instrumental idiom.

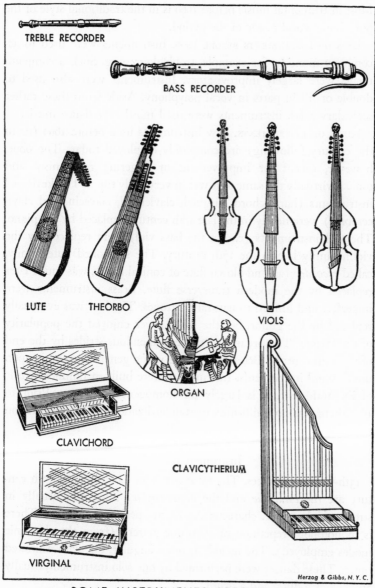

TREBLE RECORDER

BASS RECORDER

LUTE   THEORBO

VIOLS

ORGAN

CLAVICHORD

CLAVICYTHERIUM

VIRGINAL

Herzog & Gibbs, N.Y.C.

SOME INSTRUMENTS BEFORE 1600

Most instrumental music before 1600 is in the traditional style of the polyphonic vocal music of the period.

USES OF INSTRUMENTS BEFORE 1600. Instruments were used to accompany monody, for example, troubadour song. Such accompaniments were largely improvisatory. Instruments were also used to double or fill in parts in vocal polyphony. Aside from these rather secondary roles, instruments were used mostly for dance music.

KINDS OF INSTRUMENTS. Few instruments used before 1600 (or in the century following) are commonly employed today. The oboe, however, except for improvement in fingering mechanism and tone, is virtually the same as it was in very early times. The keyboard instruments (harpsichord, virginal, clavichord, clavecin, and clavicembalo) were finally in the late 18th century replaced by the piano. The viol instruments (except the bass viol) were replaced by the violin family late in the 17th century. The soft-toned flute family, called *recorder* (an end-blown flute of conical bore), was much later replaced by the modern transverse flute. Brass instruments were imperfect and limited to natural overtones. The lute was eventually replaced by the guitar, but the latter never enjoyed the popularity of the former. The organ had made tremendous strides by the end of the 16th century. Before 1600 there was a general emphasis upon use of wind instruments. Instruments were built in families. Music of the 16th century is largely for homogeneous groups. Prior to 1600 there was no uniformity or standardization of instrumentation in ensemble music.

Instrumental Forms

13th-Century Dances. The most common dances of the 13th century are the *estampie* and the *danse-royale*. These are usually in strong, triple meter, characteristic of the period in general. There is monotonous repetition of rhythmic pattern (from the rhythmic modes employed). The melody is often angular, but with a limited range. These dances were performed by one solo instrument, usually an oboe or a flute, and a drum.

14th-Century Dances. The *rota* and the *saltarello* are the two most common dances of the 14th century. They frequently employ duple as well as triple meter and the rhythmic patterns are more varied than those of the 13th century. They were played by bowed string instruments or woodwind instruments and drums.

Instrumental Forms of the Renaissance. In the 15th and 16th centuries, instrumental forms became more varied.

RENAISSANCE DANCES. In the 15th and 16th centuries dance forms were commonly in pairs, both employing the same melody, but contrasting in tempo and meter. Their combination was the result of the prevalent way of dancing. This pairing of dance forms was the prototype of the baroque dance suite. The *basse-danse* is a slow dance in three-four time, and it is followed by the *tourdion,* a lively dance in four-four time. Another dance pair is the *pavane,* slow, four-four time, followed by the *galliard* (Fr. *gaillarde*) in fast, triple time. An Italian dance pair is the *ronde* and *saltarello* which follow the general plan of the pavane and galliard. The German dance pairs were called *Tanz* and *Nach-Tanz.* These dances were written for lute, for keyboard instruments, and for instrumental ensemble.

FANTASIA. Pieces called *fantasias* were written for lute, keyboard instruments, and instrumental ensemble. They are usually polyphonic with imitative counterpoint used extensively. They have no basic structural form and are less strict in contrapuntal treatment than the ricercare (see below). In English keyboard music of the late 16th century the *fantasia* (or *fancy*) often includes display passages and figuration as well as polyphonic treatment. Fantasias are often based on folk song.

TOCCATA AND PRELUDE. In the Renaissance, free structural forms in an improvisatory style were called variously *toccata, praeludium,* or *praeambulum.* Such pieces, written for organ, harpsichord, or lute, are often characterized by virtuosity (rapid scale passages, arpeggios, etc.). They also employ polyphonic and chordal material as well.

CANTUS FIRMUS COMPOSITIONS. Instrumental compositions based upon a borrowed melody were written chiefly for the organ. The *cantus firmi* were taken variously from plainsong melody, German chorale melody, and secular melody. Such compositions, employing the title of the borrowed melody, are consistently polyphonic in character. The cantus firmus is often given prominence by long sustained notes. But coloration of the original melody is also very common.

RICERCARE. In the 16th and 17th centuries the term *ricercare* was used for various kinds of instrumental pieces. Of these the most important type is the polyphonic ricercare, primarily a church form for organ. It is virtually an instrumental motet in style, usually in a slow, dignified tempo. Like the motet, it makes use of several short themes or motives which are introduced successively and contrapuntally imitated in all voices. It is further characterized by display of contrapuntal skill: inversion, augmentation, and retrograde treatment of the thematic material. The polyphonic ricercare reveals no virtuosity and no real instrumental idiom.

CANZONA. The *canzona* is the secular counterpart of the ricercare. It is virtually an instrumental chanson. It differs from the ricercare in that it employs longer fugue-like themes which are likewise imitated in all voices. It is usually more lively than the ricercare. Various sections of the canzona in contrasting tempi and meters often employ the same melody. The ricercare and the canzona are prototypes of the fugue which gradually emerges in the 17th century.

VARIATION. The *variation* form is of special significance in that it has remained an important basis of composition down to the present day. The variation form is one of the most important contributions of the Spanish lutenists and the English virginal school of the late 16th century. The variations are usually based upon a popular melody which is repeated a number of times, each time with different figuration. Virtuosity is a notable characteristic of this form. The English *ground* is a special variation type on a composed bass theme, constantly reiterated while different figuration appears above it. Other variations on a bass theme are called *passacaglia* and *chaconne* (see page 92). These are more common in the Baroque period.

Instrumental Classes
Styles, Forms, Schools, Composers

Lute Music. From about 1450 to about 1650 the lute (a fretted, guitar-like instrument, with six strings and a long neck) was as

universal as the piano is today. It was an accompanying instrument
as well as a solo and ensemble instrument.

STYLE IN GENERAL. Most lute music displays some degree of virtuosity in the form of rapid scales and figuration. Polyphonic style
was generally attempted. Although the nature of the instrument
prevented a strict polyphonic texture, implied lines by jumping from
one voice to another were used. The third and most idiomatic style
to be found in lute music is the use of straight chordal material.

FORMS. The principal forms of lute music are the fantasia, pre-
amble or prelude, dances, variations, and arrangements of vocal
music (motets and chansons).

LUTE TABLATURE

SCHOOLS AND COMPOSERS. The principal composer of Spanish lute
music was Luis Milan (c. 1500–after 1561). In Italy Francesco Spinac-
cino and Ambrosio Dalza were the leading lute composers. In
Germany the principal names in lute music were Arnold Schlick
(d. after 1527), Hans Judenkunig (c. 1460–1526), Hans Gerl, and
Hans Neusiedler (c. 1508–1563). In France, Pierre Attaingnant
published a considerable amount of French lute music (c. 1530 ff.).
In England John Dowland (1563–1626) was the principal lutenist
composer. In Poland an important lute school was led by Albert
Dlugorai.

TABLATURE. A special notation called *tablature* was used for lute
music. It consists of letters or numbers placed on six horizontal
lines corresponding to the six strings of the lute. The letters or

numbers indicate the fret or finger position of each note to be played. Rhythm is indicated above the tablature.

Organ Music. The organ was definitely and almost exclusively associated with church service, a fact which largely determines the style of organ music.

STYLE. For the most part organ music of the Renaissance duplicates the style of vocal polyphony. Little virtuosity appears in organ music before the Baroque period, except for some toccatas (Merulo). Ornamentation and coloration are extensively employed. Organ music is mostly polyphonic.

FORMS. The principal forms of organ music are the fantasia, praeambulum, toccata, ricercare, canzona, cantus firmus compositions based upon Catholic plainsong and Protestant chorale melodies, and *verses* or *versets,* usually short pieces played by the organist between verses of a hymn sung by the congregation or choir.

SCHOOLS AND COMPOSERS. The first important composer in the German school is Conrad Paumann (c. 1410–1473), who wrote an "organ method" in 1452 entitled *Fundamentum Organisandi.* This work consists of two-part pieces in organ tablature and instructions. Other German composers, following Paumann, are Hans Buchner (1483–1538), Hans Kotter (c. 1485–1541), Leonhard Kleber (c. 1490–1556), Paul Hofhaimer (1459–1537), and Arnold Schlick (d. after 1527). The publisher Attaingnant represents the only significant contributions to organ literature in France with publications of anonymous composers around 1531. The principal name in Spain is that of Antonio Cabezon (1510–1566). In Italy a notable school of organ composition is associated with the names Claudio Merulo (1533–1604), Girolamo Cavazzoni, Annibale Padovano, and Andrea and Giovanni Gabrieli. There seems to have been little creative activity in organ music in England, where the virginal school overshadowed almost all other instrumental activity. John Redford in the early 16th century and John Bull in the late 16th century are the only names of any significance in English organ music.

Harpsichord Music. The most extensive literature for harpsichord before 1600 appears in England in the second half of the 16th century. Here the first truly independent instrumental style is extensively developed. On the Continent, harpsichord music still has little differentiation of style from that of vocal polyphony and organ music. The keyboard instrument used in Elizabethan England is called a *virginal,* a small, one-manual instrument of the harpsichord type (see page 89).

STYLE. One of the most prominent features of the English virginal school is a sheer delight in instrumental virtuosity. Musicians apparently enjoyed playing rapid scales up and down the keyboard, and using figures, arpeggios, fast repeated chords, etc. Figuration is extensively used: repeated patterns of broken chords, thirds, rapid scales, etc., ornamenting the notes of a borrowed melody. Embellishment (trills, mordents, etc.) is also employed. The English virginal music is more or less contrapuntal, but comparatively little use of imitation is to be found.

FORMS. The English virginal school was not only the first to exploit a truly instrumental style but it also was the first (along with the Spanish lutenists) to develop the variation form. These variations are usually on popular tunes of the day. The English were also fond of writing variations on a ground bass, usually an originally composed theme. A third type of variation, *hexachord variation,* is based upon six ascending or descending scale tones. These were usually given such titles as "Ut re mi fa sol la." Dances were popular forms in harpsichord music: pavanes, galliards, allemandes, etc. Cantus firmus compositions were employed. These were invariably based upon plainsong melodies and they may have been intended for performance on the organ. Pieces with descriptive titles, battle pieces, etc., and preludes are to be found among the large collections of English virginal music.

COMPOSERS AND COLLECTIONS. The principal composers of English virginal music are Hugh Aston (early 16th century), Giles Farnaby (c. 1560–c. 1600), William Byrd, John Bull (c. 1562–1628), and Orlando Gibbons. The principal collections of virginal music are the *Fitzwilliam Virginal Book, Parthenia,* and *My Ladye Nevells Booke,* the latter containing 42 pieces by William Byrd. In France Pierre Attaingnant published a collection of keyboard dances. Cabezon in Spain wrote *diferencias* (variations) for harpsichord and for lute. Elsewhere there seems to have been no distinction between harpsichord and organ music.

Ensemble Music. The problems of *Aufführungspraxis* (how early music was intended to be performed) are not yet entirely solved. This is particularly true in the field of instrumental ensemble, where there was little standardization of instrumental combinations, and where actual instrumentation was seldom indicated in manuscripts. This is because in general before 1600 it was felt that any medium of performance for a given composition would be satisfactory.

INSTRUMENTAL MEDIA. Three general classes of instruments were employed for instrumental ensemble before 1600. Ensemble music for strings employed various members of the viol family. A combination of viols was called a *consort of viols*. Members of the flute family (recorders) were frequently employed in ensemble music. In combination with viols the ensemble was called a *mixed consort*. The use of brass ensembles was particularly characteristic of the Venetian school. In Germany wind ensembles were used to sound the hours of the day by playing chorales from municipal towers or churches.

STYLE. In instrumental ensemble music there is little independent instrumental style. The pieces for ensemble are generally polyphonic and use imitation. In ensemble dance music the style is more chordal and rhythmic.

FORMS. The three principal forms in ensemble music are the fantasia, various dances, and canzonas. The latter were employed by the Venetian composers.

SCHOOLS AND COMPOSERS. In England the principal composers are Gibbons and Matthew Locke. In Germany, Melchior Franck, Valentin Hausmann, and Erasmus Widmann are the principal composers. In Italy Giovanni Gabrieli composed canzonas for brass ensembles. All these composers belong to the late 16th and the 17th centuries.

RECORDS
  Lute Music
  ARC 3078; MM 22; TEM 21.

Organ Music
HMS III 22, IV 23; MM 26; TEM 15, 29.

Harpsichord and Virginal Music
HMS IV 21; MM 21, 29; TEM 30; 2000YM 15; EA 0013, 0026.

Ensemble Music
ARC 3002, 3071; HMS II 16, 17, III 23, 24, IV 19, 20; MM 12; TEM 11, 35, 36; 2000YM 16; EA 0028.

SCORES

Lute Music
HAM 97–99, 105, 121–124, 160, 162; MM 22; SB 90, 91, 93–95, 114, 115, 138, 150, 181; TEM 21; WM 29, 32, 34.

Organ Music
HAM 84, 100, 101, 116–118, 120, 133–135, 153, 154, 157, 174, 180, 181; MM 26; SB 48, 56, 57, 82, 83, 92, 103, 105, 113, 149, 158; TEM 15, 29; WM 43, 57.

Harpsichord Music
HAM 102, 104, 134, 145b, 177, 178, 179; MM 21, 29; SB 112, 135–137, 147, 158, 174, 181; TEM 30; WM 24, 57.

Ensemble Music
HAM 88, 136, 137, 157, 162, 167b, 173, 175, 176; MM 12; SB 61, 62, 67, 75, 81, 105, 109, 119, 134, 148, 151, 153–157; TEM 11, 35, 36; WM 17, 26, 39, 40, 48, 54, 55, 56, 58–60, 63.

CHAPTER IX

Musical Notation to 1600

Our modern system of musical notation dates from the early 17th century. Prior to about 1600 various systems had been used in man's attempt to record graphically the music he heard. The evolution of musical notation is the progress toward accurate symbolic representation of two general musical factors: the pitch and the duration of a musical tone.

Neumatic Notation

Neumes. The term *neume* comes from the Greek *neuma,* meaning a nod or a sign. Neumes were probably first used about 680 A.D. At this time they did not indicate exact pitch or time value; they were merely "reminders" of melodic contour of already known plainsong melody. Neumes are derived from three basic accents: **(1)** grave (\\), a descending inflection, (2) acute (/), ascending inflection, and (3) circumflex (∧), ascending-descending. Later they were combined to form various compound neumes, called *ligatures.* At first these signs were placed above the lines of the text, a practice known as *in campo aperto,* i.e., notes "in the open field" without staff lines.

Origin of the Staff. Scribes began placing neumes above the text relative to highness and lowness of the melody. Then they used a ruled line for guidance. Gradually the line assumed meaning of actual pitch. Colored lines were later used (11th century): red for F, and yellow for C. Neumes thus began to record exact pitch.

More and more lines were added, up to ten or eleven lines. Eventually the middle C line was omitted, separating the treble from the bass registers and making the reading easier. Modern plainsong notation uses conventionalized neumes on a four-line staff.

Mensural Notation

Polyphonic music requires a system of notation conveying time values, so that various parts can keep together. This need gave rise to *mensural* (or measured) notation, which began around 1250 and was used until about 1600.

13th-Century Notation. In the 13th century, notation was dependent upon the rhythm of the text and upon the rhythmic modes (see page 12). Ternary rhythm prevailed. The system of notes employed is called *black mensural notation,* because the notes were all filled in. There were four kinds of notes used: (1) the *maxima* (▬), equal to two *longae* (▪ ▪), (2) the *longa* (▪), equal to three *breves* (▪ ▪ ▪), and (3) the *breve* (or brevis) (▪), equal to three *semibreves* (◆◆◆).

14th-Century Notation. The period from 1300 to about 1450 is characterized by great complexity in systems of notation, the rules of which varied with different localities and at different times. In this period duple and triple division of notes were recognized as equally important. Black notes, as before, indicated triple division (*perfect time*), while notes colored red indicated duple division (*imperfect time*). The relation of longa to breve was called *modus;* the relation of breve to semibreve was called *tempus;* and the relation of semibreve to minim was called *prolatio.* Each mensural relationship, then, could be either perfect (triple division of the larger note) or imperfect (duple division of the larger note).

15th- and 16th-Century Notation. The period from about 1450 to 1600 is characterized by the use of white instead of black notes. In most other respects the systems were essentially the same. In the 15th and 16th centuries only the tempus and prolatio relationships were used. Each of these was represented by a sign as shown in the following table.

Tempus perfectum: ◯ means   □ = ◇◇◇   (1 breve equals 3 semibreves).

Tempus imperfectum: ◖ means   □ = ◇◇   (1 breve equals 2 semibreves)

Prolatio major: •   means   ◇ = ♦♦♦   (1 semibreve equals 3 minims).

Prolatio minor: no dot means   ◇ = ◇◇   (1 semibreve equals 2 minims).

Thus, tempus and prolatio could be combined in the four following ways:

(1) ◉ means □ = ◇♦♦ ♦◇♦ ♦♦◇ (the equivalent of modern 9/8 time).

(2) ◯ means □ = ◇♦   ♦♦   ◇♦ (the equivalent of modern 3/4 time).

(3) ◖ means □ = ◇♦♦ ◇♦♦ (the equivalent of modern 6/8 time).

(4) ◖ means □ = ◇♦ ◇♦ (the equivalent of modern 4/4 time).

It will be observed that the last sign (C) is still employed today to indicate four-four time. Sometimes different signs were used simultaneously in different voices of a polyphonic composition. Mensural notation was further complicated by *ligatures* (combination of two or more notes into a single graph) which were subject to highly intricate rules, and by the use of *proportions* changing normal note values in arithmetic ratios. For example, the sign $\frac{3}{2}$ introduced in a part would mean that three notes of the following passage equal two notes of the preceding passage. Measure bar lines were not generally used until the 17th century.

Musical Score

A musical score means the writing of music for an ensemble so that all the parts are represented in vertical alignment. Simple scores were used in polyphonic music prior to 1225. Hence, organum, conductus, etc., were written down in this logical fashion. This practice was abandoned, however, with the advent of the 13th-century motet. In place of the score, the *choir-book* arrangement was adopted. This consisted of the parts being notated separately on one page or, more commonly, on two opposite pages. The following diagram illustrates the usual plan for a four-part polyphonic composition; the letters standing for soprano, tenor, alto, and bass, respectively:

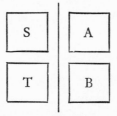

Choir books were used until about the middle of the 16th century. These were replaced by *part books*. This meant separate books for each individual part. Hence four-part polyphonic music would require four books, each including the particular part for several compositions. Finally, around the turn of the century, ensemble music again began to be written in score form. One of the first printed scores is a collection of madrigals by Cyprien de Rore (1577).

PART THREE

The Baroque Period (1600-1750)

CHAPTER X

General Considerations

General Historical Background. The century and a half between 1600 and 1750 was a period of colonization. The first half of the 17th century was dominated in Germany by religious, political wars known as the "Thirty Years' War" (1618–1648). The second half of the 17th century was dominated by the culture of Louis XIV of France (1643–1715) and his lavish court at Versailles. The principal names in science are Newton, Harvey, Galileo, Bacon, and Leibnitz. The leading thinker in the field of civil government is John Locke. The leading philosophers of the period are Descartes, Pascal, and Spinoza. In the field of literature there is an important array of English names: Milton, Dryden, Defoe, Addison, Swift, Pope, and Samuel Johnson. In France the principal literary names are Corneille, Racine, and Molière. The great names of baroque painting are Rembrandt, Rubens, Van Dyck, El Greco, and Velasquez.

THE MEANING OF BAROQUE. The painting, architecture, and music of this period are in general characterized by a certain spirit of theatricalism, of grandiose concepts, and by a rather heavy elaboration of design and magnificence of effect. Baroque spirit in general began in Italy as a result of the Catholic Counter Reformation which sought to impress the world and to re-establish the influence of the Church. Baroque style in the arts and music soon spread over all Europe and dominated the spirit of cultural creations.

General Characteristics of Baroque Music. The baroque spirit pervades the music of the period in the same ways it pervades the arts. It is manifest in large-scale productions, spectacular music, contrasts, and an over-all grandeur.

67

RELATIVE IMPORTANCE OF SACRED AND SECULAR MUSIC. Musical art, which in the polyphonic period had been developed largely by the Church, was in the Baroque period influenced more by nonecclesiastical bodies. The nobility and the upper classes everywhere took the greatest interest in music. Hence, secular music takes precedence over sacred music in the Baroque.

RELATIVE IMPORTANCE OF INSTRUMENTAL AND VOCAL MUSIC. Before 1600 vocal music predominates. In the Baroque period instrumental music comes into its own and may be said to be on a par with vocal music. An independent instrumental style is generally developed in this period.

NATIONAL SCHOOLS. Although not until the 19th century was there a conscious attempt to nationalize music, there was, nevertheless, in the Baroque period, a demarkation of national styles and schools more evident than before.

DRAMATIC ELEMENT. An important attribute of the baroque spirit, the dramatic element, is characteristic of much of the music of this period. It is manifest in the tremendous developments in opera, oratorio, and cantata. It even invaded and dominated the style of much church music.

HOMOPHONIC STYLE. In the early 17th century a new importance was attached to homophonic music. It dominated the whole period but it did not completely replace polyphonic music, which continued to develop to a new height, reached at the hands of J. S. Bach at the end of the period.

TONALITY. Clearer concepts of key feeling are apparent in the music of the Baroque. Major and minor as we know it today replace the old church modes. However, influence of the latter was to be felt throughout the period.

HARMONY. For the first time in music history attention to chord structure and chord progressions is evident. The harmonic or vertical approach to music tends to overshadow the older contrapuntal or horizontal approach. Chromaticism, the extensive use of altered tones, plays an important role in baroque harmony. It furnished a means of harmonic experimentation; it provided increased harmonic color, and, more than any other factor, it broke down modality.

FIGURED BASS. The characteristic importance of harmony in the Baroque period is reflected in an entirely new device, the *figured bass,* which is generally employed throughout the period. In fact, the entire Baroque period is sometimes referred to as the Figured Bass period. Figured bass is a sort of musical shorthand in which chords are indicated by placing numbers below the bass part played by a keyboard instrument. Its origin and development will be discussed in the following chapter.

NEW FORMS. Clarification of formal structure and more clearly defined formal concepts characterize the music of the Baroque period in comparison with that of the Renaissance. New forms are developed. The new instrumental forms of the Baroque are: the dance suite, the solo sonata, the trio sonata, the solo concerto, the concerto grosso, the overture, and the fugue. The latter is also a choral form. In vocal music the new forms are the aria, arioso, and accompanied solo song. Recitative, an innovation of the early 17th century, should be mentioned here, although it is more a style of dramatic declamation than a structural form. Three large vocal forms come into being in the Baroque: the opera, the oratorio, and the cantata. All three make use of the new ideas of the period: dramatic declamation (recitative), accompanied solo song (arias and ariosos), chorus and orchestra.

Important Composers. Further evidence of the growth of musical art is to be seen in the enormous increase in the number of first-rank composers.

ITALY. Claudio Monteverdi (1567-1643) wrote madrigals and operas. Alessandro Scarlatti (1660-1725) was the chief figure in Neapolitan opera. Domenico Scarlatti (1685-1757) wrote sonatas for keyboard. Arcangelo Corelli (1653-1713) and Antonio Vivaldi (c. 1680-1743) wrote chamber and concert music for strings.

FRANCE. Jean Baptiste Lully (c. 1632-1687) wrote opera and ballet. François Couperin (1668-1733) worked principally in the field of keyboard music. Jean Philippe Rameau (1683-1764) wrote operas, ballets, keyboard music, and he was the most important theorist of the period.

ENGLAND. Only one name of first rank belongs to England in this period. It is that of Henry Purcell (1658–1695), who wrote much fine dramatic music and instrumental music of various kinds. Because of his many years of creative activity in England, George Frederick Handel (Georg Friedrich Händel) is said to belong to the English school, although he was German by birth and Italian by training.

GERMANY. A long list of illustrious names comes from Germany, chiefly in the fields of instrumental and church music. Johann Hermann Schein (1586–1630) wrote keyboard music, as did Samuel Scheidt (1587–1654). The most important German composer of vocal music in the 17th century is Heinrich Schütz (1585–1672), who wrote choral music, cantatas, oratorios, and Passion music. Johann Jakob Froberger (1616–1667) wrote keyboard music. Michael Praetorius (1571–1621) wrote choral music in renaissance and baroque styles. Dietrich Buxtehude (1637–1707) and Johann Pachelbel (1653–1706) were the immediate predecessors of J. S. Bach in the fields of organ music and church cantatas. Finally, J. S. Bach (1685–1750) and George Frederick Handel (1685–1759) are the culminating figures of baroque music. Bach worked in the fields of church music and instrumental music, while Handel contributed principally to opera and oratorio (see Chapter XV).

CHAPTER XI

Nuove Musiche

THE term *nuove musiche*, meaning "new music," is used to apply to the revolutionary aspects of early 17th-century music that show a radical departure from the practices of the polyphonic period. The term originated from a collection of accompanied solo songs by Giulio Caccini, entitled *Nuove Musiche*, published in 1602.

Three Essentials of Nuove Musiche. The basic innovations of the early 17th-century revolt against polyphony dominated the entire period. (1) Perhaps the most revolutionary of the three innovations is the use of dramatic declamation in music, called *recitative*. Recitative follows the free rhythm of prose text. Its melodic line and accompaniment are of secondary importance. (2) The *solo song* (in connection with opera, called *aria*) is a homophonic vocal composition with accompaniment intended for performance by a lute or keyboard instrument, with or without additional instruments. In the nuove musiche period the solo songs, arias, and especially the recitatives had the simplest kind of chordal accompaniments. (3) The third essential innovation of the early 17 century is the *figured bass* (see page 72). It was used throughout the entire Baroque period for accompanied song and recitative, and for vocal and instrumental ensemble.

The Origin of Nuove Musiche. The "new music" of the early 17th century was a natural reaction against the old polyphonic art which had reached its culmination in the Renaissance. It represents a desire for new dramatic expressions.

THE FLORENTINE SCHOOL. Shortly before 1600 a group of noblemen in Florence, Italy, calling themselves the *Camerata*, began meeting for the purpose of reviving the art of Greek tragedy. But the result of their activities was the emergence of a new concept in music: opera and dramatic music. The Camerata was chiefly concerned with problems of appropriate dramatic declamation. The Florentine school avoided polyphonic treatment of any sort, made little use of the aria as such, and little use of the chorus. The important names connected with the Florentine movement are Giovanni Bardi, the patron and sponsor of the group; Vincenzo Galilei (the father of Galileo, the scientist), who made an early case against polyphony (1581), upholding the ideals of homophonic simplicity; Ottavio Rinuccini, a poet and librettist of the earliest extant opera, *Euridice;* Peri, a musician and the composer of *Euridice;* Giulio Caccini, the composer of *Nuove Musiche* and of operas; and Jacopo Corsi, nobleman and later patron of the Camerata.

The Figured Bass. The practice of using figures below the bass line to indicate harmony probably originated from a similar practice in the late 16th century known as *organ bass*. When an organ was used to accompany a polyphonic vocal composition it was necessary for the organist to make some sort of improvised score. To do this he used the bass or lowest-sounding part and inscribed numbers to indicate the harmonies produced by the other parts. It was only a step from this practice to the idea of originally indicating the harmonies of a composition by using figures (i.e., numerals, with sharp, flat, and natural signs to indicate alterations). The part in ensemble music which carries the figures is called *basso continuo* or *thorough-bass*. The basso continuo part was almost invariably performed by at least two instruments. A string bass instrument or a group of string basses would play the bass melody as written. A keyboard instrument, usually organ or harpsichord, would also play the same bass melody with the left hand, and with the right hand fill in the implied harmonies of the figured bass. This allowed considerable latitude to the keyboard artist, although there were elaborate rules as to how the figured bass should be *realized* (i.e., performed by filling in the parts). The improvisatory art of realizing a figured bass was highly developed in the baroque period and has since been lost.

Important Works of Nuove Musiche. An early opera, probably the earliest prototype of real opera, *Dafne*, written in 1597 by Rinuccini and Peri, has been lost. The work usually referred to as the earliest opera is *Euridice*, produced in 1600 by Rinuccini, Caccini, and Peri on the occasion of a festival for the wedding of Maria de' Medici and Henry IV of France. In the same year, 1600, an allegorical play by Cavalieri and Guidicioni called *La Rappresentazione di anima e di corpo* was presented. It is related to the origin of Roman oratorio and opera. Two additional operas of the period should be mentioned: *Orfeo* by Monteverdi (1607), and *Dafne* (1608), a lyrical tragedy by Gagliano. The most important early use of figured bass belongs to a collection of church pieces for from one to four voice parts with basso continuo, entitled *Cento concerti ecclesiastici* (1602) by Viadana. Finally, the collection of solo songs with figured bass accompaniment entitled *Nuove Musiche* by Caccini has been mentioned as one of the important works of the early 17th century.

RECORDS
    ARC 3035, 3036; HMS IV 25, 26a; MM 30; TEM 37.

SCORES
    HAM 182–185, 187; MM 30; SB 168–173, 175–177; TEM 37; WM 52, 53.

CHAPTER XII

Dramatic Music of the Baroque Period

THE forms and styles of nuove musiche were first conceived in Florence, where opera and other dramatic forms were born. These new ideas were soon taken up in other Italian cities and eventually spread over all of Europe.

Italian Opera Schools

Roman Opera. The innovations of the Florentine school (see page 71) were soon taken up by musicians in Rome, which was the second city to develop opera. Special features of opera in the Roman school are (1) the more extensive use of choruses, and (2) the use of comic scenes, called *intermezzi*, interpolated among the scenes of the serious drama. The latter feature is important in that it later led to Italian comic opera, called *opera buffa*.

COMPOSERS AND OPERAS. The principal composers and operas of the Roman School are Domenico Mazzochi, who wrote *La Catena d'Adone* (1626); Michel Angelo Rossi, who wrote *Erminia sul Giordano* (1637); Loreto Vittori, who wrote *La Galatea* (1639); Steffano Landi, who wrote *Santo Alessio* (an oratorio); and Luigi Rossi, who wrote another *Orfeo*.

Venetian Opera. The Venetian school, following the Roman school, flourished around the middle of the 17th century. It was in Venice that the first public opera was established (Teatro San Cassiano) in 1637. Venetian opera is characterized by considerable use of canzonas and popular tunes. There are short, singable melodies and fewer endless arias. The Venetian composers made use of instrumental pieces and instrumental sections within arias called *ritor-nelli*. They also wrote short overtures to operas in the style of fan-fares. In the Venetian school recitative and aria became completely distinct.

COMPOSERS AND OPERAS. The principal composers of the Venetian school are Francesco Cavalli (1602-1676), who wrote *Giasone;* Marc Antonio Cesti (1623-1669), who wrote *La Dori* and *Il Pomo d'oro;* and Giovanni Legrenzi (1626-1690), who wrote operas but was more important in church music and instrumental music.

MONTEVERDI. The greatest Italian musician of the first half of the 17th century is Claudio Monteverdi (1567-1643). He may be said to belong to the Venetian school of opera, but his contributions to music are such that special consideration needs to be given him. Monteverdi took up the innovations of the Florentines and devel-oped them, adding his own genius of dramatic expression. Monte-verdi had what may be called a dual style: (1) He retained the old contrapuntal styles of which he was a master throughout his life. He wrote many madrigals. (2) He also became a master of the new homophonic, dramatic style which he mastered equally well. His specific innovations in the instrumental field are the violin tremolo and the string pizzicato. Monteverdi's harmonies are radical and expressive. His important operas are *Orfeo* (1607); *Arianna* (1608), now lost except for the famous aria, "Lament"; *Il Combattimento di Tancredi e Clorinda* (1624), in which he made the first use of tremolo and pizzicato; *Il Ritorno d'Ulisse* (1641); and his last great opera, *L'Incoronazione di Poppea* (1642).

Neapolitan Opera. Naples was the last of the Italian cities to de-velop opera, late in the 17th century, but this school came to dom-inate opera not only in Italy but everywhere in Europe. The Neapoli-tan school developed a sense of musical form rather than dramatic truth. The principal musical form of the school is the *da capo aria* which follows a simple ternary plan, represented by the structural formula, *A B A,* i.e., a section, a contrasting section, and a return to the first section with embellishment. The melodic style of the Neapolitan school is characterized by vocal embellishment, florid writing, and coloratura, much of which was improvised by the singer. In addition to the ornamental melodic style, virtuosity was of great importance to the Neapolitans. Excess of display of technique over dramatic truth led to a decline of operatic art and to the reforms of Gluck in the 18th century. Hand-in-hand with the love for virtuosity were the *castrati* (male altos and sopranos), who were the stars of the day and whose vocal pyrotechnics were of more interest to the public than the opera itself. The Neapolitans made little use of the chorus.

ITALIAN OVERTURE. A final contribution of the Neapolitan school was the new form of overture, called *sinfonia*. It consists of three movements, the first fast, with strong rhythm, and in canzona style. The second movement is slow, short, and usually thordal in style. The third movement is again fast and usually dance-like.

COMPOSERS AND OPERAS. Francesco Provenzale (d. 1704) is considered the founder of the Neapolitan school. The greatest figure is Alessandro Scarlatti (1660–1725), whose principal operas are *La Rosaura* (c. 1690), *Teodora* (1693), *Tigrane* (1715), and *Griselda* (1721). In addition to operas Scarlatti wrote some six hundred cantatas, a hundred and fifty oratorios, and a great quantity of church music.

French Opera and Ballet

Italian opera spread to France and flourished there before an indigenous French opera appeared. Luigi Rossi's *Orfeo* was one of the first to be performed in Paris (1647). In the second half of the 17th century French opera came into its own with the works of Cambert and Lully.

Characteristics of French Opera. French opera was dominated by the classical tragedy of Corneille and Racine. The high quality of poetry and the greater importance of the drama are considerable features of French opera. There is more importance of melody and of dramatic expression in recitative as well as in aria. French opera made more use of short airs than of extended and elaborate arias. The French predilection for the dance is shown in the use of chaconnes, bourées, menuets, gavottes, etc. In the 17th century there was much use of fantastic stage machinery. In general the French made greater use of instrumental music in their operas. Five-part string orchestration characterizes the instrumental music of the French baroque opera.

FRENCH OVERTURE. French opera under Lully developed a special overture. The first movement is in a slow, stately style and is especially characterized by the use of dotted rhythms. The second movement is fast, lively, and fugal. The third movement, which was not always used, returns to the plan of the first movement. This form was employed outside of France, and even as a form separate from opera. Bach used it extensively, as did Handel (e.g., the overture to the *Messiah*).

BALLET. Court dances with costume and scenery but without singing or spoken dialogue were common in the Burgundian and French courts of the 15th century. The earliest extant music for ballet is that of the *Ballet comique de la reine* (1581). The highest development of ballet was reached in the Baroque period in the Versailles Court of Louis XIV. Royalty often participated in these, as did Louis XIV. One of the most important court ballets (*ballet de cour*) was the *Ballet de la nuit* (1653) by Lully. Later, Lully and Molière collaborated to create the *comédie-ballet,* a combination of play and ballet. *Le Bourgeois gentilhomme* (1670) is perhaps the most famous of these. Later, Lully introduced ballets into his operas and called these productions *tragédies,* or *opéra-ballets. Armide* and *Cadmus et Hermione* are examples of this type of opera.

COMPOSERS AND LIBRETTISTS. The first opera in the French language was called *Pastorale,* written by Abbé Pierre Perrin (librettist) and Robert Cambert (composer) in 1659. This is of additional interest because it marks the opening of the Académie Royale de Musique, an institution in Paris that still lives as the Grand Opera. Jean Baptiste Lully (1632–1687) is the most important composer of French opera in the 17th century. His librettist was Philippe Quinault. Jean Philippe Rameau (1683–1764) carried on the great traditions of ballet and opera established by Lully. His principal operas are *Hippolyte et Aricie* (1733) and *Castor et Pollux* (1737).

Opera in Germany

During the Baroque period there was very little indigenous opera in Germany. This was principally because of the tremendous impact of Italian opera, but in part also because of the disruption of the Thirty Years' War. Furthermore, there was a dearth of libretto literature of any quality.

Italian Opera in Germany. Aside from an early opera by Heinrich Schütz, *Daphne* (1627), now lost, nearly all operatic activity in Germany consisted of Italian operas performed by Italian companies. Even German composers were content to write in the Italian style and to Italian texts. Some of these composers are Fux, Hasse, and, later, Gluck and Mozart. The principal cities in Germany where opera flourished were Vienna, Munich, and Dresden. In Hamburg the first German opera began. An opera house opened in 1678 with Johann Theile's *Adam und Eva.* The most important names connected with Hamburg are Georg Philipp Telemann (1681–1767) and Reinhard Keiser (1674–1739).

Opera and Dramatic Music in England

Similar to the situation in Germany, there was very little real English opera in the Baroque period. The first genuine opera in English is John Blow's *Venus and Adonis* (c. 1685). The only great figure in English opera is Henry Purcell who wrote *Dido and Aeneas* (c. 1689).

Types of Dramatic Music in England. In addition to Italian opera which flourished in England as it did on the Continent, there were certain types of dramatic production that tended to take the place of opera.

MASQUE. The *masque* is a dramatic form of entertainment produced for the nobility, based upon an allegorical or mythological subject, and consisting of poetry, vocal and instrumental music, scenery, stage machinery, costumes, and dancing. Famous literary names connected with writing of masques are Ben Jonson and John Milton. Henry Lawes wrote the music to Milton's masque *Comus.* Other composers of masques are John Blow, Matthew Locke, William Lawes, and Henry Purcell. *Acis and Galatea* (c. 1720) is a famous masque by Handel.

BALLAD OPERA. In the second quarter of the 18th century there arose in England a type of comic opera, known as *ballad opera*. These were parody operas burlesquing the mannerisms of Italian grand opera. They were composed by setting words to already existing popular tunes or folk songs. Heroic characters of grand opera were replaced by beggars, thieves, pickpockets, prostitutes, etc. The best-known example of ballad opera is *The Beggar's Opera* by Gay and Pepusch (1728). The popularity of ballad opera in England, lasting throughout the century, had much to do with Handel's failures in his productions of Italian opera in England.

INCIDENTAL AND ENTR'ACTE MUSIC. English composers were fond of writing music to go with already existing plays. *Incidental music* was composed as background or atmosphere music used during the action of a play. Examples of incidental music are Purcell's *The Fairy Queen* and *King Arthur*. *Entr'acte music* was composed for performance between the scenes and acts of a play. Examples of entr'acte music (often called *act-tunes* or *curtain tunes*) are Matthew Locke's *Instrumental Musick Used in "The Tempest,"* Henry Purcell's *Dioclesian* and *Collection of Ayres Composed for the Theatre*.

Comic Opera

Early in the 18th century a new type of opera began to appear in various forms in Europe and England. The type is referred to generally as comic opera, although it should be noted that the humorous element is not necessarily prominent.

General Characteristics of Comic Opera. Comic opera in general differs from serious opera in several respects. (1) Light, frivolous, often humorous subjects are used. (2) Commonplace characters replace exalted personages of serious opera. (3) Spoken dialogue replaces lengthy recitatives of serious opera. (4) Light, popular melody instead of heavy dramatic arias is characteristic. (5) On the whole the use of chorus is more important in comic opera. Choral finales are usually employed. (6) Comic opera often takes on the nature of parody: parody of character, or frivolous tunes set to words of a well-known serious aria, or frivolous words set to the melody of a well-known aria of a serious opera.

Types of Comic Opera. In Italy, France, Germany, and England comic opera had somewhat different origins and developed along somewhat different lines.

ITALIAN OPERA BUFFA. Comic opera in Italy is called *opera buffa*. Its origin was in the comic intermezzi used between acts of serious opera. Early in the 18th century it emerged as a separate form in Naples. Its popularity as entertainment increased throughout the century. It is generally characterized by full chorus finales, popular tunes, lively action, and witty dialogue. An example of opera buffa is *La Serva padrona* by Pergolesi (1733). Other composers of buffa opera are Logroscino, Paisiello, Cimarosa, Piccini, Galuppi, and Mozart.

FRENCH OPÉRA-COMIQUE. In France comic opera originated in the early 18th century as a farce, satire, parody on serious opera. Short satirical poems sung to already existing popular airs, called *vaudevilles*, were commonly employed. Poets of early parody opera in France are Lesage and Favart. Composers of opéra-comique are Duni, Jean Jacques Rousseau (*Le Devin du village*), Philidor, Monsigny, and Grétry.

BALLAD OPERA. The English counterpart of comic opera on the Continent is the ballad opera (discussed on page 79).

GERMAN SINGSPIEL. The term *Singspiel* (drama with music) was at first used for serious and comic opera alike. Later it came to designate comic opera. Singspiel began as an offshoot of English ballad opera. Coffey's ballad opera *The Devil to Pay* was translated into German and set to new music by Standfuss about 1750. Principal developments of Singspiel took place in the second half of the 18th century. The most important composers are Johann Adam Hiller (1728–1804) and Mozart.

Oratorio, Cantata, Passion

Along with opera, other important dramatic forms developed from the innovations of nuove musiche. They are oratorio, cantata, and Passion.

Definitions. *Oratorio* is a dramatic production on a large scale, usually dealing with a Biblical subject, and produced without staging, costuming, or scenery. Oratorio makes use of a narrator, vocal soloists, chorus, and orchestra. The forms used in oratorio are overture, aria, recitative, and diverse choral ensembles. The *cantata* is similar to the oratorio except that it is a short, lyric form. It deals with varied subject matter, either religious or secular. Cantatas are written for a small number of performers, often limited to soloists with few accompanying instruments. A special dramatic form is the *Passion* which is a dramatic presentation of the story of Easter (see page 82).

Oratorio. Early prototypes of the oratorio are to be found in the liturgical dramas of the late Middle Ages and in the miracle plays and mystery plays of the 14th and 15th centuries. Music in some form was usually employed in these early religious dramas, which were based upon scenes from the Bible, hagiology, and allegory. Late in the 16th century, under the leadership of Saint Philip Neri (d. 1595), a group of Romans, calling themselves *Oratorians,* congregated for quasi-evangelical meetings. Among other things they sang laudi spirituali and performed religious allegorical or morality plays which included dialogue-laudi performed by different groups of singers. This movement gave rise to the oratorio proper. One of these allegorical plays is *La Rappresentazione di anima e di corpo* (1600) by Emilio Cavalieri (c. 1550–1602). It makes use of all the innovations of nuove musiche.

Two Types of Oratorio. In the 17th century there were two types of oratorio: (1) *Oratorio Latino* was based upon a Biblical text and was sung in Latin. Oratorio Latino was real church music. (2) *Oratorio volgare* was based upon a free text, was sung in Italian, and tended toward a more secular approach. The distinction between these two types disappeared in the late Baroque.

Composers and Oratorios. Steffano Landi wrote *Il Santo Alessio* (1632). Giacomo Carissimi (1605–1674) wrote *Jephtha*. Carissimi may be said to have established the true oratorio form and style in the Roman oratorio of the 17th century. One of Alessandro Scarlatti's important oratorios is *I Dolori di Maria sempre vergine* (1693). The most important contributions to German oratorio in the 17th century are Heinrich Schütz's *Historia der Auferstehung* ("Story of Resurrection," 1623) and *Die sieben Worte Jesu Christi am Kreuz* ("Seven Last Words," c. 1645), both in the nature of Passion music. Undoubtedly the most important composer of oratorio in the entire Baroque period is Handel. The following are the characteristics of his oratorios: (1) They have an "earthy" quality, less worshipful than similar works by Schütz and Bach. (2) Handel wrote imposing choruses. (3) Biblical history and decorous love interest are to be found in most of Handel's oratorios. (4) Operatic influence on Handel's oratorios is to be found in his use of three acts instead of the conventional two acts of oratorio. The famous *Messiah* (1741) is a special case in that it is reflective rather than narrative. Some of Handel's oratorios are *Athalia, Semele, Samson, Israel in Egypt, Belshazzar, Judas Maccabaeus,* and *Solomon.*

Cantata. The cantata, a third product of nuove musiche, in its earliest form was a musical recitative or short drama in verse, without action, and with a simple accompaniment of one instrument.

SECULAR CANTATA. Secular cantata (*cantata da camera* in Italy, *Kammerkantate* in Germany) was developed before sacred cantata. It predominates in the 17th century, especially in Italy. The most important composers in Italy are: Carissimi, Cesti, A. Scarlatti, and Stradella. In France the leading composers are Charpentier, Campra, Bernier, Clérambault, and Rameau.

CHURCH CANTATA. The church cantata (called *cantata da chiesa* in Italy, *Kirchenkantate* in Germany) developed later than the secular cantata and mostly in Germany. It had an important function in connection with the Lutheran service. It makes use of soloists and instrumental sections and sometimes chorus. Also important to the church cantata is the use of chorale melody and text. This type of cantata, then, belongs to the category of church music. The principal composers of church cantatas are Schütz, Buxtehude, Telemann, Kuhnau, and J. S. Bach.

Passion Music. Presentation of the story of Easter according to the gospels of St. Matthew, St. Mark, St. Luke, and St. John has a long history, going back into the early Christian era. Five stages in its development can be traced.

GOSPEL RECITATION. From about 300 A.D. to 1100 it was common practice in the Church to have the gospels of the Evangelists recited during Holy Week.

PLAINSONG PASSION. In the 12th century the Passion story was presented as a sort of play in which the part of Christ was sung in a low register by a priest, the part of the Evangelist or narrator was sung in a middle register by another priest, and the part of the crowd (*turba*) was sung in a high register by still another priest. Most of this was done in a psalmodic style, except for the words of Christ, "Eli, Eli, lama sabachthani," which were given a more expressive melody.

POLYPHONIC PASSION. In the Renaissance period composers began using polyphonic settings of the story, at first setting only the exclamations of the turba, in a motet style. One of the earliest of these was a setting of the St. Matthew gospel by A. Longueval in the late 15th century. Polyphonic Passions were composed by most of the 16th-century masters, including Palestrina.

ORATORIO PASSION. With the advent of the 17th century and the nuove musiche styles the presentation of the Passion story was inevitably affected. Recitative for the Evangelist and other principal characters was then employed, as were also chorus, orchestra, and arias. The basic gospel story was adhered to but free texts were also interpolated.

CHORALE PASSION. The importance of the chorale in the Lutheran service was bound to affect settings of the Passion. Early in the 18th century Protestant chorales were added as reflective elements in the narrative of the Easter story. In Bach's *St. Matthew Passion,* four-part harmonizations of chorales are used reflectively throughout the work, especially the famous "Passion Chorale" by Hassler ("O Sacred Head").

Accompanied Solo Song

In addition to the late-Renaissance lute songs of Spain and England, the accompanied monodies and solo madrigals in Italy, and the "airs" from operas, oratorios, and cantatas, the solo song with continuo accompaniment developed throughout the baroque period, principally in Germany. This category of music is more lyric than dramatic. The leading composers in this field were Heinrich Albert (1604–1651), Andreas Hammerschmidt (1611–1675), Adam Krieger (1634–1666), Philipp Heinrich Erlebach (1657–1714), John Blow (1647–1708), and Henry Purcell (1659–1695).

RECORDS

Italian Opera

ARC 3035, 3036, 3039; HMS IV 25, 26, V 1–6; MM 31, 44; TEM 50; 2000YM 18; Monteverdi, *Combattimento di Tancredi e Clorinda:* Period 551. Monteverdi, *Lamento d'Arianna:* Angel 35667. Alessandro Scarlatti, *Trionfo dell' Onore:* Cetra 1223. Pergolesi, *La Serva Padrona:* Victor LM 2321. Pergolesi, *The Music Master:* Westminster 18262.

French Opera

HMS V 7, 8; MM 41. Lully, operatic arias: Lyrichord 16. Rameau, *Diane et Acteon* and *L'Impatience:* Lyrichord 44. Rameau, *Platée:* Pathé DTX 223/4. Rameau, operatic excerpts: Decca 9683.

English Dramatic Music

HMS V 9; *Beggar's Opera:* 2 Westminster OPW 1201; Purcell, *Dido and Aeneas:* Period 546; *Fairy Queen:* 3 Oiseau-Lyre 50139–41; *King Arthur:* Oiseau-Lyre 50176/7; *Ode for St. Cecilia's Day:* Bach 559; songs from *The Tempest* and *Dioclesian:* Oiseau-Lyre 600021.

German Opera

HMS V 10; TEM 46.

Oratorio, Cantata, Passion

ARC 3005, 3006, 3008, 3011, 3123; HMS II 8 (medieval liturgical drama), V 11, 12, 18, 21, 22, VI 2, 3; MM 32, 45, 46, 48, 49; TEM 5 (medieval liturgical drama), 37, 42, 49. Carissimi, *Judicium Extremum; Suscitavit Dominus; Militia est Vita Hominis:* Westminster 18835. Schütz, *St. John Passion: Renaissance* X–26; *St. Matthew Passion:* Westminster 18590. Handel, *Belshazzar:* Bach 534/5; *Israel in Egypt:* Angel 3550–B; *Judas Maccabaeus:* Westminster 3310; *Messiah:* London Z4403.

SCORES

Italian Opera

HAM 187, 189, 206, 208, 209, 221–223, 259, 262, 286, 300; MM 31, 44; SB 171, 175, 177, 178, 199–204, 223, 224, 226, 227, 231, 258, 259, 278, 298; TEM 50.

French Opera

HAM 223–225, 276, 291; MM 41; SB 222, 232–234, 261, 296, 298.

English Dramatic Music

HAM 204, 243, 255, 264; SB 247, 281.

German Opera

HAM 228, 267, 282; SB 195, 236, 250, 266, 268, 269, 293, 309; TEM 46.

Oratorio, Cantata, Passion

HAM 183, 201, 203, 207, 214, 218, 226, 235, 254, 258, 266, 272, 279, 281; MM 32, 45, 46, 48, 49; SB 169, 170, 180, 191, 192, 197, 198, 212, 225, 230, 242, 260, 267, 280, 284, 308; TEM 5 (medieval liturgical drama), 37, 42, 49.

Solo Song

HAM 184, 205, 228, 254; MM 30; SB 172, 173, 193, 194, 197, 209a, 210, 211, 217, 235, 256, 262, 288, 289, 299, 300; WM 49, 50, 51, 63–66.

CHAPTER XIII

Church Music of the Baroque Period

Pʀɪᴏʀ to 1600 church music was largely vocal. In the Baroque, however, the use of instruments became important and separate instrumental forms for church performance, such as the church sonata for strings and organ and the chorale prelude for organ, were used. These will be considered separately in the chapter on baroque instrumental music. The distinction between religious music and liturgical church music should also be pointed out: the oratorio was usually based upon religious subjects but it was not generally intended for performance in church services. The German cantatas, on the other hand, were expressly written for performance in the Lutheran service and are therefore real church music.

General Characteristics of Baroque Church Music. The nuove musiche styles permeated nearly all church music. There was a general abandonment of the renaissance *a cappella* choral style. In its place we find the use of soloists, figured bass accompaniment (basso continuo) and a large use of independent instrumental material: introductions, interludes, ritornelli, etc. Furthermore, there was a general prevalence of the characteristic dramatic style of the new music. The church music of the Baroque was more generally in the vernacular language (French, Italian, German, etc.), replacing the almost universal use of Latin in the Renaissance. The old church modes were abandoned for major and minor keys. Chromaticism was widely used. The pure *a cappella* style of the Renaissance was not completely abandoned, however. The Roman school continued the traditions of Palestrina well into the 17th century. The Sistine

Chapel in Rome was particularly strict in keeping alive the worshipful, nondramatic style of church polyphony.

Principal Schools and Composers. Whereas in the Renaissance,
church music had an almost universal style, in the Baroque there is
a sharper distinction of nationalistic styles.

ITALIAN CHURCH MUSIC. It has been pointed out above that much
of the renaissance tradition was kept alive in Italy. But Italy was
also the birthplace of nuove musiche, and so this naturally affected
much of the church music written there. Viadana's *Cento concerti
ecclesiastici* was the first important collection of church music in
the Baroque. Church music was composed by most of the operatic
composers of the period: Carissimi, Monteverdi, Cavalli, Legrenzi,
A. Scarlatti, etc. Francesco Durante (1684–1755) was almost exclusively a church composer. Mention should be made of a cantata-
like work by Pergolesi, *Stabat Mater* (c. 1730), sung to a Latin text.
This work may be taken as an example of the fine church music
written in Italy in the Baroque. Another work, a fifty-three-voice
Mass (1628) by Orazio Benevoli, which makes use of vocal and
instrumental choirs, is a continuation and expansion of the Venetian
technique, and it represents very well the baroque ideals of the
grandiose and magnificent.

FRENCH CHURCH MUSIC. French church music of the Baroque is
on the whole rather superficial. It, too, conformed to the new styles
in music. Cantata-like forms, called "motets," were written. These
used soloists, chorus, and orchestral accompaniment. The most important French church composers of the Baroque are Lully, who
retained the *a cappella* style of writing, Charpentier, Campra, La-
lande, and Rameau.

GERMAN CHURCH MUSIC. The nuove musiche techniques were
employed in Germany in various forms in the 17th century. There
was a general tendency, however, toward a crystallization in the
church cantata, which was fairly standardized by Bach's time. The
German church cantatas make extensive use of chorale melodies,
and employ soloists, chorus, and orchestral accompaniments with
basso continuo. The most important figure in German church music in the 17th century is Heinrich Schütz. His music incorporates

the old Venetian style and the new dramatic forms of the period; in this respect Schütz resembles Monteverdi. Schütz wrote many cantata-like forms called *Cantiones sacrae, Geistliche Gesaenge, Symphoniae sacrae,* and *Geistliche Konzerte.* The most important composers between Schütz and Bach are Tunder, Weckmann, Fux, Buxtehude, Telemann, and Kuhnau.

ENGLISH CHURCH MUSIC. The English composers of the Restoration continued to use the verse anthem as the principal form in the Anglican Church. It became more lengthy and more cantata-like, taking on the general aspects of nuove musiche. The hallelujah chorus, usually as the finale, was quite common. The principal composers are John Blow and Henry Purcell.

RECORDS
   Italian Church Music
   ARC 3091; HMS V 14.

   French Church Music
   ARC 3097; HMS V 13.ᐟ

   German Church Music
   ARC 3040, 3041, 3096, 3098, 3103, 3108, 3122, 3133; HMS V 17,
      19, 20, 23, 24; MM 33; TEM 38; 2000YM 19, 20.

   English Church Music
   ARC 3038, 3133; HMS V 15, 16; TEM 43.

SCORES
   Italian Church Music
   HAM 185; SB 159, 168, 273, 275.

   French Church Music
   HAM 226, 257, 266.

   German Church Music
   HAM 201, 202, 213, 218, 235, 272; MM 33; SB 161–163, 189, 190,
      212, 271, 284; TEM 38.

   English Church Music
   HAM 242, 268, 279; SB 246; TEM 43.

CHAPTER XIV

Instrumental Music of the Baroque Period

INSTRUMENTAL music rivals vocal music for the first time in the Baroque. Its importance is seen in the development of new instrumental forms and new independent instrumental styles, in the improvement of instruments, and in the greater amount of instrumental music written.

General Considerations

Instruments of the Baroque Period. With a few exceptions, most of the instruments used in the Renaissance period were still used throughout the Baroque; there were some important improvements in instruments but no new instruments were invented.

KEYBOARD INSTRUMENTS. The harpsichord was the most important keyboard instrument of the period. It usually had two *manuals* (i.e., two keyboards). Its basis of tone production is the string plucked mechanically by a quill when the key is depressed. The harpsichord was used for basso continuo parts as well as for solo forms. The clavichord has a weak, delicate tone, and was used only in small rooms. Its tone is produced by a string struck by a tangent when the key is depressed. The organ was still inseparably connected with church music. In the Baroque period its mechanism was greatly improved, and the literature for organ increased proportionately.

STRING INSTRUMENTS. In the late Baroque the violin was added to, but did not replace, the older viol instruments. A distinct violin idiom was developed, particularly by the Italians. The bowed instru-

ments were used for both solo and ensemble music. The lute became less important as an instrumental medium in the late 17th
century, but production of lute literature continued throughout
the Baroque period.

WIND INSTRUMENTS. The oboe and the bassoon (double-reed woodwinds) were the standard wind instruments in the Baroque. The
clarinet and the English horn did not appear in general orchestral
usage until about the 19th century. The French horn, or hunting
horn, was commonly employed. It was without valves until the 19th
century. Instruments of the trumpet and trombone class were not
yet standardized in the Baroque, and the former were also limited
to the natural overtones. In the late Baroque the transverse flute
superseded the recorder type of instruments.

General Characteristics of Baroque Instrumental Music. (1) A
distinct instrumental style was developed. (2) Many new instrumental forms appeared. (3) Instrumental virtuosity was an important feature of style. (4) On the whole, instrumental music tended
to be more polyphonic than homophonic. (5) Instrumentation for
ensemble music was still far from becoming standardized, but
strings predominated and the harpsichord or organ was consistently employed for the basso continuo part. (6) The bass is more
prominent in instrumental music of the Baroque than in any other
period. It functions both as harmonic bass and contrapuntal (i.e.,
melodic) bass. (7) Late in the Baroque period *equal-tempered tuning* of keyboard instruments (i.e., division of the octave into twelve
equi-distant tones—the modern system) replaced the older *just in-
tonation* (i.e., tuning in perfect fifths, resulting in unequal half-steps
in the octave).

Lute Music

Lute music in the Baroque was less extensive and less important
on the whole than it had been in the Renaissance. It persisted mainly
in France and Germany. In Italy and Spain popular guitar music
took the place of the sophisticated art music for the lute. The lute
literature of the 17th century consists mainly of preludes and stylized dances and dance suites. The most important composers of

17th-century lute music are Denis Gaultier (d. 1672) in France, and Reusner and Weiss in Germany. J. S. Bach wrote a few pieces for lute.

Harpsichord Music

Forms. The distinction between harpsichord forms and styles on the one hand and those of the organ on the other became more marked in the 17th century, but there was still a good deal of overlapping. In general, harpsichord music was secular, whereas organ music was largely in the realm of church music.

DANCE SUITE. Groups of stylized dances (i.e., nonfunctional dance music), called *suites,* began to be written around the middle of the 17th century. They evolved from the 16th-century dance pairs (bassedanse and tourdion, pavane and galliard, etc.). The style of the baroque suite in general is contrapuntal, usually limited to two or three parts. Ornamentation is particularly characteristic of harpsichord dances. There are four standard dances of the suite: *allemande, courante, sarabande,* and *gigue.* In addition to these, various optional dances are included in the suite.

a. *Allemande.* The allemande is usually moderately fast, in duple time. It usually begins with an eighth-note or sixteenth-note pickup.

b. *Courante.* The courante of the dance suite is in triple meter, a combination of three-two and six-four meter. It also uses the pickup note and frequent dotted rhythms.

c. *Sarabande.* The third basic movement of the suite, the sarabande, is in slow, triple time. It makes use of the dotted rhythms: ♩.♩ ♩ and ♩ ♩.♩.

d. *Gigue.* The last movement of the dance suite is the gigue. It is in lively six-eight or nine-eight time and in a fugal style (i.e., making use of imitation). Often the theme in the second half is an inversion of the opening thematic material.

e. *Optional Dances.* Most of the optional dances employed in the baroque suite originated in the French ballets of the late 17th century. In the Bach suites they usually appear between the sarabande and the gigue. The suite of the late Baroque often begins with a prelude. The optional dances are: *gavotte,* a dance in four-four time, beginning phrases on the third beat of the measure; *bourrée,* a dance in four-four time, as a rule beginning on the fourth beat; *menuet* in three-four time; *loure, air, polonaise, rigaudon,* and *passepied.*

f. *Structure of Dance Movements.* The conventional structure of the dance movements is *binary,* i.e., in two sections. The first section, ending with a double bar and repeat sign, modulates to the dominant key (a fifth above the tonic key) or if the suite is in a minor key it modulates to the relative major key (a minor third above the tonic key). The second half of the dance movement modulates from the contrasting key back to the tonic key, and it also concludes with a double-bar repeat.

SONATA. In the Baroque period the term "sonata" was used for various keyboard pieces as well as for other instrumental music. This term should not be confused with the later classical sonata form. No clear or consistent structural principles were established. The principal composer of baroque keyboard sonatas is Domenico Scarlatti (1685–1757), who wrote virtuosic pieces called *esercizii* (exercises).

VARIATION FORMS. Different types of variations continued to be popular in baroque keyboard music. These are the *partita* (a term also applied to the dance suite), the *chaconne,* the *passacaglia,* and the *ground.*

DESCRIPTIVE PIECES. The use of descriptive titles for various kinds of music was commonly employed. Such music attempts some sort of word painting, or imitation of sounds. The "Combat between David and Goliath" in Kuhnau's *Biblical Sonatas,* and Rameau's "La Poule" ("The Hen") are examples of descriptive keyboard music. In baroque keyboard and lute music one often runs across the title *Tombeau* (Fr. "Tombstone"). Such pieces, intended as eulogy for some famous deceased person, are of a decidedly expressive character.

PRELUDE AND FUGUE. Pieces in various free styles and forms, called preludes, were often combined with the strict fugue in the late 17th and first half of the 18th centuries. The prelude-fugue combination was more common in organ literature than in harpsichord music. The most important collection of preludes and fugues for the harpsichord is J. S. Bach's *Well-Tempered Clavier (Das wohltempe-*

rierte Clavier). It consists of two sets of 24 preludes and fugues in all keys, major and minor, illustrating the advantages of the new equal-tempered tuning. The term "clavichord" in this case was probably meant to imply any keyboard instrument.

MISCELLANEOUS FORMS. In addition to the principal forms of keyboard music listed above, such terms as "toccata," "prelude," and "fantasia," and various dance forms are to be found.

Schools and Composers. The most important schools of harpsichord music were in Italy, France, and Germany.

ITALY. In the first half of the 17th century the most important names in Italian keyboard music are Trabaci, Valente, and Girolamo Frescobaldi (1583–1643). The latter wrote outstanding variations (called "partitas") for the *cembalo* (Italian harpsichord). In the second half of the 17th century Bernardo Pasquini composed toccatas, suites, and sonatas. The most important Italian keyboard composer of the Baroque is Domenico Scarlatti (1685–1757), a contemporary of J. S. Bach. He wrote virtuosic, one-movement sonatas, usually binary in form, and displaying all sorts of scale and arpeggio figuration with characteristic repetition of short phrases or figures. Figuration is more important than counterpoint in Scarlatti's sonatas.

FRANCE. Jacques Champion de Chambonnières (c. 1602–1672) was the first important composer in the French school of *clavecin* music (French harpsichord). Henri d'Anglebert (1635–1691) was a pupil of Chambonnières. François Couperin (1668–1733) is perhaps the most important composer of baroque harpsichord music. He wrote suites (called *ordres*) and many descriptive pieces. The French school reaches its culmination with Jean Philippe Rameau (1683–1764). In general, the French clavecin school is characterized by a fondness for dance pieces and descriptive music, for rich ornamentation, characterization, and dramatic surprise. The French school considerably influenced the harpsichord style of the German school, particularly that of Bach's keyboard music.

GERMANY. Johann Jakob Froberger (1616–1667), a pupil of Frescobaldi, was largely instrumental in establishing the order of the suite movements. His keyboard music shows further development of the Frescobaldi trait of freely adding or taking away contrapuntal parts and filling in chords (*Freistimmigkeit*). J. K. F. Fischer (1650–1746) wrote a collection of preludes and fugues in all keys, called *Ariadne musica* (1715), possibly for organ. Johann Kuhnau (1660-1722) wrote keyboard sonatas of a descriptive nature. J. S. Bach wrote suites (sometimes called partitas), preludes and fugues for the harpsichord.

ENGLAND. The two principal composers of baroque harpsichord music in England are Henry Purcell (1658-1695), who wrote numerous suites and single dance pieces and grounds, and Handel, who wrote suites and a few fugues for harpsichord.

Organ Music

Forms. Organ music, which is generally vocal in style in the Renaissance, becomes more idiomatic and more instrumental in the Baroque. Four main categories of organ forms are: (1) free forms, (2) fugal forms, (3) chorale prelude forms, and (4) variation forms.

FREE FORMS. This classification includes a wide variety of styles and involves no standard structural principles. The baroque *toccata* is characterized by a display of virtuosic material (rapid scales, arpeggios, broken chords, etc.), the use of full chordal sections, and the use of polyphonic sections or *fughettas*. The toccata is usually in a free rhythm and has a rhapsodic character, especially in North Germany (Buxtehude and Bach). Special types of toccatas are to be found in the *perpetuum mobile* style, which consists of rapid, consistent, étude-like material, and in the *liturgical toccata*, which is a short prelude in a restrained, dignified style. The *fantasia* or *fantasy* is similar to the toccata in its indeterminate, free, improvisatory style. It is usually less virtuosic than the toccata, often more polyphonic. The *prelude* also includes a wide range of styles and structures. It is usually shorter than the fantasia and the toccata, and frequently precedes a fugue. The *capriccio* in the 17th century is more contrapuntal, more fugal than the others. It is often based on a pre-existing theme. Because of its decidedly contrapuntal nature, the capriccio is sometimes considered as one of the ancestors of the fugue.

FUGAL FORMS. Although imitative counterpoint is employed in many forms in the Baroque, there are three forms which are primarily based upon imitation: the *ricercare* (see page 54), the *canzona* (see page 54), and the *fugue*. The fugue emerges in the second half of the 17th century. It differs from the ricercare and canzona chiefly in its monothematic basis and its economy of material derived from the subject. A fugue subject may resemble the lively canzona style or the slow ricercare style. The fugue gradually replaced the canzona and the ricercare in the late Baroque period.

CHORALE PRELUDE. The chorale prelude is essentially a cantus firmus type of composition, based upon a chorale melody or sometimes a plainsong. Six types of chorale prelude can be distinguished.

a. *Simple Cantus Firmus Treatment.* When the chorale melody is stated in long notes against a faster-moving counterpoint the chorale prelude belongs to the simple cantus firmus type.

b. *Coloration.* When the original chorale melody is highly ornamented by melismatic treatment this is called coloration and constitutes an important style in chorale prelude writing.

c. *Fugal Chorale.* When fragments of the chorale melody are used imitatively the chorale prelude belongs to the fugal type.

d. *Trio Chorale.* When three distinct polyphonic parts are used (one for each of two hands and pedals), this is designated as a trio type of chorale prelude. The material is derived from the original chorale melody.

e. *Chorale Variations.* This type consists of polyphonic variations on the chorale melody, which is then somewhat altered.

f. *Chorale Fantasy.* Free, rhapsodic use of material derived from the chorale melody is sometimes made. This type, as well as the fugal and trio types, is not strictly a cantus firmus composition because the chorale melody is not continuous throughout.

VARIATIONS FOR ORGAN. In addition to chorale variations, other terms indiscriminately applied to variations are *passacaglia, chaconne,* and *ground* (English). These are all continuous variations based either upon a recurrent bass theme (ostinato bass) or else upon a recurrent harmonic progression.

Schools and Composers. Germany led in the field of baroque organ music. Less important contributions were made by Italy, France, and England.

GERMANY. A continuous line of German organ composers and

organ music extends from Paumann in the 15th century to Bach in the 18th century. German organ music expanded enormously in the 17th century and eclipsed that of all other schools. The German school of organ music of the 17th century begins with the Dutchman, Jan Pieters Sweelinck (1562–1621), who applied English virginalist technique to his organ chorale variations. Samuel Scheidt (1587–1654), a pupil of Sweelinck, was perhaps the most important German organ composer in the first half of the 17th century. Dietrich Buxtehude (1637–1707) and Georg Böhm (1661–1735) are the most significant predecessors of Bach in North Germany. They developed particularly the free forms of organ music and the fugue. Heinrich Bach (J. S. Bach's grandfather), Johann Krieger, Johann Pachelbel, and Johann Kuhnau, all Middle-German composers, contributed to the development of the chorale prelude and the variation forms. From South Germany the composers Hassler, Erbach, Steigleder, and Froberger developed the Italian contrapuntal styles of organ music, particularly the ricercare and the fugue. The achievements of the German organ school are summed up in the crowning works of J. S. Bach, who, writing in all the forms and styles, wrote the greatest organ music of all time.

ITALY. The Italian organ school flourished chiefly in the first half of the 17th century. After 1650 there is a marked decline in the quality and quantity of its organ music. Its traditions were largely passed on to the South German school, from Frescobaldi to Froberger. Girolamo Frescobaldi (1583–1643), a famous organist at St. Peter's in Rome, was undoubtedly the greatest of Italian organ composers. He wrote toccatas, canzonas, ricercares, capriccios, and a collection of church pieces for organ entitled *Fiori musicali*. His style is notable for its daring harmony and chromaticism, for virtuosity and contrapuntal ingenuity.

FRANCE AND ENGLAND. Organ music in France and England was of little consequence. The French are noted for contributions to organ registration and colorful stops. Jean Titelouze (1563–1633) wrote liturgical organ music (mostly cantus firmus compositions on plainsong) in Renaissance style. Other names connected with French baroque organ music are Dumont, Nivers, Gigault, Le Bègue,

Raison, Marchand, Couperin, and Daquin. Organ music in England is even less significant than that in France. _Voluntaries_ and similar short pieces to be used in the church service were composed by John Blow, Purcell, Clark, and Croft. Special mention should be made of Handel's 12 organ concertos intended for performance between the acts of oratorios.

Chamber Music

Music designated as chamber music is written for small combinations of instruments, and usually one instrument to a part.

Media. Although, as has been pointed out, there was little or no standardization of instrumentation in ensemble music in the Baroque, still there was a growing tendency toward certain chamber music media. There were two of these: the _solo sonata_ and the _trio sonata_.

SOLO SONATA. The solo sonata of the Baroque was a composition in several movements for a solo instrument, usually with a figured bass accompaniment. The violin was by far the most common solo instrument, but solo sonatas were also written for the viol, viola da gamba, flute, and oboe. Somewhat less common was the unaccompanied solo sonata for some bowed string instrument which, in lieu of a keyboard accompaniment, filled in harmonies by double and triple stopping.

TRIO SONATA. Like the solo sonata, the trio sonata is a composition in several movements. But it was written for two solo instruments, usually violins, and a basso continuo part. The trio sonata, then, was usually performed by four instruments: two violins, a low string instrument (cello or viola da gamba) playing the continuo part, and a keyboard instrument (harpsichord or organ) also playing the continuo part and filling in the indicated harmonies of the figured bass.

Forms. In addition to renaissance ensemble forms such as the fantasia for viols which continued to be written in the 17th century, two new forms arose in the second half of the 17th century: the _chamber sonata_ and the _church sonata_. Both forms were written for solo sonata and trio sonata media.

CHAMBER SONATA. The chamber sonata (*sonata da camera* in Italy, *Kammersonate* in Germany) is a dance suite usually consisting of the conventional four dance movements (allemande, courante, sarabande, and gigue) and one or more optional dances.

CHURCH SONATA. The church sonata (*sonata da chiesa* in Italy, *Kirchensonate* in Germany) is a more dignified and more abstract form than the chamber sonata, because it was actually used in the church. It is usually in four movements following the plan of tempo contrast: slow, fast, slow, and fast. The fast movements are usually fugal, the slow movements more cantabile in style, or sometimes chordal. Although not so labeled, the last movement is very often a lively gigue. There is no definite plan of key contrasts between the movements, although occasionally the third movement is in a relative key. It is not uncommon for one movement to end on the dominant, leading directly into the following movement.

Style. It should be kept in mind that the term "sonata" in the Baroque period designates an entirely different form and style from that of the 18th-century classical sonatas of Haydn, Mozart, and Beethoven. The conventional thematic material, the "tune element," is not present in the baroque sonata. Nor is there any thematic development, so important to the classical sonata. Furthermore, the movements are generally in a binary form similar to that of the dance suite movements. A definitely instrumental violin idiom is developed in the baroque sonata. This is shown by the extensive use of violin figuration and double stopping.

Schools and Composers. Chamber music in the Baroque period was developed chiefly in Italy and Germany.

ITALY. The Italian school was the first to develop the baroque sonata forms and styles, principally for strings. Perhaps the first important composer to be named is Giovanni Vitali (c. 1644–1692). He was followed by Giuseppe Torelli (c. 1650–1708). The greatest figure in the 17th century is Arcangelo Corelli (1653–1713), who wrote solo and trio sonatas of the church and chamber types, as well as much fine orchestral music for strings. Antonio Vivaldi (c. 1680–1743), a contemporary of Bach, is noted for his strength and vigor which undoubtedly had considerable influence upon Bach.

Giuseppe Tartini (1692–1770) was particularly noted for advances in bow technique and for virtuosity of style. Less important composers of the Italian school are: Marcello, Pergolesi, Veracini, Pugnani, Nardini, and Locatelli.

GERMANY. In Germany Johann Rosenmüller (1620–1684) wrote solo and trio sonatas. A special feature of the sonatas of Heinrich von Biber (1644–1704) was the use of *scordatura* (different tuning of the violin strings for the purpose of obtaining special effects in double stopping). Georg Philipp Telemann (1681–1767) wrote trio sonatas, solo sonatas, and ensemble music called *Tafelmusik,* i.e., "table music" to be performed at a banquet. Again, in the field of chamber music, the works of J. S. Bach reveal the assimilation of forms and styles. He wrote 3 sonatas for harpsichord and flute; 6 sonatas for harpsichord and violin (3 church sonatas and 3 chamber sonatas); 3 sonatas for harpsichord and viola; one trio sonata for flute, violin, and basso continuo; 1 sonata for 2 violins and basso continuo; 6 sonatas for violin; and 6 sonatas for cello.

ENGLAND. Henry Purcell wrote four-part fantasies in the old polyphonic style. He also wrote baroque trio sonatas, the most famous of which is the *Golden Sonata.* Handel wrote solo sonatas for flute, oboe, and violin without much idiomatic distinction between the specific instruments.

FRANCE. François Couperin wrote some chamber music. The principal name in the French school, however, is Jean Marie Leclair (1697–1764), who is considered the founder of the French school of violin playing.

Orchestral Music

In distinction from chamber music, orchestral music is for a larger body of instruments, and it involves the use of several instruments to a part.

Media. There was less standardization of instrumentation in large ensembles than in chamber music. A typical feature of baroque orchestration is that there was little or no attempt to bring out instrumental colors as such. As in the Renaissance, various instruments double on parts of a polyphonic composition with no regard to blending, just so long as the part is within the range of the instrument. The strings invariably predominate in orchestras of the Baroque. The bass part, particularly prominent in baroque orchestras, is invariably basso continuo. Orchestras were generally conducted from the harpsichord, the harpsichordist having the dual function of playing the continuo part and leading the ensemble. Timpani (kettle drums) were rarely used, and brass instruments were used only sparingly.

Forms. The baroque orchestra was used considerably in connection with large vocal forms: operas, cantatas, oratorios, and choruses. But it also developed special forms of its own.

Overture. The Italian sinfonia (see page 76) and the French overture (see page 77) became important orchestral forms in the late Baroque. They were employed as overtures not only to operas but to oratorios and cantatas, and even as opening movements to orchestral suites.

Orchestral Suite. The form of the dance suite was also employed as an orchestral form. It used the same form and the same types of dance movements as those found in keyboard suites and in the chamber sonatas of the Baroque. It is often introduced by an elaborate prelude, overture, or sinfonia.

Concerto Grosso. The most important orchestral form of the Baroque period is the *concerto grosso*. It has a characteristic instrumentation. In addition to the main body of the orchestra, called *tutti* or *ripieno,* from two to four solo instruments, called *concertino,* are employed. The most characteristic feature of style of the concerto grosso is the dynamic contrast of alternating sections of tutti and concertino. Concerti grossi usually follow the plan of the four-movement sonata: slow, fast, slow, fast. However, this plan is variable. Sometimes numerous shorter movements are used (Corelli), and later a three-movement plan (fast, slow, fast) is to be found (Vivaldi, Bach). The last movement, as in the church and chamber sonatas, is often gigue-like in character, and it is apt to be more fugal than the other movements.

Solo Concerto. Music for orchestra with one or two solo instruments, usually violins, is called a *solo concerto*. It differs from the concerto grosso in that the solo instrument is more prominently featured, plays more continuously, and does not provide the contrast between tutti and concertino that is so characteristic of the concerto grosso.

TURMSONATE. A less significant form of instrumental ensemble, called *Turmsonate* or *tower sonata,* was developed in Germany. It arose from the current practice of sounding the hours of the day from church or municipal towers. Chorales were often used for this purpose. Tower music was played mostly by brass instruments. The tower sonata consists of several movements of varying character, some dance-like, some chordal, others contrapuntal. Johann Pezel (or Petzold) (1639–1694) is the principal composer of Turmsonaten.

Schools and Composers. Orchestral music of one sort or another was written in all countries where dramatic forms flourished. Special orchestral forms such as the orchestral suite and concerto grosso were developed principally in Italy and Germany.

ITALY. The principal composers of orchestral music, chiefly the concerto and concerto grosso, are Stradella (c. 1645–1682), Corelli, Torelli, Geminiani (1674–1762), and Vivaldi.

GERMANY. The principal German composers of orchestral music are Abaco, Fux, Telemann, and J. S. Bach, whose six *Brandenburg Concertos* are among the finest orchestral music of the period.

ENGLAND. Little orchestral music was written in England. Handel wrote concerti grossi patterned after the Corelli plan. He also wrote two extended works for wind instruments intended for outdoor festival performance, *Fireworks Music* and *Water Music.* These consist of a large number of movements in varying forms and styles.

FRANCE. Separate orchestral music was not extensively employed in France. The greater portion of French orchestral music is that written for French opera and ballet, including instrumental dances of all kinds.

RECORDS

Organ Music

ARC 3013–3030, 3037, 3054, 3107; HMS IV 24, VI 9–11; MM 34, 37, 47; TEM 41; EA 0022.

Harpsichord Music

ARC 3056, 3068–70; HMS IV 22, VI 6, 7, 8; MM 35, 38, 40, 42; TEM 40; EA 0013, 0022, 0026, 0032, 0033.

Lute Music

TEM 39.

Chamber Music

ARC 3007, 3008, 3043, 3056, 3103; HMS VI 12–20; MM 39, 50; TEM 36, 48; 2000YM 21, 22.

Orchestral Music

HMS VI 21–24; MM 36, 43, 44; TEM 44, 45, 47.

SCORES

Organ Music

HAM 190, 191, 193, 194, 195, 215, 217, 231, 234, 236, 237, 239, 240, 249, 251; MM 34, 37, 47; SB 158, 185, 196, 243, 249, 263, 265, 283, 291, 292, 302; TEM 41.

Harpsichord Music

HAM 192, 196, 199, 212, 216, 229, 232, 247, 248, 250, 261, 265, 274, 280, 284, 288, 289, 296, 297, 302, 308; MM 35, 38, 40, 42; SB 205, 207, 218, 244, 253, 264, 279, 282, 296; TEM 40.

Lute Music

HAM 211, 233; SB 181b, 215, 216; TEM 39.

Chamber Music

HAM 197, 198, 199, 210, 219, 220, 230, 238, 245, 246, 252, 253, 256, 269, 271, 275, 278, 304; MM 39, 50; SB 155–157, 182–184, 219, 228, 229, 237–241, 245, 251, 294, 295, 307; TEM 36, 48.

Orchestral Music

HAM 208, 223, 224, 246, 259, 260, 270, 294, 295; MM 36, 43, 44;
   SB 213, 214, 220, 221, 224, 232, 233, 252, 257, 276, 277, 278; TEM
   44, 45, 47.

CHAPTER XV

Bach and Handel

THE culmination of the Baroque period is represented in the works of two great German masters: Johann Sebastian Bach (1685–1750) and George Frederick Handel (1685–1759). Unlike the masters of the early 17th century, Bach and Handel perfected rather than invented forms and styles. Although both were German by birth, their music, taken as a whole, reflects an amazing amalgamation of all national schools and styles—an important factor in their universal greatness.

Bach and Handel Compared

Lives. A comparison of the biographies of Bach and Handel shows many striking differences and a few similarities. (1) Bach was provincial in the sense that he spent his entire life within a geographical area of about a forty-mile radius; whereas Handel was cosmopolitan, spending large parts of his life in Germany, Italy, and England. (2) Bach was very much of a family man, who by two successive wives had twenty children. Handel never married and never seemed to need domestic life. (3) Bach's life was largely concerned with small ventures and commonplace problems, whereas Handel's life centered around big ventures. (4) Whereas Bach had a long line of musical ancestors (to such an extent that in Germany any musician was apt to be referred to as "a Bach"), Handel had virtually no musical ancestry. (5) It is a curious coincidence of fate that both these great masters ended their last years in blindness.

Character, Personality. Bach and Handel were both devoutly religious, but Handel was more mundane. Handel was pompous and lordly, whereas Bach, although on occasions willful, was generally more humble and even obsequious.

Kinds of Music. (1) Bach's musical output was chiefly in church music (church cantatas and sacred organ music); Handel dealt in large dramatic forms (opera and oratorio). (2) Bach's music is utilitarian for the most part, written for specific occasions or functions, whereas Handel wrote music on a grand scale and often for no particular occasion or function. (3) Whereas Bach used the chorale extensively in his music, Handel made virtually no use of it. (4) Bach's output and greatness in organ music are well known, a contrast to the fact that Handel, although a great organist, wrote very little organ music. (5) Both composers were great masters of choral music. (6) Whereas Bach's music is of an impersonal nature, it may be said that Handel is the first composer to reveal his personality through his music.

Differences of Musical Style. (1) Bach's music is predominantly polyphonic; Handel's music is predominantly homophonic, although both were great masters of baroque polyphony. (2) Bach's vocal music shows a strong tendency toward instrumental idiom, whereas Handel displays a more idiomatic vocal writing. (3) Although both composers were fond of regular rhythms, Bach often has a stronger, more driving rhythm. (4) Bach's harmony, on the whole, is richer and more ingenious than that of Handel.

Bach

Style. (1) Bach's contrapuntal ingenuity has never been surpassed, rarely equalled. The beauty of contrapuntal lines and the mastery with which they are combined in polyphonic textures are evident in such works as the fugues for organ and for harpsichord, the *Art of Fugue* (*Die Kunst der Fuge*), and the *Musical Offering* (*Das musikalische Opfer*). (2) The driving rhythm of many of the organ toccatas, some of the fugues, and most of the orchestral works is a characteristic of Bach's style. (3) Bach's harmonic ingenuity is on a par with his great contrapuntal skill. Richness, variety of progression, and considerable chromaticism are generally evident in his music. (4) Bach's instrumentation, characteristic of baroque instrumental music in general, is unidiomatic and rather uncolorful. (5) Bach had an extraordinary architectural sense of form, and subtlety and continuity of phraseology are everywhere manifest.

PICTORIAL EXPRESSION. According to Albert Schweitzer, an important aspect of Bach's music is his use of pictorial and symbolic expression. This is evident in his vocal music where the general meaning or mood of the text is brought out by various devices. For example, grief is often expressed by a descending chromatic line, as in the "Crucifixus" of the *B Minor Mass*. Joy, on the other hand, is often expressed in long, continuous lines of eighth or sixteenth notes as in the well-known choral setting "Jesu, Joy of Man's Desiring." Expressive words, such as "eternity," "still," "quiet," "pain," "fall," "ascend," etc., are pictorially treated. Such expression is to be found in the chorale preludes as well as in the vocal music. It was not an original idea with Bach, but he probably employed it more extensively than any of his contemporaries or predecessors.

Origins of Bach's Style. Bach's style, an assimilation of baroque practices in general, can be traced to various sources.

ORGAN MUSIC. The principal features of Bach's organ music are derived from the great and numerous German masters before him. He seems to have derived his fugal style from Pachelbel. The trio sonata and the trio chorale preludes come from Hofhaimer, Buchner, Kotter, and Kleber of the 16th century. His style of coloration comes from the 15th-century style of Paumann, through Finck, Isaac, and Schlick in the 16th century. Variation technique comes from the English virginal school, through Sweelinck and Scheidt. The toccata style is traced from Frescobaldi in Italy, through Froberger, and more immediately from Buxtehude.

HARPSICHORD MUSIC. The style of Bach's partitas and suites for harpsichord comes directly from the French clavecin school. This is noticeable in the contrapuntal treatment and in the use of embellishment.

ORCHESTRAL AND CHAMBER MUSIC. A direct Italian influence on Bach's instrumental ensemble music is to be seen in the use of string figuration, sequence, and clear phraseology. The driving rhythm of his orchestral music comes from Corelli and more from Vivaldi.

CHORAL MUSIC. Bach's choral technique comes from the Venetian school of Giovanni Gabrieli through Schütz (a pupil of Gabrieli's) to Buxtehude and Telemann.

HARMONY. Bach's harmony is solidly German.

Summary of Works. Bach's great versatility can be seen from the following classified summary of his music.

VOCAL CHURCH MUSIC. Bach wrote some 300 church cantatas of which only about 200 have been preserved, and several secular cantatas. In addition to the famous *St. Matthew Passion* he wrote Passion music to the St. John gospel, 4 short Masses, the great *B Minor Mass,* a setting of the Magnificat, and several choral compositions called "motets." He harmonized nearly 400 chorales in four-part harmony.

HARPSICHORD MUSIC. Bach's harpsichord music includes 15 two-part inventions (short, imitative contrapuntal pieces), 15 "symphonies" (three-part inventions), 6 partitas (suites), 6 English suites, 6 French suites, 48 preludes and fugues (*The Well-Tempered Clavier*), miscellaneous suites, toccatas, preludes, fugues, etc., and the *Goldberg Variations.*

ORGAN MUSIC. Bach's organ music includes 6 trio sonatas, numerous preludes and fugues, toccatas, fantasias, a passacaglia and fugue in C minor, the *Orgelbüchlein* (a set of short chorale preludes for the liturgical year), various sets of 6, 18, 25, and 28 chorale preludes, and chorale variations (called "partitas").

CHAMBER MUSIC. Bach's chamber music includes 3 sonatas for harpsichord and flute, 6 sonatas for harpsichord and violin (3 church sonatas and 3 chamber sonatas), 3 sonatas for harpsichord and viola, one trio sonata for flute, violin, and basso continuo, 1 sonata for 2 violins and basso continuo, 6 sonatas for violin alone, and 6 sonatas for cello alone.

ORCHESTRAL MUSIC. His orchestral music includes 1 concerto grosso for harpsichord, flute, and violin, 6 *Brandenburg Concertos* (concerti grossi), 3 concertos for violin and orchestra, 1 concerto for 2 violins, 4 orchestral suites, 2 concertos for harpsichord, 3 concertos for 2 harpsichords, 2 concertos for 3 harpsichords, and 1 concerto for 4 harpsichords.

COLLECTIONS. Bach wrote several collections that are of great historical as well as musical interest. The *Musical Offering* is a collection of contrapuntal pieces (various canons, ricercares, fugues, and a trio sonata) all based on a theme by Frederick the Great and presented to him by Bach. *Anna Magdalena Bach's Music Notebook* is a collection of rather simple pieces presumably for the musical edification of his second wife. It consists of two volumes of diverse pieces for harpsichord and some songs. *The Art of Fugue* was Bach's last great work. It is a collection of fugues and canons all based on one thematic idea. The final piece is an incomplete quadruple fugue one of the themes of which spells out Bach's name, *B A C H* (the letter *H* in German stands for B natural, while *B* stands for B flat).

Handel

Style. (1) Handel's style is a mixture of national elements: Italian, German, and English. (2) His style includes most of the traits generally characteristic of the late Baroque: formal, strict structures, ornamentation, artificiality of stereotyped cadences and harmonic progressions, and certain melodic formulae. (3) Handel's music is predominantly homophonic. (4) Handel's harmony is conventional, more diatonic than Bach's. Specifically, Handel makes extensive use of tonic and dominant progressions and of first inversion chords. (5) Handel's rhythm is generally strong, and he favors dotted rhythm patterns. (6) Handel is fond of contrasts of tempo, material, polyphonic and homophonic sections, range, and timbre. (7) Handel's phrases are more clearly definite on the whole than those of Bach; they are also inclined to be long. (8) Cantabile melody, often beginning with a long sustained note, is characteristic of his melodic style. (9) In his choral music he often gains a special effect by writing tenor and bass parts high and soprano and alto parts low. (10) Handel frequently makes use of a special final cadence: a pause or complete rest in all parts following a climax, and then a few solid cadential chords.

Summary of Works. Handel's principal contributions are in opera, of which he wrote forty-three, mostly in Italian style, and in oratorio, of which he wrote twenty-seven, mostly in his later life after his operatic ventures had failed.

OTHER VOCAL WORKS. Handel's other vocal works consist of 22 Italian duets, numerous anthems, a masque (*Acis and Galatea*), Italian cantatas with basso continuo and other instruments, and Italian, German, and English songs.

INSTRUMENTAL MUSIC. Handel's instrumental music includes 17 harpsichord suites, 12 harpsichord pieces of varying nature, 6 fugues for harpsichord, 15 solo sonatas for violin, oboe, flute, and recorder, all with figured bass accompaniment, 6 trio sonatas for 2 oboes and basso continuo, 15 sonatas for 2 violins, 6 oboe concertos, 12 organ concertos, 22 orchestral concertos (concerti grossi), *Water Music, Fireworks Music,* and both French and Italian types of overture to his 43 operas and 27 oratorios.

PART FOUR

The Classical Period (1750–1820)

CHAPTER XVI

General Considerations

THE second half of the 18th century and the first quarter of the 19th century is a period marked by momentous events in general history, and by significant changes in musical form and style.

THE MEANING OF CLASSICISM. The term "classical" in music conforms to the ideals of the Apollonian cult of Ancient Greece: objectivity, emotional restraint, clarity of form, and adherence to certain structural principles. Classical ideals in music are not confined to the late 18th century. They appear in the ars antiqua; they are manifest in certain aspects of the 20th century. Classicism is also characteristic of the late baroque music of Bach and Handel, for example. To distinguish the classicism of the early 18th century from that of the late 18th century, the latter is often referred to as the *Viennese Classical* period, because Vienna was the musical capital of Europe at that time.

General Historical Background. The period between 1750 and 1820 is generally marked by the rise of the lower and middle classes in a democratic spirit which asserted itself in the French Revolution. The French Revolution and the Napoleonic Wars dominate the period. Before the French Revolution, a widespread conflict, known as the Seven Years' War (1756–1763), in which Prussia, allied with England, fought against Austria and France, spread through Europe, India, and America (the French and Indian Wars). The American Declaration of Independence (1776) and the American Revolution belong to this period. The predominant philosophy was rationalist; it is manifest in the works of the German Kant and of the French

Diderot and the Encyclopedists. Voltaire and Rousseau are important names in literature and philosophy. In sociology Adam Smith's *The Wealth of Nations* (1776) is a milestone. Important artists of the period are Goya, David, Reynolds, Gainsborough, and Copley. *Rococo* is the term applied to the general spirit and style of the art and music of this period.

THE MEANING OF ROCOCO. *Rococo* is defined in Webster as "a florid style of ornamentation characterized by curved lines and decoration of pierced shellwork, popular in Europe in the 18th century." The term has come to have a somewhat broader meaning and application. It is used to connote a sort of preciosity, overrefinement, and delicacy that pervades not only decoration but also painting, architecture, literature, poetry, and music. At best the rococo is a delicate, polished, restrained, and somewhat superficial art; at worst it is a degeneration of the baroque spirit.

General Musical Characteristics of the Classical Period. In general, classical music can be described as objective, showing emotional restraint, polish, refinement, and a certain amount of superficiality. The classical spirit is more clearly manifest in instrumental music than it is in opera and other dramatic forms.

FORM. Clarification of formal structure is generally evident. Modern sonata form emerges in the Classical period.

MELODIC STYLE. A new type of melody is developed. It has an individual and compact character, and it is often folk-like in its clarity and simplicity. It replaces the long lines and the figuration styles of baroque polyphony.

HOMOPHONIC STYLE. A new importance of distinct thematic material gives homophonic style a decided precedence over polyphonic style. A special aspect of this characteristic is the *Alberti bass,* a special type of broken-chord accompaniment.

COUNTERPOINT. Counterpoint is still employed, especially in thematic development, but it is of secondary importance. Contrapuntal forms are generally abandoned.

HARMONY. Classical music generally shows a remarkable simplicity. On the whole, there is less harmonic complexity and ingenuity than in the works of J. S. Bach, for example. No significant harmonic

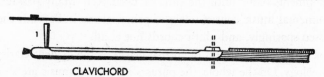

CLAVICHORD

1. Tangent which strikes string when key is depressed.

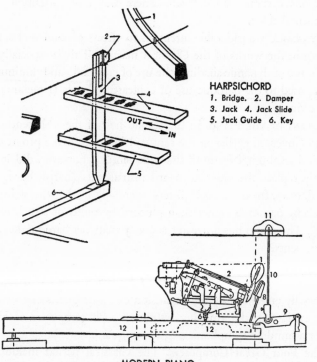

HARPSICHORD

1. Bridge. 2. Damper
3. Jack 4. Jack Slide
5. Jack Guide 6. Key

OUT
IN

MODERN PIANO

1. Hammer Head. 2. Hammer Shank and Butt. 3. Repetition Lever. 4. Tack. 5. Set-off Button. 6. Capstan Screws. 7. Repetition Spring. 8. Check Head and Wire. 9. Damper Body. 10. Damper Wire. 11. Damper Head. 12. Key.

Harpsichord reprinted by permission of the publishers from Willi Apel, Harvard Dictionary of Music, Cambridge, Mass.: Harvard University Press, 1945. Clavichord and Piano reprinted by permission of the publishers from Grove's Dictionary of Music and Musicians, New York: The Macmillan Company.

Herzog & Gibbs, N. Y. C.

ACTION OF KEYBOARD INSTRUMENTS

developments occur until the time of Beethoven. Many passages in instrumental music consist solely of principal triads. Seventh chords are used sparingly, and ninth chords not at all.

PHRASEOLOGY. An aspect of formal clarity is the evident clarity of phraseology. On the whole, the phrases in classical music are shorter and more regular than those in the Baroque period.

ORCHESTRATION. The basis of modern orchestration and instrumentation was established in the Classical period. Instrumental combinations became standardized. There was more attention to instrumental color.

DYNAMICS. Considerable attention to effects of loud and soft are shown in the works of the Classical masters. This is especially true in the use of dynamic shading, the use of crescendo and diminuendo, as opposed to the baroque use of contrasting levels (ripieno against concertino).

ADVENT OF THE PIANO. In the second half of the 18th century the piano (invented earlier in the century) began to make progress as a musical medium. Not until the 19th century, however, did it completely replace the older keyboard instruments (harpsichord, clavichord, etc.), from which it differs essentially in that the strings are struck by hammers rather than plucked by quills or struck by tangents. The piano has a greater sonority than the baroque keyboard instruments.

MUSICAL OUTPUT. There was an enormous increase in the production of all kinds of music in the Classical period. This was undoubtedly enhanced by the expansion of music publishing business. It is evident in the amazing output of such composers as Haydn (over a hundred symphonies, 83 string quartets, etc.).

The Four Great Composers. The Classical period includes the lives and works of four first-rank composers: (1) Christoph Willibald Gluck (1714–1787), noted for his operas and for opera reform, (2) Franz Joseph Haydn (1732–1809), who wrote symphonies, chamber music, and oratorios, and who is credited with having established the basis of modern orchestration and sonata form; (3) Wolfgang Amadeus Mozart (1756–1791), who was equally great in symphonic music, chamber music, and opera; and (4) Ludwig van

Beethoven (1770–1827), who, in his great symphonies, chamber music, piano music, Mass, opera, and oratorio, represents the culmination of the classical styles and forms and the transition to 19th-century romanticism. Beethoven will be taken up separately in Part Five, Chapter XXI.

RECORDS

An interesting comparison of classical and baroque music can be made in the study of Haydn's *Surprise Symphony* (No. 94, in G major), and Handel's *Concerto Grosso,* No. 1, in G major. There are excellent recordings of both these works.

CHAPTER XVII

Instrumental Music of the Classical Period

In the Classical period instrumental music became more important than vocal music. With certain reservations, it may be said that the most important developments in style and form took place in the field of instrumental music. Objectivity, clarity of form, and other aspects of classicism are generally more apparent in the instrumental music of the period than they are in dramatic music.

Classical Sonata Form

The most significant structural principle evolved and established in the Classical period is *sonata form*. Subject to certain modifications, it is the basis for nearly all instrumental music of the period: the symphony, the concerto, chamber music, and the keyboard sonata. It was eventually established as a group of three or four movements which follow certain structural plans.

First Movement. As opposed to the baroque sonata which usually begins with a slow movement, the classical sonata opens with an allegro movement. Occasionally, as with Haydn symphonies, a slow introduction is used. The first movement usually follows a basic structural plan known as *sonata-allegro form,* which consists of three principal sections: *exposition, development,* and *recapitulation*.

Exposition. The exposition consists of the presentation of two principal thematic materials in the following manner: (1) The first theme is presented in the key of the sonata (tonic key). (2) An *episode* or *bridge passage* modulates to a contrasting key (the dominant key if the sonata is in major, the relative major key if the sonata is in a minor key). (3) The second theme (sometimes called *subordinate theme*) is then presented in the contrasting key. It is usually more lyric and less dynamic and forceful than the first theme. (4) The exposition frequently has a closing section called *codetta* or *closing theme*. The classical exposition always ends with a double bar and repeat sign, although in performance the exposition is no longer repeated.

DEVELOPMENT. The middle part of the sonata-allegro form is called the development section. It consists of free treatment or development of any or all of the thematic material presented in the exposition. There is no set plan of organization in the development section. It usually passes through several keys according to the fancy of the composer.

RECAPITULATION. The recapitulation consists of a restatement of thematic material similar to that of the exposition, except that normally all themes are in the tonic key. The development and recapitulation were repeated in classical sonata-allegro form.

Second Movement. The second movement of the classical sonata is in a slow tempo (andante, largo, etc.). It is usually in the subdominant key (four degrees above the tonic key), or it may be in the relative major key (three degrees above the tonic in minor keys), or in the dominant key. A variety of structural plans are employed for the second movement. The most common of these are: (1) *first rondo,* in which the form, according to contrast of thematic materials, is *A B A,* (2) *song form,* which includes the use of shorter themes in variously related plans (*A A B A, A A B A' B A',* etc.), (3) variations, (4) sonata-allegro form, and (5) sonatina form, which is sonata-allegro form abridged by omission of the development section in favor of a brief transition.

Third Movement: Minuet. In the Classical period this movement is optional. It is used in all four-movement symphonies, quartets, and in a relatively few keyboard sonatas. But it is omitted in the concerto and in all three-movement symphonies and sonatas. It is in a moderate or fast tempo, and in three-four time. The minuet movement uniformly follows a structural plan called *song form with trio,* or *minuet and trio*. Each of the three main sections is a song form, so that the whole plan may be represented in a formula as follows:

$$A{:}\|{:}BA'{:}\|\quad C{:}\|{:}DC'{:}\|\quad ABA'\|$$

minuet   trio   minuet

The middle section, called trio, is often in a contrasting key.

Fourth Movement: Finale. The last movement of sonata form is in a lively tempo (allegro or presto). It is in the tonic key. It is often a rondo form, following the plan of thematic materials: *A B A C A* (second rondo form), or *A B A C A B A* (third rondo form). Not infrequently the finale is in sonata-allegro form, as in the first movement.

The Classical Symphony

Perhaps the most important single contribution of the Classical period is the symphony. It embodies not only a new formal principle, the classical sonata form, but also new concepts of orchestration.

Origin of the Symphony. The term "sinfonia," from which the word symphony is derived, was used almost indiscriminately in the 17th century to apply to various kinds of instrumental music. It is similar in its broad application to the term "sonata." It was also applied to interludes and ritornelli in opera. Late in the 17th century its meaning came to be narrowed to the Italian overture. From the latter form the basic plan of movements of the symphony was derived (fast, slow, fast). By the middle of the 18th century the Italian sinfonia was developed as an independent instrumental form, not connected with opera. Haydn added the minuet between the second and last movements of the symphony. The four-movement symphony became standard by the end of the 18th century, although the minuet was sometimes omitted. The internal structure of the movements appears to have developed first in the first movement sonata-allegro plan. The bithematic scheme of sonata-allegro form emerged during the first half of the 18th century, largely in connection with keyboard sonatas and the sinfonia. Thus the classical symphony of the second half of the 18th century replaced the concerto grosso and the orchestral suite of the late Baroque period as the most important type of orchestral music.

Instrumentation and Orchestration. The Classical period established the basic plan of instrumental grouping for the symphony orchestra: strings, woodwinds, brass, and percussion.

STRINGS. The string instruments are divided into five parts: first violins, second violins, violas, cellos, and basses. The first and second violins often double in passages for emphasis. The cellos and basses usually double. Double and triple stopping is used for special chordal emphasis, particularly in final cadences. There is no subdivision of string parts in classical orchestration.

WOODWINDS. The instrumentation for the woodwind section is more variable in the Classical period. The most common plan is one flute, two oboes, and a bassoon. The clarinet is added or else it replaces the oboe in the later classical symphony (e.g., Haydn's *London Symphony* and Mozart's *E–Flat Symphony*).

BRASS. Two French horns (without valves) are generally used in the classical orchestra. Trumpets are occasionally used; and tubas and trombones are not employed in classical symphonies.

TIMPANI. Timpani or kettle drums are used in pairs, tuned to the tonic and the dominant tones of the key.

Schools and Composers. The development of the classical symphony took place at many different places and by many different composers exploring the new form and style. The principal activities were in Italy and Austria.

MILAN. A large school of talented musicians was centered in Milan. The principal figure among the preclassical symphonic composers is G. B. Sammartini (1701–1775), the teacher of Gluck, J. C. Bach, Wagenseil, and Mozart. Sammartini was chiefly responsible for the cultivation of the bithematic plan of sonata-allegro form.

VIENNA. Milan was under Austrian rule and so Austrians became conversant with the new style. The principal composers of the Viennese school are Georg Matthias Monn (1717–1750) and Georg Christoph Wagenseil (1715–1777). Among these composers the prototypes of Haydn's classical symphonies are to be found.

MANNHEIM. In Mannheim further developments leading to the classical symphony took place. The school centered around a famous court orchestra of that city. The principal contribution of the

Mannheim composers seems to have been new dynamic effects (forte, piano, sforzando, crescendo, diminuendo, etc.). The leading composers of this school are Johann Stamitz (1717-1757), his two sons, Karl and Anton, Ignaz Holzbauer (1711-1783), F. X. Richter (1709-1789), and Christian Cannabich (1731-1798).

OTHER COMPOSERS. Bach's sons, Carl Philipp Emanuel Bach (1714-1788) and Johann Christian Bach (1735-1782), contributed chiefly to the development of the sonata. Other composers of preclassical and classical symphonies are Michael Haydn (1737-1806, brother of Franz Josef), François Gossec (1734-1829), Karl Ditters von Dittersdorf (1739-1799), and Luigi Boccherini (1743-1805). The great masters of the classical symphony are Franz Josef Haydn, Mozart and Beethoven (see Chapter XXI).

Style. The classical symphony is homophonic in style. Counterpoint is employed, but it is usually incidental to the style as a whole. Each theme is brought into prominence, and the themes are the nucleus of the music. The basso continuo and the use of the harpsichord disappear in the Classical period. Clear and regular phraseology is characteristic of the thematic material, which is compact rather than continuous and extended as with Bach and Handel. The harmony is in general simple, conventional. Effective use of dynamics is evident in a greater dynamic range, and there is more gradation and contrast between loud and soft. Form becomes conventionalized with standard relationship of thematic material and keys.

HAYDN AND MOZART. Although in similar fashion Haydn and Mozart represent the full realization of classical ideals in their symphonies, sonatas, chamber music, and concertos, and although each composer influenced the style of the other to some extent, still, there are some individual traits that should be pointed out. Haydn makes extensive use of slow introductions to the first movements of his symphonies, which Mozart seldom does. Haydn's themes are, on the whole, characteristically lively, folk-like in style, cheerful, and robust. Mozart's themes are more subtle, less folk-like. A cantabile style of melody is particularly characteristic of Mozart. Whereas Haydn has clear phraseology, Mozart's phraseology is more irregular, subtle, and extended. Haydn's melody and harmony are usually simple and diatonic, whereas Mozart is more inclined toward chromaticism. Ornamentation is more prominent with Mozart, and there is a greater delicacy of style, a sort of "laciness" characteristic of his music.

The Classical Concerto

The classical concerto developed directly from the baroque solo concerto. In a general sense it resembles the baroque concerto in that it is based upon the exchange of material between a solo instrument and the entire orchestral ensemble (tutti).

Form. The classical concerto is a three-movement form as is the baroque solo concerto. The minuet movement of the classical symphony is not used in the concerto. The formal structure of the movements differs considerably from that of the baroque concerto, making use as it does of a modified classical sonata form.

First Movement. The first movement of the classical concerto is a modified sonata-allegro form. The exposition usually consists of three main parts: (1) The opening tutti, in which principal themes are introduced, ends in the tonic key. (2) The solo instrument then enters either with a brilliant introduction or immediately with the principal subject. There follows an exchange of material (first and second subject) between the solo instrument and the orchestra. (3) The exposition closes with a short tutti section. The solo instrument and the orchestra then take part in a short development section, which leads through various keys back to the tonic. The recapitulation begins with a tutti section corresponding to the first tutti section, but shorter. Then, there is a solo section corresponding to the first solo section of the exposition. A short tutti section, corresponding to the second tutti section in the exposition, ends on a six-four chord (tonic chord with the fifth in the bass). The solo instrument alone then plays a *cadenza*. This is a brilliant, virtuosic display of thematic material, freely and elaborately developed. Cadenzas are either written by the composer of the concerto, composed separately by the performer or someone else, or, most often in the classical period, improvised by the performer. The cadenza is followed by a brief tutti section, either with or without the solo instrument, concluding the movement.

SECOND MOVEMENT. The second movement is less virtuosic and more ornamental than the first movement. It is usually in some sort of enlarged song form, a first rondo, or a variation form. The cadenza is rarely employed in the andante movement.

FINALE. The third and last movement of the concerto is again in fast tempo. It is usually some form of rondo, resembling the last movement of the classical symphony. Occasionally a short cadenza is used.

Composers. The transition from the baroque solo concerto to the classical concerto is attributed mainly to Bach's sons, Carl Philipp Emanuel Bach and Johann Christian Bach. The Italians, Locatelli and Tartini, also show a departure from baroque methods.

HAYDN AND MOZART. Haydn wrote 20 piano concertos, 9 violin concertos, 6 cello concertos, and numerous other concertos for various instruments (flute, baryton, horn, clarino, etc.). Mozart wrote 25 piano concertos, 8 violin concertos, and concertos for other instruments: violin and viola, bassoon, flute, flute and harp, horn, and clarinet.

Small Orchestral Forms

In the second half of the 18th century large quantities of music were written for small orchestral ensembles. Such music was variously called *serenade* (*Nachtmusik*), *cassation,* and *divertimento*. These terms apparently were used interchangeably. They are the counterpart of the baroque orchestral suite in that they consist of from four to ten movements, many of which are dances such as minuets, gavottes, etc. They were written for small orchestras of highly diverse instrumentation, and they usually employed only a few instruments on a part. Haydn wrote about 65 of these, Mozart wrote about 30.

Chamber Music

Media. Music written for a small group of solo instruments continued to be important in the classical period. The chief difference between classical and baroque chamber music is that the former abandoned the use of the figured bass or continuo part. It is also more homophonic than the baroque chamber music. The instrumental combinations differ somewhat from those employed in earlier periods.

STRING QUARTET. By far the most important medium in classical chamber music is the string quartet, consisting of two violins, a viola, and a cello. It replaced the string fantasy ensemble of the Renaissance and the trio sonata of the Baroque. The music written for this ensemble, as well as the medium itself, is called *string quartet*. The form of the string quartet (as with the symphony) is the classical sonata form. The principal composers of string quartets in the Classical period are Luigi Boccherini (91 quartets), Haydn (83 quartets), Mozart (26 quartets), and Beethoven (16 quartets).

OTHER CHAMBER MEDIA. Combinations less extensively employed in the Classical period are the mixed quartet (three strings and one other instrument, usually piano, flute, or oboe), string trio, mixed trio, string quintet, and mixed quintet (string quartet plus piano, flute, or oboe).

THE VIOLIN SONATA. The violin sonata is the least important of classical chamber music media. Haydn wrote 12 violin sonatas, and Mozart wrote some 35 sonatas for violin and piano.

THE KEYBOARD SONATA. The keyboard sonatas of Haydn and Mozart are usually three-movement works; some are in two movements. Not until Beethoven is the four-movement sonata form usually employed. The structure of movements in the classical sonata is somewhat variable. Many of Haydn's earlier sonatas are in the older binary plan of movement rather than in sonata-allegro form. The same is true with many of the contemporary classical composers of keyboard music. A preclassical sonata form, showing transition from the older baroque binary plan of movement to the classical developed ternary (sonata-allegro) is exhibited in 12 keyboard sonatas by Domenico Paradisi (1710–1792). The sonatas of Carl Philipp Emanuel Bach, Wilhelm Friedemann Bach (1710–1784), and Johann Christian Bach, constitute an important literature in the development of the classical keyboard sonata. The sonatas of Muzio Clementi (1752–1832) lead up to the more advanced sonata style of Beethoven, whose 32 piano sonatas are the culmination of that form.

CHAPTER XVIII

Opera in the Classical Period

THE distinction between the baroque and the classical style in dramatic music is less clearly marked than in the field of instrumental music. The field of opera music expands enormously in the 18th century, and yet relatively few operas of this period are included in standard operatic repertory today.

Prevailing Types of Opera in the 18th Century. Italian opera seria dominated the 18th century. Opera buffa rivaled opera seria in the second half of the 18th century. In the same period opéra-comique predominated in France. In Germany Singspiel became increasingly important, although it never rivaled opéra-comique or opera buffa.

Italian Opera Seria. The Neapolitan school of opera, which began in the late 17th century, flourished and spread over all Continental Europe during the first half of the 18th century. As it became the model, or at least the point of departure, for all opera, it also became decadent, so that reform was inevitable as was the rise and growth of other operatic styles, particularly in the field of comic opera.

CHARACTERISTICS. 18th-century Italian opera was marked by characteristics most of which were the object of attack and reform in the second half of the 18th century: (1) Opera plots were overcomplex and artificial; they centered around intricate love intrigues and impossible situations. (2) There were usually six characters, representing three of each sex. (3) Dramatic truth was generally neglected. (4) From the dramatic standpoint, the overemphasis on arias was objectionable. Most of the operas consisted of chains of arias. Nevertheless, arias selected from 18th-century opera constitute an important repertory of vocal music; many of them are exceedingly fine and beautiful. Arias were artificially classified into various types and there were strictly observed rules concerning where, when, and by whom they could be sung. (5) There was little use of chorus. (6) There was an almost exclusive use of *castrati* (male sopranos and altos); women were generally barred from leading roles. (7) There was prominence of *parlando style* of recitative (i.e., rapid dialogue, half spoken, half sung). This was even more extensively employed in buffa opera.

COMPOSERS. The principal composers of Italian opera in the Classical period are: Niccolò Jommelli (1714–1774), Tommaso Traetta (1727–1779), Baldassare Galuppi (1706–1785), Antonio Sacchini (1730–1786), Christoph Willibald Gluck (1714–1787), Giuseppe Sarti (1729–1802), Nicola Piccini (1728–1800), Domenico Cimarosa (1749–1801), Giovanni Paisiello (1740–1816), who represents a transition from 18th- to 19th-century opera, Antonio Salieri (1750–1825), and Mozart.

Gluck and Opera Reform. Because of his attempts to simplify and purify opera, Christoph Willibald Gluck (1714–1787) represents the classical spirit in opera as no other contemporary did. With Mozart, he is one of the two greatest opera composers in the Classical period.

RECOGNITION OF DEFICIENCIES IN NEAPOLITAN OPERA. Gluck was not the first to recognize the decadent aspects of Neapolitan opera. In 1720 Benedetto Marcello wrote a satire on opera, entitled *Il Teatro alla moda*. Another treatise by Count Algarotti, entitled *Saggio sopra l'opera in musica* (1755) sets forth principles similar to those later advanced by Gluck. Opera reform was further recognized in a work by Arteaga, entitled *Rivoluzioni del teatro musicale italiano* (1783–1788). These treatises, reflecting to some extent a growing antipathy to operatic trends, would have been of little avail were it not for the intrinsic greatness of Gluck, who put theories into actual practice.

GLUCK'S CONTRIBUTIONS AND STYLE. Gluck's importance to opera can be seen from the following list of his contributions: (1) Entirely apart from its historical significance, Gluck's music is great. (2) In general, his music represents the classical spirit by a return to simplicity of style. (3) Gluck improved the libretto by eliminating complex love intrigue and by returning to classical Greek mythology for the basis of his librettos. (4) He strove for dramatic truth by eliminating superfluous virtuosity and by creating music that follows the emotional and dramatic situations. (5) He placed more emphasis upon recitative and made less stylistic difference between recitative and aria. (6) He made dramatic use of the chorus. (7) Character delineation is an important attribute of Gluck's operas. (8) Effective instrumentation adds to successful characterization. (9) Gluck's overtures present the general mood of the work and are closely related to the opera.

GLUCK's MOST IMPORTANT WORKS. Gluck began his career by writing some 20 typical Italian operas. The first important opera in the reformed style was *Orfeo ed Euridice* ("Orpheus and Eurydice"), produced in Vienna in 1762. It was not a success there, being generally misunderstood, but it was translated into French and successfully produced in Paris. Despite certain concessions to Italian operatic practices (the title role is for an alto castrato, and the story is altered to have a happy ending), it reveals most of the points in Gluck's reform. *Iphigénie en Aulide* (1774), *Armide* (1777), and *Iphigénie en Tauride* (1779) were all produced in Paris. The latter was the crowning work of Gluck's career. It was also the victorious work in a controversy between Gluckists and Piccinists, which was an outgrowth of the "war" between Italian buffonists in France and the French anti-buffonists. *Alceste* was produced in Vienna, 1767.

GLUCK's INFLUENCE AND SUCCESSORS. Gluck's influence was probably not of very considerable extent outside of Paris. At least for the time being, Italian tradition continued as before. Gluck's influence can be shown in Mozart's *Idomeneo*. Gluck's followers were Sacchini, Cherubini, Méhul, and Spontini.

Mozart Opera. Mozart was not a reformer. He wrote in the prevailing forms and styles of the day. His operas are considered great because they are musical masterpieces in themselves. In fact, Mozart's operas are the only 18th-century operas remaining in the standard repertory today.

STYLE. Mozart's operas show predominating Italian influence. He uses the parlando style extensively and highly complex plots (*Figaro* and *Don Giovanni*). Mozart's operas are greater than contemporary Italian operas (1) because of the greatness of Mozart's music and its importance to the dramatic work, (2) because of Mozart's great melodic genius, and (3) because of his ability in character delineation.

TYPES AND EXAMPLES OF MOZART OPERA. Mozart opera falls into three categories: Singspiel, opera seria, and opera buffa.

a. *German Operas, Singspiel Type.* The two principal German operas by Mozart are: *Die Entführung aus dem Serail* ("The Seraglio," 1782) and *Die Zauberflöte* ("The Magic Flute," 1791).

b. *Opera Seria.* Two Mozart operas which may be classed as Italian operas of the seria type are *Idomeneo* (1781) and *La Clemenza di Tito* (1791).

c. *Opera Buffa.* Most of Mozart's important operas belong to the opera buffa class. They are *La Finta giardiniera* (1775), *Le Nozze di Figaro* ("The Marriage of Figaro," 1786), which is probably Mozart's best-known opera, *Don Giovanni* ("Don Juan," 1787), called *dramma giocosa,* a mixture of opera seria and opera buffa elements, and *Così fan tutte* (1790).

CHAPTER XIX

Religious Music of the Classical Period

THE least significant developments in music in the Classical period are in the field of religious music, including oratorio and church music. They are decidedly overshadowed by opera and instrumental music.

Oratorio

Principal Composers and Works. A transition from the cantata style of J. S. Bach to the late 18th-century oratorio style of Haydn is shown in the works of Carl Philipp Emanuel Bach (*The Resurrection* and *The Israelites in the Wilderness*). By far the most important classical composer of oratorios is Haydn, whose oratorios fall in the late 18th century. His most important oratorio is *The Creation* (1798), which is based upon Genesis and upon an early adaptation of Milton's *Paradise Lost. Il Ritorno di Tobia,* an early work written in 1774, is the best example of 18th-century Italian oratorio. Haydn's last oratorio, *The Seasons* (1801), is a secular oratorio with very little religious content. Mozart's work in oratorio is negligible.

Church Music

In general, the church music of the Classical period is inferior. It is mostly of a dramatic nature and it appears to have been conceived for concert purposes rather than liturgical usage.

Forms of Church Music. The principal forms of 18th-century church music are: (1) The Mass, concert-like settings of the Ordinary of the Mass, with orchestra, soloists, and chorus, (2) Requiem

Mass, (3) motets, for chorus, solo voices, and instrumental accompaniment, (4) litanies, short choral pieces including responses, and (5) vespers, music for the penultimate Catholic canonic hour, and the only one permitting music other than plainsong. It includes antiphons, psalms, hymns, and settings of the Magnificat.

Composers. As in other fields of music of the classical period, Haydn and Mozart are the greatest composers of church music.

HAYDN. Haydn wrote 14 Masses, 13 offertories, and miscellaneous religious choral music: motets, Salve Reginas, Ave Reginas, etc.

MOZART. Mozart wrote 15 Masses, 4 litanies, 2 vespers, a *Requiem Mass,* which is probably his most famous work in this field, and miscellaneous smaller works including motets, offertories, etc.

OTHER COMPOSERS. In Italy there is a long list of church composers who turned out enormous quantities of church music, mostly mediocre. The most notable of these are Galuppi, Paisiello (some 103 church compositions), Zingarelli (over 500 church compositions), Sarti, and Cherubini. To this list should be added the names of early 19th-century composers: Spohr, Schubert, and Beethoven, whose *Missa Solemnis* is a great festival Mass.

PART FIVE

The Romantic Period (1820–1900)

CHAPTER XX

General Considerations

General Aspects of Romanticism. The 19th-century romantic point of view, expressed in philosophy, literature, arts, and music, may be summed up according to the following points: (1) individualism, (2) emotionalism, (3) subjectivity, largely replacing classical objectivity, (4) favorite subjects: the ancient (particularly medieval), the supernatural (magic, witches, fairies, ghosts, etc.), the weird, and the mystic, and (5) nationalism.

Historical Background. The cultural, economic, political, and social order was greatly affected by momentous progress in science and mechanics (electromagnetic induction, photography, food canning, the railway and steamboat, steel production, electric light, telephone, telegraph, etc.). The Industrial Revolution brought on new social and economic problems, and the rise of capitalism and socialism. Important wars of the 19th century are: the Crimean War (1854–1856), the Civil War in the United States (1861–1865), and the Franco-Prussian War (1870). The most important development in art is French impressionism by the painters Manet, Degas, Renoir, and the sculptor Rodin. Whistler is considered one of the great 19th-century painters. The outstanding philosophies of the period belong to the Germans: Schopenhauer, Nietzsche, and Hegel. In literature and poetry there is a long list of illustrious names. In England, Byron, Wordsworth, Scott, Thackeray, Dickens, Hardy, Carlyle (Scottish essayist and historian), Coleridge, and Keats are the most outstanding. In Germany, Goethe, Richter, Heine, and E. T. A. Hoffmann (author, musician, and painter) are the principal writers in addition to the philosophers named above. In France, Hugo, Flaubert, Lamartine, and Musset are the leaders. The United States produced some great writers, chief among whom are Emerson, Longfellow, Poe, Hawthorne, and Mark Twain.

General Musical Aspects of the 19th Century. All of the five general aspects of romanticism apply to the music of the 19th century. Individualism is manifest in the great diversity of styles of individual composers. Emotional expression, personal feeling, and sentimentality are everywhere present in 19th-century music. Romantic subjects are evident in the songs and operas of the period. Nationalism in music becomes one of its marked characteristics in the second half of the century, when countries consciously fostered their own styles centered around folk music. And, in general, subjectivity replaced objectivity in music. There was great expansion of instrumental music, particularly for the orchestra and for the piano. The choral music of the period is comparatively unimportant. In the 19th century, program music is more important than at any other period in the history of music. Virtuosity became a marked characteristic; the virtuoso composer-performer in piano and violin became a phenomenon typical of the century. Germany and Austria were the leading countries in the Romantic period.

Specific Musical Characteristics. The 19th century reveals marked changes in musical style and in formal concepts, both of which are highly diverse in comparison to style and form in the Classical period.

MELODY. Romantic melody is characterized by warmth of personal feeling. It is less regular in phraseology than classical melody.

HARMONY. The 19th century sees an important expansion of harmonic idiom: new chords and new chord progressions are to be found. There is a greater use of chromaticism than in the 18th century. More altered chords and seventh and ninth chords are employed. A freer use of nonharmonic or non-chordal tones is manifest. Modulation becomes more of an end than a means, used more for its own effect than as a function to get from one key to another.

TONALITY. The basic concept of key feeling is still intact in the 19th century, but there is more tonal obscurity, fluid modulations obscuring the key feeling of whole passages. More remote keys and more varied key schemes are employed. In the late 19th century there are definite signs of departure from conventional tonal concepts.

COUNTERPOINT. Contrapuntal forms as such hold virtually no place at all in 19th-century music. Counterpoint is seldom used other than in a very secondary role, and it is even more rarely strict.

FORM. There is a great expansion of formal concepts and of formal freedom in the 19th century. Extremes of formal dimensions are characteristic of the period: great popularity of small forms in piano and song literature, and the growth to enormous lengths in symphony and opera. The essentially new forms of the period are numerous. (1) New stylized dances are the waltz (the slow Ländler and the fast Viennese waltzes), mazurka, polonaise, etc. (2) The *étude,* a technical study for any instrument, glorified for concert usage, becomes an important form. (3) In piano music the classical sonata form is largely replaced by various free forms called romanza, fantasy, arabesque, nocturne, ballad, etc., and also by descriptive pieces. (4) Symphonic music shows an expansion of classical symphonic form, and there are new symphonic forms: the symphonic poem, the symphonic suite, the program symphony, and the concert overture. (5) The most important formal development in opera of the 19th century is the Wagnerian music drama.

PREDOMINATING MEDIA. The 19th century is dominated by four principal media: (1) piano, (2) orchestra, (3) solo song with piano accompaniment, and (4) opera. Chamber music and religious and secular choral music are of less importance.

INSTRUMENTATION AND ORCHESTRATION. The 19th century sees an expansion of the orchestration. Three important names in this connection are Berlioz, Wagner, and Rimsky-Korsakov. Instrumental color is developed. Symphony orchestras are large and greater sonority is created by more extensive employment of brass, woodwinds, and percussion. Mechanical improvements and innovations had a great deal to do with the growth of the orchestra. The English horn added a new color to the orchestral palette. The invention and widespread use of valves for brass instruments greatly increased the usefulness of those instruments. The Böhm key systems applied to woodwind instruments greatly increased their effectiveness.

CHAPTER XXI

Beethoven

LUDWIG VAN BEETHOVEN (1770–1827) represents the end of the Classical period and the beginning of the Romantic period. Along with Palestrina, Bach, Haydn, and Mozart, he is one of the greatest masters of all time.

Beethoven's Place in Music History. Beethoven's music is of consummate greatness. Beethoven was a great individualist. More than any other master he freed music and musicians from servile status. He broke the confines and the artificial restraint of the Classical period by giving his own profound spirit free expression. Beethoven's early music is definitely classical, based upon the style of Haydn. His music of the middle and late periods reveals the subjectivity, emotionalism, and freedom of romanticism.

Beethoven's Style. Because he was the first great individualist in music history, Beethoven's music, though a product of his times, shows many remarkable features of style that reflect his character and at the same time set his music apart from that which went before and that which followed.

GENERAL FEATURES. There are four general features of Beethoven's music. (1) The most important of these is the profoundness of emotional content. This has been aptly called the "appassionata spirit," in reference to the great piano sonata, Opus 57, which so definitely reveals this quality. (2) Beethoven had a great sense of humor; but unlike Haydn's cheerful, light-hearted humor, his is gruff, rustic, and profound. The scherzo of the Fifth Symphony and the peasant dance of the Sixth Symphony are good examples of this characteristic. (3) Beethoven's impulsiveness and sudden changes of emotion are well known to readers of biography. These traits are clearly manifest in his music. (4) Closely associated with Beethovenian humor and impulsiveness is the element of surprise in his music. This is created by prolonged passages of suspense, then sudden changes of rhythm, key, dynamics, and by tremendous climaxes followed by abrupt introduction of a simple, naïve tune.

SPECIFIC FEATURES. The more specific aspects of Beethoven's style may be considered under five headings: thematic material, counterpoint, form, choral music, piano music.

a. *Types of Thematic Material*. Beethoven is a great master of thematic material. He employs two broad types of melody: (1) short motival first themes in sonatas, symphonies, etc. (e.g., the "fate motive" of the Fifth Symphony), and (2) beautiful cantabile melody (e.g., the adagio cantabile movement of the piano sonata, Opus 13).

b. *Counterpoint*. In his early- and middle-period works counterpoint is masterful but it is definitely subordinate. In his late works, however, at a time when elsewhere counterpoint was generally abandoned, Beethoven returned to the old contrapuntal practices and revealed a great mastery of this art (e.g., the fugue for string quartet, Opus 133).

c. *Form*. Beethoven is one of the greatest masters of form. He is a master of thematic development. He expanded sonata-allegro form to include more than two principal thematic materials and he even occasionally introduced new material in the development section or in the recapitulation. He greatly varied the plan of movement in the sonata: (1) He used variation form as an opening movement (Opus 26), or (2) a free fantasy as in the opening movement of the *Moonlight Sonata*. (3) He replaced the third movement minuet with a scherzo, a change of style rather than of formal structure. (4) He varied the number and type of movements in late works (e.g., the string quartet in C sharp minor, Opus 131, and the Ninth Symphony with a choral finale).

d. *Choral Music*. Beethoven's choral music is great because of the greatness of Beethoven's musical ideas and the profoundness of his expression, but he exceeds the limits of choral idiom, and treats his chorus as additional instrumental color.

e. *Piano Style.* In addition to the general features of style which apply to his piano music, there are several minor traits peculiar to his style in that medium. He creates a special effect of texture by the use of widely separated hands. Heavy thick chords in the low register of the piano are frequently noticeable. Occasional long sweeping chromatic scales, usually ascending, often lead to an emphatic objective in the music. He uses thirds moving in opposite directions.

Principal Contributions to Music Literature. In addition to three large vocal works, Beethoven worked principally in the fields of piano, orchestra, and chamber music.

PIANO LITERATURE. Beethoven's contributions to piano literature are chiefly 32 sonatas and 21 sets of variations.

ORCHESTRAL WORKS. Beethoven's 9 symphonies are among the greatest in the literature. The Ninth Symphony is notable for its finale, a setting of Schiller's *Ode to Joy* for vocal soloists and chorus. Equally famous are his overtures to *Egmont, Coriolanus,* 4 overtures to his opera *Fidelio* (*Leonore Overtures I, II,* and *III* and *Overture to Fidelio*), and the *Prometheus* ballet music. A violin concerto and 5 piano concertos should be added to the list of Beethoven's great orchestral music.

CHAMBER MUSIC. Beethoven's chamber music, with that of Brahms, is the greatest of the 19th century. He wrote 16 string quartets, 9 piano trios, and 10 violin sonatas. These are his most important contributions in the field of chamber music.

VOCAL WORKS. Three great vocal works by Beethoven are the opera *Fidelio,* the oratorio *Christus am Ölberg* ("Christ on the Mount of Olives"), and the *Missa solemnis in D.* In addition, Beethoven wrote some songs which are less important than the contemporary song literature of Schubert, although his song cycle, *An die ferne Geliebte,* should be mentioned.

CHAPTER XXII

19th-Century Opera

Nineteenth-century opera was developed chiefly in Italy, France, and Germany. The 19th century also saw the rise of nationalism, which is particularly manifest in operatic production. Opera reached a peak of development in the second half of the century.

Italian Opera

Italy, which had led the field since the beginning of opera in the early 17th century, still held a front rank in opera in the 19th century, although its prominence was shared almost equally by the developments in France and in Germany.

General Characteristics of Italian Opera. In the 19th century, virtuosity for its own sake is less prominent. Dramatic profundity is hardly to be found until Verdi late in the century. The bel canto style of song prevails, as does also the rapid parlando style of recitative. The chorus is more often and more prominently used, but the orchestra still plays a secondary role. Realism becomes an important aspect of opera in the late 19th century.

Composers, Styles, Works. Italian opera in the 19th century is dominated by four composers: Rossini, Bellini, Donizetti, and Verdi.

Rossini. Gioacchino Rossini (1792–1868) was more successful in the comic opera style than in opera seria. He had great facility. His sparkling wit, the vivacity of his music, and the rapid parlando style are characteristic. His principal works are *L'Italiana in Algeri* (1813), *Il Barbiere di Siviglia* ("The Barber of Seville," 1816), *La*

Gazza ladra ("The Thieving Magpie," 1817), *Mosè in Egitto* (1818), *Semiramide* (1813), and *Guillaume Tell* ("William Tell," 1829). The latter, produced in Paris, is typical French grand opera.

BELLINI. Vincenzo Bellini (1801–1835) reveals a generally high quality of emotional content. He employs appropriate libretti (by Romani). Sentimentality of his melodies, warm and flowing, is characteristic of his style, and they influenced Chopin's melody. His principal operas are *La Sonnambula* (1813), *Norma* (1832), and *I Puritani* (1834).

DONIZETTI. Gaetano Donizetti (1797–1848) is the third and last important Italian opera composer of the first half of the 19th century. He was less gifted and less original than Bellini but his superior training and technique are shown in his operas. His principal operas, among some 65 that he wrote, are *Lucrezia Borgia* (1833), *Lucia di Lammermoor* (1835), *La Favorita* (1840), *La Fille du régiment* ("The Daughter of the Regiment," Paris, 1840, opéra-comique), and *Don Pasquale* (Paris, 1843, opera buffa).

VERDI. Giuseppe Verdi (1813–1901) is the greatest Italian composer of opera in the entire century. He developed great power of characterization and dramatization. His late works show a greater profundity of spirit than those in the first half of the 19th century. The orchestra is more important than it is with his predecessors. He is truly Italian in spirit, not an imitator of his German contemporary, Wagner. His principal operas are *Rigoletto* (1851), *Il Trovatore* (1855), *La Traviata* (1855), *Aida* (1871–1872), which is characterized by its colorful pageantry, and *Otello* ("Othello," 1887), on a libretto by Boito, faithful to the Shakespearian drama. *Falstaff* (1893), his last great opera, is a return to buffa style but with greater profundity.

OTHER COMPOSERS. Realism, or *verismo,* is typical of other late 19th-century works by Pietro Mascagni (1863–1945) (*Cavalleria rusticana,* 1890), Ruggiero Leoncavallo (1858–1919) (*I Pagliacci,* 1892), and Giacomo Puccini (1858–1924) (*La Bohème, Madama Butterfly,* and *Tosca,* 1900).

French Opera

Whereas in the 18th century there was a clear demarcation between the comic opera and serious opera types, this distinction gradually became less evident during the 19th century, until in the second half of the century they merge. In France, in the first half of the 19th century, opéra-comique and grand opera exist side by side.

Opéra-Comique. The comic opera tradition which was paramount in the 18th century continues to flourish during the first half of the 19th century. It gradually began to develop in two directions. On the one hand it became more purely entertainment of the operetta type. On the other hand, it approached the style, form, and subject matter of serious opera, so that in the second half of the 19th century it grows into lyric opera.

COMPOSERS AND WORKS. The principal composers and opéras-comiques are François Boïeldieu (1775-1834) (*La Dame Blanche,* 1825); Daniel Auber (1782-1871) (*La Muette de Portici,* 1828, and *Fra Diavolo,* 1830); Louis Hérold (1791-1833) (*Le Pré aux clercs,* 1832); Victor Massé (1822-1884) (*Les Noces de Jeannette,* 1853); and Charles Gounod (1818-1893) (*Le Médecin malgré lui,* 1857).

Grand Opera. New developments took place in French grand opera in the first half of the 19th century which made it a rival of opéra-comique. This is often referred to as the "grand spectacle opera," which describes its general character, featuring grandiose schemes, heroic or historical subjects, extravagant characters and situations, demons and men in conflict, plainsong or chorale juxtaposed with ballet tunes, and great choral masses. The chief exponent of this style of opera was Giacomo Meyerbeer (1791-1864), whose principal works are *Robert le Diable* (1831), *Les Huguenots* (1836), *Le Prophète* (1849), and *L'Africaine* (1860). In the second half of the 19th century the French leaned toward a lyric style of opera as well as retaining some aspects of the grand spectacle opera. Charles Gounod's *Faust* (1859) and *Roméo et Juliette* (1867), Thomas' *Mignon* (1866), and Massenet's *Manon* (1884) reveal a tender sentiment and no great heights of passion, characteristically French refinement of style, good declamation, and good stage orchestration.

COMPOSERS AND WORKS. In addition to the composers and works already mentioned, there is a long list of operatic works belonging to the second half of the 19th century: Jacques Halévy (1799-1862), an imitator of Meyerbeer, wrote *La Juive* (1835); Hector Berlioz (1803-1869), *Les Troyens* (1858); Georges Bizet (1838-1875), *Carmen* (1875); Edouard Lalo (1823-1892), *Le Roi d'Ys* (1876-1888); Léo Delibes (1836-1891), *Le Roi l'a dit* and *Lakmé* (1883); Jacques Offenbach (1819-1880), *Les Contes d'Hoffmann* (1881); Camille Saint-Saëns (1835-1921), *Samson et Dalila* (1877); Gustave Charpentier (1860-1956), *Louise* (1900); Jules Massenet (1842-1912), *Manon* (1884); Alexis Chabrier (1841-1894), *Gwendoline* (1886), resembling Wagner's *Tristan;* Vincent d'Indy (1851-1931), *Fervaal* (1895); and, finally, Debussy, the impressionistic opera *Pelléas et Mélisande* (1902).

German Opera

In Germany two significant developments in opera took place in the 19th century. The first is the rise of German romantic opera in the first half of the century. The second is the *music drama* of Richard Wagner.

German Romantic Opera. German romantic opera springs from the German Singspiel of the late 18th century and the early 19th century. It has even been said that all German opera from Mozart's *Entführung* and *Zauberflöte* to Wagner's music dramas are merely enlarged Singspiele in style. New elements come into German opera in the first half of the century.

CHARACTERISTICS. The fundamental characteristics of German romantic opera are: (1) The subjects are derived from German folklore and legend. (2) There is a romantic treatment of nature and natural phenomena. (3) There is an important use of supernatural agencies to heighten dramatic interest. (4) German folk song, or folk song style, is used along with more conventional operatic styles of aria.

COMPOSERS. The most important representative of German romantic opera is Carl Maria von Weber (1786-1826). In addition to the general characteristics of romantic opera, Weber's operas point toward Wagner in the attempt to fuse the arts, and to gain dramatic realism by avoiding repetition of lines or verses in arias. His principal operas are *Der Freischütz* (1821), *Euryanthe* (1823), and *Oberon* (1826). Other composers are Beethoven, *Fidelio* (1805); Ludwig Spohr, *Faust* (1818) and *Jessonda* (1823); E. T. A. Hoffmann, whose *Undine* (1816) forms a connecting link between literature and music; Heinrich Marschner (1795–1861), *Der Vampyr* (1828) and *Hans Heiling* (1833); Robert Schumann, *Genoveva* (1850); Konradin Kreutzer, *Nachtlager von Granada* (1834); Reissinger, *Felsenmühle* (1833); Friedrich von Flotow, *Martha* (1847); Albert Lortzing (1801–1851), *Czar und Zimmermann* (1837) and *Der Wildschütz* (1842); Otto Nicolai (1810–1849), *Die lustigen Weiber von Windsor* ("The Merry Wives of Windsor," 1849); and Richard Wagner's *Der fliegende Holländer* ("The Flying Dutchman," 1841).

Wagner and the Music Drama. The most important figure in 19th-century opera is Richard Wagner (1813–1883), who achieved a fusion of the arts in his music dramas. He is one of the greatest geniuses of all time.

CHARACTERISTICS. The fully developed music drama shows marked departure in general concept, style, and form from all other operatic production.

a. *Fusion of Arts.* Wagner conceived the music drama as a work in which music, poetry, and stagecraft are fused to form a new dramatic whole. He believed that no one art should at any time dominate the drama. This resulted in dramatic unity and dramatic truth surpassing anything in the operatic field.

b. *Libretto.* Wagner wrote his own libretti. They are perfectly conceived literary works for his music dramas. Three fundamental bases of his libretti are (1) German folklore, mythology, and legend, (2) romantic mysticism, the supernatural, and the medieval, and (3) the idea of redemption, often associated with some religious implications.

c. *Continuity.* One of the most notable features of Wagnerian music drama is continuity. This is achieved in part by the important innovation of abandoning the distinction between recitative and aria. The continuous melodic line, the nonperiodic rhythm, and the constant use of the orchestra all contribute to the over-all aspect of continuity.

d. *Leitmotif.* Another significant aspect of Wagnerian music drama is the use of themes, called *leitmotifs,* throughout the opera. These thematic ideas are connected with a particular person, idea, situation, or mood, and they are variable according to the dramatic requirement of the moment. They are developed symphonically throughout the opera. By their use Wagner attained musical unity and dramatic coherence.

e. *The Wagnerian Orchestra.* The orchestra is highly important to Wagnerian music drama, carrying as it does its share of dramatic content in a continuous flow of music. Aside from operatic considerations, important developments in instrumentation and orchestration are found in the music drama. Wagner generally increased the size of the orchestra. He used complete choirs of instruments (e.g., three clarinets and bass clarinet). Brass choirs are used more extensively than heretofore. The strings are often divided, and special ethereal effects are obtained by using them in high registers and with tremolo. The significance of Wagner's orchestral music is reflected in the fact that considerable portions of it are used in concert form.

f. *Other Aspects of Style.* Wagner's harmony is characteristically chromatic. Chromaticism also plays an important part in the melodic style. Wagner makes a significant use of counterpoint, an element heretofore neglected in opera. On the whole, he makes little use of the chorus (*Die Meistersinger* is a notable exception).

WORKS. Wagner set forth his ideas in several treatises on the subject of music and drama. The principal ones are *The Artwork of the Future* (1850), and *Opera and Drama* (1851). These were written during a period of political exile (1849–1864). His operas are: *Die Feen* (1833); *Das Liebesverbot* (1836); *Rienzi* (1840), which is a spectacle opera reminiscent of Meyerbeer; *Der fliegende Holländer* (1841); *Tannhäuser* (1845); *Lohengrin* (1845), which is the last work Wagner called romantic opera; *Das Rheingold* (1854), which is Part I of the great operatic tetralogy entitled *Der Ring des Nibelungen; Die Walküre* (1856), which is Part II of the *Ring; Tristan und Isolde* (1859); *Die Meistersinger* (1867); *Siegfried* (1871), which is Part III of the *Ring; Götterdämmerung* (1874), which is Part IV of the *Ring;* and *Parsifal* (1882), Wagner's last opera.

Other 19th-Century Opera

The major developments in opera in the 19th century have been outlined under the three nationalities, Italian, French, and German. In addition there are a few outstanding works in other countries to be mentioned.

Russian National Opera. Nationalism in Russian music is said to begin with the opera by Michail Glinka (1804–1857), *A Life for the Tsar* (1836), which nevertheless shows strong Italian influence. *Russlan et Ludmilla* (1842) is a second important opera by Glinka. Other Russian composers and operas are: Alexander Dargomijski (1813–1869), *Roussalka* (1856) and *The Stone Guest* (1872); Modest Moussorgsky (1839–1881), *Boris Godunov* (1874), a highly important Russian work; Alexander Borodin (1833–1887), *Prince Igor* (completed and produced posthumously, 1890); Tschaikovsky (1840–1893), *Eugen Onegin* (1877), romantic but not nationalist; and Nicolai Rimsky-Korsakov (1844–1908), who produced a great number of Russian operas: *May Night* (1878), *Snow Maiden* (1881), *Mlada* (1895), *Sadko* (1896), *Tsar's Bride* (1898), *Tsar Saltan* (1900), *Pan Voyevoda,* and *Le Coq d'or* (before 1908).

Bohemian National Opera. National opera in Bohemia is chiefly represented by *Prodana nevesta* ("The Bartered Bride"), a comic opera by Bedřich Smetana (1824–1884). Anton Dvořák's *King and Collier* (1874) is also an example of Bohemian national opera.

Opera in England. Operatic production in England in the 19th century is of little consequence, with the exception of the famous Gilbert and Sullivan operettas in the last quarter of the century. The wit, humor, rollicking tunes, and clever satire of these creations are peculiarly English. The principal Gilbert and Sullivan operettas are: *Trial by Jury* (1875), *H. M. S. Pinafore* (1878), which ran for over 700 consecutive nights, *The Pirates of Penzance* (1880), *Patience* (1881), *Iolanthe* (1882), *Princess Ida* (1884), *The Mikado* (1885), *The Yeomen of the Guard* (1888), *The Gondoliers* (1889), and *Utopia Limited* (1893).

CHAPTER XXIII

19th-Century Oratorio and Choral Music

DESPITE the fact that oratorio in the 19th century was overshadowed by opera, and that choral music was less popular than other media, there were some notable contributions to both fields.

Oratorio

Little oratorio of consequence was written from the time of Handel, who overshadowed all consequent attempts in the field of oratorio, until Mendelssohn's *St. Paul* and *Elijah,* which represent the peak of artistic creation in that form in the 19th century.

Mendelssohn Oratorio. The greatest 19th-century composer of oratorio is Felix Mendelssohn (1809–1847).

STYLE. The greatness of Mendelssohn's oratorios rests primarily upon his outstanding choral technique. His style in general is reminiscent of Handelian technique plus the addition of romantic elements. He wrote melody of high quality. He was skilled in instrumentation, and he had a great sense of form. All these factors combined to make his oratorios the principal masterworks of the century in that field.

PRINCIPAL WORKS. Mendelssohn wrote a symphony-cantata called *Lobgesang* ("Song of Praise"). His oratorio, *St. Paul,* makes use of chorales. *Elijah* (1846) is Mendelssohn's greatest oratorio. *Die Walpurgisnacht* (1842) is a secular cantata on a text by Goethe.

Other 19th-Century Oratorio. The first important oratorio of the 19th century is Beethoven's *Christus am Ölberg* ("Christ on the Mount of Olives," 1800). A work which enjoyed popularity until the appearance of Mendelssohn's oratorios is Spohr's *Das letzte*

Gericht ("The Last Judgment"). Other oratorios of the 19th century are: Schumann's *Das Paradies und die Peri* (1844), Berlioz' *Damnation de Faust* (1846), a secular oratorio, and *L'Enfance du Christ* (1854), which is a cantata trilogy, Liszt's *St. Elizabeth,* a concerto-oratorio with Wagnerian leitmotifs, and *Christus* (1873). Some important English oratorios of the late 19th century are: Stainer's *The Crucifixion* (1887), Hubert Parry's *Judith* (1888), *Job* (1892), and *King Saul* (1900), Elgar's *The Dream of Gerontius* (1900) and *The Kingdom* (1906).

Sacred Choral Music

Much of the sacred choral literature in the 19th century assumes the romantic operatic spirit, making it difficult to distinguish between cantata and oratorio on the one hand and liturgical church music on the other.

Principal Forms of Church Music. Settings of the Catholic Ordinary of the Mass and the Requiem continued to be made in the 19th century. Most of these were for concert rather than liturgical purposes. In addition there were numerous settings of the Psalms.

Composers of Religious Choral Music. Mendelssohn and Brahms are the two greatest choral composers of the 19th century. Mendelssohn's *Psalms* for chorus and orchestra, his *Lauda Sion* for chorus and orchestra, and his Opus 39, motets for female voices and organ, are his chief contributions to sacred choral literature. Brahms's *Deutsches Requiem* ("German Requiem") is his greatest work in sacred choral literature. It is based upon Biblical selections rather than upon the Catholic Requiem text. In addition, he wrote *Ave Maria* for female voices, orchestra, and organ, and settings of the Psalms. Other composers and works in this field are: Schumann, *Mass in C Minor;* Berlioz, *Requiem* and *Te Deum;* Liszt, *Graner Mass* and *Ungarische Krönungs-Messe* ("Hungarian Coronation Mass"); Cherubini, *Mass in D Minor;* Beethoven, *Missa solemnis;* Schubert, 6 Latin Masses, 1 German Mass, 5 Salve Reginas, 2 Stabat Maters, etc.; Verdi, *Requiem;* Gabriel Fauré, *Requiem;* César Franck, *Les Béatitudes* (an oratorio) and *Psalms;* and Bruckner, *Te Deum, Mass in F Minor,* and other Masses.

Secular Choral Music

The 19th century produced a dearth of high quality choral music. With a few exceptions, the secular choral music was of a decidedly cheap and popular nature. Notable exceptions are the fine part songs of Mendelssohn and numerous larger works by Brahms: the *Alto Rhapsody,* for alto solo, male chorus, and orchestra, *The Song of Destiny* for chorus and orchestra, *The Song of Triumph* for eight-part chorus, and *Nänie* for chorus and orchestra. Anton Bruckner also wrote some solid works for male chorus. The choral finales of Beethoven's Ninth Symphony and Liszt's *Faust Symphony* are notable examples of 19th-century symphonic works using chorus.

CHAPTER XXIV

The Solo Song

T̶HE accompanied art song, as opposed to folk song, popular song, and operatic aria, is one of the most significant developments of the 19th century. The chief contributions to this form of music come from Germany, where the lied (German art song) was developed. Song composition in France and Russia in the second half of the century is also important. In Italy, where opera always eclipsed every other kind of musical activity, and in England, the solo song literature is negligible.

General Considerations. The rise of great German romantic poetry is an important factor in the development of the lied. Another factor is the rise of the piano in the early 19th century. Its increased sonority over earlier keyboard instruments provided an adequate support for the solo voice. Greater attention was given to appropriate musical setting of the text than ever before.

SONG CYCLE. Songs of a related character and subject, usually composed to the verses of one poet, were written. Such groups are called *song cycles* or *Liederkreise*. Important examples of song cycles are Beethoven's *An die ferne Geliebte* (1816), Schubert's *Die schöne Müllerin* (1823) and *Winterreise* (1827), Schumann's *Frauenliebe und Leben* (1840) and *Dichterliebe* (1840), Brahms's *Magelone* (1861–1868), Fauré's *La Bonne chanson* (1892), and Debussy's *Chansons de Bilitis* (1897).

FORM. Two structural plans are used in the accompanied solo song. One is the *strophic song* in which the same music is used for each stanza. The other plan is called *through-composed* (or *durchkom-*

poniert) in which the music changes with each stanza according to the nature of the text. The latter plan came to be used more extensively in song literature.

German Lied Composers. Early romantic song composers in Germany are Beethoven, Reichardt, Zelter, and Zumsteeg.

FRANZ SCHUBERT. Franz Schubert (1797–1828) is the greatest master of the lied. He is one of the greatest melodic geniuses of all time. His melodies and accompaniments show sensitivity to the text. He was one of the first to employ the through-composed plan of text setting. He wrote over 600 songs and two famous song cycles.

FELIX MENDELSSOHN. The song literature of Felix Mendelssohn (1809–1847) is characterized by its excellence of melody but a lack of variety, and a rather loose connection between music and text. He usually employed the strophic plan.

ROBERT SCHUMANN. The songs of Schumann (1810–1856) are typically romantic. The importance of the piano is to be seen in that the accompaniment is often more important than the melody. His songs are also sometimes declamatory in style. He is best in settings of Heine poems.

KARL LOEWE. Karl Loewe (1796–1869) was a master of 19th-century ballad form.

HUGO WOLF. Absorption in the text and great power in bringing out the mood of the text are characteristics of Wolf (1860–1903). Richness of harmony is also typical. Wolf was almost exclusively a song composer.

JOHANNES BRAHMS. The songs of Johannes Brahms (1833–1897) show characteristic attention to formal considerations. They are mostly strophic, and often strongly flavored with German folk song style. Richness and moodiness are generally typical of Brahms harmonies.

ROBERT FRANZ. Robert Franz (1815–1892) was exclusively a song composer. He limited his songs to subjects of extreme emotion and wrote only for the mezzo-soprano voice.

French Song Composers. All French opera composers contributed to some extent to song literature. The poets Verlaine and Baudelaire had a great deal to do with the excellence of French song literature in the second half of the 19th century. Refinement and taste are characteristic of the French song literature of this period. The principal composers of French songs are: Gounod, Duparc, Fauré, Chausson, and Debussy.

Russian Song Composers. The principal contributors to song literature in Russia in the 19th century are: Glinka, Tschaikovsky, Rachmaninoff, Grechaninov, Glière, and Moussorgsky.

CHAPTER XXV

19th-Century Piano Music

Piano music is one of the most important developments of the 19th century. Interest in piano music from the middle of the century eclipsed even interest in the orchestra.

General Characteristics. The piano came into general use early in the 19th century. Its sonority, greater than that of earlier keyboard instruments, opened the way for new developments in idiom, and its warmth of tone and its power were an inspiration for the expression of romantic ideas. Keyboard technique reached new heights and this resulted in the prominence, excesses, and even extremes of virtuosity. The pianist-composer was a phenomenon of the Romantic period.

Form. The new medium of the piano plus the currents of romanticism combined to produce entirely new styles. Short pieces for piano were generally characteristic of the period. Pieces with descriptive titles were also popular. Stylized dances of the 19th century were the waltz, the mazurka, and the polonaise. Eighteenth-century dances, such as the minuet, gavotte, bourée, etc., disappeared early in the 19th century. Numerous free forms came into being, works with no predetermined structural principles: romanza, fantasy, nocturne, ballade, novelette, etc. The variation form was employed throughout the century, but it often revealed shallow virtuosity rather than artistic skill. The étude is a piece based upon one or more aspects of technique, it is often openly virtuosic, and it is glorified for concert performance. Sonata form was generally neglected after Beethoven and Schubert. The suite and contrapuntal forms are virtually absent from 19th-century piano literature.

Principal Composers. Nearly all the important piano music of the 19th century belongs to Germany.

BEETHOVEN. The first quarter of the 19th century is characterized by the expansion of classical forms in the hands of Beethoven. His 32 piano sonatas and his 21 sets of variations are the greatest achievements in these forms. Details of his style are discussed on page 140.

SCHUBERT. Schubert's piano music is a mixture of classical and romantic elements. He wrote sonatas based on classical patterns. He also wrote fantasies, impromptus, and numerous pieces of a decidedly romantic nature. Schubert was a genius of melodic invention but not of thematic development. His music is poetic and lyric rather than clever or profound.

SCHUMANN. Schumann is the arch-romanticist in all his music. In his piano music he wrote exclusively in romantic forms and in a completely romantic style. His piano works consist of the romantic free forms and, most extensive of all, pieces with descriptive titles. He wrote collections of short, descriptive pieces: *Davidsbündlertänze, Papillons,* and *Carnival.* Schumann's music for piano is seldom brilliant, seldom excessively virtuosic. His longer piano compositions seem to be constructed by joining together several smaller forms.

MENDELSSOHN. Mendelssohn's piano music is less significant than that of his principal contemporaries and less significant than his own music in other media. He wrote capriccios, scherzos, and concert variations in a style more virtuosic than that of Schumann. He also wrote short pieces of a poetic, lyric nature, such as the *Songs without Words.*

CHOPIN. Frédéric Chopin (1810-1849) was almost exclusively a composer for the piano. More than any other 19th-century composer he developed piano idiom through his astute awareness of the possibilities of the instrument. Chopin's music depends to a great extent upon the use of the sustaining pedal, or, more properly, the damper pedal. This mechanism enables the production of greater sonorities than can be sustained by the two hands alone, and it also paves the way to more modern effects of mixed harmonies. Chopin's melodic style is a lyric, cantabile style with melismatic variation, used principally in the nocturne type of composition. Virtuosity is characteristic of the études and preludes particularly. Chromaticism and fluctuating tonality are marked characteristics of Chopin's style. His music represents Polish nationalism in the use of polonaises and mazurkas. His style in general is a mixture of French and German romanticism. He wrote polonaises, ballades, mazurkas, waltzes, nocturnes, preludes, études, impromptus, and freely romantic sonatas. He was essentially a piano composer, and his attempts in other media (e.g., 2 piano concertos) are less successful, less idiomatic.

LISZT. Franz Liszt (1811–1886) is the great virtuoso pianist-composer of the 19th century. Virtuosity is prominent in nearly all of his piano compositions. He is fond of frequently introducing cadenza-like material. Chromaticism and unusual progressions characterize his harmonic style. His melodies are often romantic, sentimental. His music has a certain formal looseness. In addition to much piano music, Liszt is noted for his numerous difficult and sometimes unidiomatic transcriptions for piano of works by Paganini, Bach, Verdi, Wagner, etc.

BRAHMS. Johannes Brahms wrote a considerable amount of piano music, less idiomatic than that of Chopin, but he shows great attention to structural form. Rich, dark harmony, and special textures are characteristic of his music. His variations especially show a more important use of counterpoint than is typical of the 19th century in general. Brahms wrote intermezzi, variations, capriccios, sonatas, rhapsodies, fantasies, ballades, and romances. His sonatas are more reminiscent of the nobility and greatness of Beethoven than are any other sonatas of the 19th century.

OTHER COMPOSERS. Other composers of 19th-century piano music are Grieg, MacDowell, Albéniz, Granados, Reger, Busoni, and Fauré.

CHAPTER XXVI

Instrumental Ensemble Music

THE instrumental ensemble music of the 19th century may be considered under two main categories: symphonic music which expanded enormously in the century, and chamber music which was one of the least popular fields.

Symphonic Music

General Considerations. During the 19th century the symphony orchestra and symphonic form show tremendous expansion. The technique of orchestration grew accordingly. The greatest names in this field of development are Beethoven, Berlioz, Wagner, and Rimsky-Korsakov.

Symphonic Forms and Styles. Whereas sonata form was largely abandoned in piano music after Beethoven, it was retained as the basic form of the symphony throughout the 19th century. Other forms were added.

SYMPHONY. Beethoven expanded the classical symphony with new freedom of expression. Romantic composers following Beethoven replaced classical style with romantic style and romantic treatment of thematic material. Although retaining the broad outlines of the classical symphonic structure, the romantic symphony handles the thematic material much more freely. Programmatic aspects of symphonic music were soon adopted by many romantic composers, Berlioz being the chief exponent of this idea.

CONCERTO. All the features of the romantic symphony except the programmatic aspects apply to the romantic concerto. Concertos were written principally for piano and for violin. Here is a notable extension of virtuosity, with characteristically elaborate and brilliant cadenzas.

SYMPHONIC POEM. The symphonic poem, developed in the second half of the 19th century, was an outgrowth of the earlier program symphony. It was originated by Liszt. It is a large, free form in one movement. It is usually programmatic: (1) either on a narrative basis (e.g., Strauss's *Till Eulenspiegel*) or (2) pictorial or descriptive but not narrative (e.g., Debussy's *L'Après-midi d'un faune* and Liszt's *Les Préludes*).

SYMPHONIC SUITE. The symphonic suite of the 19th century has no affinity with the baroque orchestral suite. The symphonic suite consists of several movements of a related programmatic nature but descriptive rather than narrative (e.g., Debussy's *La Mer* and Rimsky-Korsakov's *Scheherazade*). The symphonic suite also includes incidental music for drama (Grieg's *Peer Gynt Suite*) and ballet music (Tschaikovsky's *Nutcracker Suite*).

CONCERT OVERTURE. The overture not connected with opera was a form employed moderately often by 19th-century composers. It is usually in a modified sonata-allegro form, with more structural definitude than the symphonic poem. Several diverse examples of concert overture may be cited: (1) Beethoven's *Coriolanus Overture* and *Egmont Overture* are incidental or entr'acte music to plays. (2) Mendelssohn's music to "A Midsummer Night's Dream" belongs to the category of incidental music. The whole work, including the overture, is an orchestral suite because of its several movements and its descriptive nature. (3) Mendelssohn's *Hebrides Overture* is descriptive and programmatic. (4) Brahms's *Academic Festival Overture* is occasional music, i.e., written for a particular event or occasion.

SYMPHONIC VARIATIONS. Though not completely abandoned in the 19th century, variation form was not one of the most extensively employed for the symphony orchestra. Notable examples of symphonic variations are: Brahms's *Variations on a Theme by Haydn,* César Franck's *Symphonic Variations* for piano and orchestra, D'Indy's *Istar Variations,* and Elgar's *Enigma Variations.*

POPULAR TYPES OF ORCHESTRAL MUSIC. Considerable quantities of a more popular type of orchestral music were written in the 19th century. The most important of these are the Viennese waltzes of Johann Strauss (1825–1899). Other types of orchestral entertainment music, replacing the classical serenades of the 18th century, were the ballet suites and opera suites, and potpourri overtures from stage works.

Principal Composers, Works, Styles. The principal contributions to symphonic literature in the Romantic period came from Germany. In the second half of the century, however, France, Russia, and other countries began to contribute to the enormous literature of that period.

BEETHOVEN. 19th-century symphonic literature begins with Beethoven. (See Chapter XXI.)

SCHUBERT. Schubert wrote 8 symphonies and 8 overtures. He employs a conventional orchestration of the late Classical period, and classical symphonic form. His melodies are great, showing the typical lyric, songlike quality so characteristic of Schubert. But there is a deficiency of technical resources in his music and no abundance of thematic development, his themes usually being merely repeated or transposed. His music is full of ingenious harmony and modulations.

SCHUMANN. Schumann wrote 4 symphonies, 4 concert overtures, and a piano concerto. His orchestration is romantic but rather uninspired in its thick, drab texture with almost constant mixing of strings, woodwinds, and brass. His melodic style is definitely romantic as is also his freedom with the symphonic form. Strong rhythmic traits are noticeable, especially his use of syncopation and dotted rhythms.

MENDELSSOHN. Mendelssohn wrote 5 symphonies, concert overtures, 1 violin concerto, and 2 piano concertos. His symphonic music leans rather heavily upon programmatic ideas. His orchestration is clear and bright, particularly in the very characteristic scherzo style he developed by the use of woodwinds and light strings in high registers playing rapid figures.

BERLIOZ. Berlioz, the most famous French symphonist of the first half of the 19th century, wrote 4 program symphonies and 5 dramatic concert overtures. His chief contribution to symphonic music is in the field of instrumentation and orchestration. In addition to advancing a more colorful orchestration in his music, he wrote a treatise on orchestration that in many respects is still standard today. He is one of the chief exponents of symphonic program music, an example of which is his *Fantastic Symphony*. In this and other works he uses the *idée fixe,* a sort of leitmotif recurrent throughout the work. His *Roman Carnival* is a concert overture.

BRAHMS. Brahms is generally considered the greatest symphonic composer in the second half of the 19th century. He wrote 4 symphonies, 2 symphonic overtures, symphonic variations, 2 serenades, 1 violin concerto, 1 double concerto for violin and cello, and 2 piano concertos. Rich, full, and varied color characterizes his orchestration. His harmony is likewise rich and full, and often somber. Brahms is a great formalist and his symphonies show mastery of architectural proportions. Other prominent features of his style are the use of wide-range thematic material, important contrapuntal qualities, use of cross-rhythms and rhythmic modification of thematic material, and the use of root and third without the fifth in chords and themes.

LISZT. The principal contribution of Liszt to symphonic literature is the symphonic poem, in which form he wrote 13 works. In addition he wrote a *Faust Symphony* for orchestra, tenor solo and male chorus. Virtuosity plays an important part in Liszt's orchestral style. This is, of course, also evident in his concertos for piano in E♭ and A. His melodies are often romantic, sentimental. His rhythmic style is often influenced by Hungarian patterns. His harmony is characteristically chromatic. His formal structures are rather loose, rhapsodic, and improvisatory.

BRUCKNER. The symphonic works of Anton Bruckner (1824–1896) consist of an early overture and 11 symphonies, 2 of which are incomplete. Austrian romanticism and Schubertian style of melody are characteristic of his symphonic music. He uses Wagnerian orchestration and harmonic style. The great length of his formal structures is notable.

MAHLER. Gustav Mahler (1860–1911) wrote 10 symphonies (the last incomplete), of which No. 8 (the *Symphony of a Thousand*) is the most famous, as well as *Das Lied von der Erde,* a song cycle for symphony orchestra, tenor, and alto. Romantic sentimentality is present in most of his music. Like Bruckner, he employs a Wagnerian style of orchestration and harmony. He makes considerable use of solo instruments and solo voices (in Symphonies 2, 3, 4, and 8). His symphonies, like those of Bruckner, are of extraordinary length.

STRAUSS. Richard Strauss (1864–1949) is a transitional figure whose music represents a continuation of Wagnerian orchestral traditions and the symphonic poem into the realm of modern neoromanticism. (See page 172.) His principal orchestral works are: *Till Eulenspiegel, Don Juan, Also sprach Zarathustra* ("Thus Spake Zarathustra"), *Don Quixote* (fantastic variations for violoncello and orchestra), *Ein Heldenleben* ("A Hero's Life"), and *Symphonia Domestica.*

French Symphonic Literature. Except for Berlioz, French symphonic composition was not extensively developed until the second half of the 19th century. To summarize the principal composers and works represented in standard symphonic repertory: Saint-Saëns wrote 5 symphonies, symphonic poems, and 2 orchestral suites. Lalo is noted primarily for his *Symphonie espagnole* for violin solo and orchestra. César Franck's *Symphony in D Minor* continues to be popular. His pupil, Chausson, wrote 1 symphony. D'Indy wrote program symphonies, symphonic poems, and 3 symphonic overtures. Bizet's *L'Arlésienne Suite* is his most popular orchestral work.

Russian Symphonic Literature. Russian symphonic literature begins in the last quarter of the 19th century. Its expansion parallels the development of Russian nationalism.

TSCHAIKOVSKY. The highly romantic works of Peter Ilich Tschaikovsky (1840–1893) have enjoyed a popularity out of proportion to their artistic merits. Tschaikovsky wrote 7 symphonies (including the *Manfred Symphony*), 6 orchestral suites, 11 symphonic poems and overtures, 3 piano concertos, the best known of which is that in B-flat minor, and the violin concerto in D. His melody is romantic, and only partly Russian in quality. His harmony and orchestration are basically German. His symphonic works all reveal structural weaknesses, particularly in long passages of aimless padding and repetition. In all his works there is to be found brooding melancholy and noisy ebullience.

RIMSKY-KORSAKOV. Of all symphonic works by Rimsky-Korsakov (1844-1908), the orchestral suite *Scheherazade* is the best known. He wrote 3 symphonies, of which *Antar* is the most famous, as well as symphonic poems, and overtures. His most significant contribution is his masterful and brilliant orchestration. His treatise on orchestration is standard. His music is characterized by Orientalism, and exotic harmony and subjects. He is also one of the most prominent exponents of Russian nationalism.

MOUSSORGSKY. The symphonic music of Modest Moussorgsky (1839-1881) is not extensive, but it is important in that it shows signs of departure from romantic styles toward a more modern Russian idiom. His principal orchestral work is the symphonic poem *Night on Bald Mountain.*

OTHER RUSSIAN COMPOSERS. Alexander Borodin (1833-1887) wrote 3 symphonies, a few symphonic poems, the best known being *The Steppes of Central Asia.* Balakirev (1837-1910) wrote 2 symphonies, 3 symphonic poems, 3 overtures, and 1 orchestral suite. These are rarely performed on symphony programs.

Other Symphonic Works of the 19th Century. A few additional composers and works should be mentioned: Dvořák's *Symphony from the New World,* Grieg's *Peer Gynt Suite,* Smetana's symphonic cycle, *My Fatherland,* Albéniz's *Iberian Suite,* originally written for piano, and Elgar's *Enigma Variations.*

Chamber Music

Chamber music, on the whole, was one of the least popular media during the 19th century. The limitations of chamber music media point toward the absolute rather than the emotional or programmatic, toward the objective rather than the subjective, toward the classical rather than the romantic spirit. Nevertheless, some great chamber music was composed in the 19th century.

Summary of Principal 19th-Century Chamber Music Composers.
Beethoven and Brahms are the two greatest masters of 19th-century
chamber music. The following summary of the works of the principal composers of chamber music shows a variety of instrumental
combinations.

BEETHOVEN. Beethoven wrote 10 violin sonatas, 5 cello sonatas,
9 piano trios, 4 string trios, 1 horn sonata, 1 string quintet, and 16
string quartets.

SCHUBERT. Schubert wrote 14 string quartets, 2 piano trios, a quintet, a string quintet, and an octet.

SCHUMANN. Schumann wrote 3 string quartets, a piano quartet,
a piano quintet, 3 piano trios, 2 violin sonatas, and numerous ro-
manzas, fantasies, etc., for various instruments with piano.

MENDELSSOHN. Mendelssohn's output in chamber music was 7
string quartets, 3 piano quartets, 2 string quintets, 2 string trios,
a violin sonata, 2 cello sonatas, an octet, and concert variations for
cello and piano.

BRAHMS. Brahms wrote 3 string quartets, 2 string quintets, 3 piano
quartets, a piano quintet, 3 piano trios, a clarinet quintet, a *Horn
Trio* (for French horn, piano, and violin), a clarinet trio, 2 clarinet
sonatas, 3 violin sonatas, 2 cello sonatas, and 2 sextets. In addition
to the extensive literature for chamber ensembles, Brahms also wrote
some significant organ music: fugues and chorale preludes.

FRANCK. César Franck wrote 1 string quartet, 4 piano trios, and
a piano quintet. His organ music is of substantial value.

FAURÉ. Gabriel Fauré wrote 2 piano quintets, 2 piano quartets,
and a piano trio.

CHAPTER XXVII

Summary of Principal Composers

THE principal composers of the 19th century have been mentioned in the foregoing chapters of Part Five in connection with each of the principal fields of musical development. The following summary lists the great masters of the period according to country and the fields of musical activity and chief contributions to musical development.

Germany. Germany is the leading country of the 19th century, and is represented in all fields of music.

BEETHOVEN: transition from classical to romantic; symphony, sonata, and chamber music.

WEBER: romantic opera and symphonic works; some piano music.

SCHUBERT: song, piano music, and symphony.

SCHUMANN: song, piano music, and symphony. Schumann is also the most noted 19th-century critic. As editor of the *Neue Zeitschrift für Musik* ("New Musical Journal") he wrote many essays and valuable criticisms championing the cause of good music and musicians through the fictitious "Davidsbündler" (i.e., the society of David against the musical Philistines).

MENDELSSOHN: choral music, oratorio, symphony, piano music, and organ music. Mendelssohn was also one of the leading conductors of the first half of the 19th century. In this connection his greatest contribution was the revival of Bach's *St. Matthew Passion* in 1829, marking the beginning of a great revival of interest in Bach's music which had been forgotten for nearly a century.

BRAHMS: symphonic music, chamber music, choral works, song, piano and organ music.

LISZT: piano virtuosity in composition and performance, symphonic poem, numerous transcriptions. Although Hungarian by birth, Liszt really belongs to the school of German romantic composers.

WAGNER: music drama, opera.

STRAUSS: symphonic poem, opera, songs.

Italy. The sole contribution of Italy in the 19th century is opera, instrumental fields being almost totally neglected.

ROSSINI: opera; especially excelled in buffa opera.

BELLINI: romantic Italian opera.

DONIZETTI: romantic Italian opera.

VERDI: the greatest master of 19th-century Italian opera.

France. The chief contribution of France in the 19th century is opera. In the second half of the century instrumental music and the solo song were developed.

MEYERBEER: romantic French opera.

BERLIOZ: orchestration, program symphony.

CHOPIN: exclusively a composer of piano music. Although Chopin was Polish by birth and exhibits Polish nationalist traits in some of his music, he may be considered as belonging to the French school because of his residence and associations in Paris.

SAINT-SAËNS: symphony, opera, oratorio.

GOUNOD: opera, romantic church music.

FRANCK: symphonic works, chorus, organ. Although Franck was Belgian by birth, he, like Chopin, spent almost his entire life in Paris.

FAURÉ: song, piano music, *Requiem*.

England. English music, which had been eclipsed by Continental activities since the time of Purcell, did not again rise to a position of eminence until the 20th century. In the 19th century it was largely under the influence of German romanticism and later of French impressionism, despite certain nationalistic and individual traits that appear here and there.

SAMUEL WESLEY (1766–1837): organ music, church music.

SAMUEL SEBASTIAN WESLEY (1810–1876): English church music.

JOHN FIELD (1782–1837): piano music (nocturnes predating Chopin style).

WILLIAM STERNDALE BENNETT (1816–1875): piano and orchestral music.

JOHN STAINER (1840–1901): *Crucifixion,* cantatas, anthems.

ARTHUR SULLIVAN (1842–1900): operettas.

CHARLES H. PARRY (1848–1918): oratorios, anthems, cantatas.

CHARLES STANFORD (1852–1924): Irish nationalism, church music, oratorios, operas, and chamber music.

EDWARD ELGAR (1857–1934): oratorios, cantatas, orchestral works.

Russia. Russia came into the group of prominent musical nations in the second half of the 19th century when the strong current of Russian nationalism began.

GLINKA: Russian nationalist opera.

"THE FIVE": a group of Russians who consciously fostered the spirit of Russian nationalism in music: Moussorgsky, Borodin, Balakirev, César Cui, and Rimsky-Korsakov.

MOUSSORGSKY: symphony, opera, song.

BORODIN: symphony, opera.

BALAKIREV: symphony, songs, piano.

RIMSKY-KORSAKOV: brilliant orchestration, symphonic poem, opera, orientalism, and Russian nationalism.

TSCHAIKOVSKY: romantic symphonic works, opera, song.

RACHMANINOFF: romantic symphonic works, piano concertos, songs. He was perhaps the last of the great pianist-composers of the romantic tradition.

Norway. Norway boasts of one famous composer: Grieg, who was a champion of Norwegian nationalism in his piano music, piano concerto, and numerous songs.

Bohemia. The two Bohemian nationalists of the 19th century are Smetana in the fields of opera and symphonic works, and Dvořák in symphony and chamber music.

Spain. Working principally in the fields of orchestral and piano music, the Spanish nationalists are Albéniz, Granados, and De Falla, the last named representing 20th-century Spanish nationalism.

Music in the United States. Music in America before 1700 was largely confined to Psalm singing, partly because of the rigors of pioneer life and partly because of the severe attitudes of the Puritans.

THE 18TH CENTURY. Concert life began in the second quarter of the 18th century in Boston, Charleston, New York, and Philadelphia. Francis Hopkinson (1737-1791) may be considered the first native American composer. He wrote songs in the current English style. Musical activities were virtually halted by the period of the American Revolution, and the development of native American talent was arrested by the influx of European musicians and composers who had the advantages of tradition and better training.

THE 19TH CENTURY. In the 19th century the influx of European musicians continued to increase. This was particularly true of Germans, musicians and teachers, whose romantic German culture colored the American musical point of view. The result was that not until the 20th century was there any considerable development of indigenous American art music. A native American style did develop, however, in the field of entertainment: the minstrel show with its strongly flavored Negro style. The folk-like songs of Stephen Foster (1826-1864) are also truly American, although somewhat limited to Southern melodic style and subject matter. In the second half of the 19th century there was a beginning of a real school of American composition which was to flower in the 20th century. The principal names connected with the development of American composition in the late 19th century are: John Knowles Paine (1839-1906), whose symphonies are basically German and solid in workmanship; his pupils, Arthur Foote, Frederick Converse, John Alden Carpenter, and Daniel Gregory Mason; others of the New England group, Chadwick, Parker, Whiting, Kelley. Because of his individuality of style Edward MacDowell (1861-1908) is considered one of the most important American composers of the 19th century. He is noted primarily for his piano music and his second piano concerto.

PART SIX

The Twentieth Century

CHAPTER XXVIII

General Considerations

THE first three decades of the 20th century represent a revolutionary period in the history of music, comparable to the Ars Nova of the 14th century and the Nuove Musiche at the beginning of the 17th century.

General Historical Background. Two global wars overshadow the first half of the century: World War I (1914–1918) and World War II (1939–1945). Great scientific and technological progress has affected civilization, beginning with accelerated advances in the physical sciences and engineering. The airplane, radio, and, more recently, jet propulsion, radar, atomic energy, and exploration of outer space have created a new civilization. The arts reflect this materialistic and mechanized age. The modern spirit is represented by a return to objectivity, expressionism, and functionalism.

The Problems of Contemporary Music History

The study of contemporary music poses problems more severe than does the music of earlier periods.

Quantity of Music Composed and Performed. Contemporary music is a subject so vast that no one person can hope to become familiar with all its facets. Not only is more music being composed and performed than in any previous period of music history, but it is also being made accessible to untold millions through new and expanded channels of publication, recording, concert performance, and educational resources.

Historical Perspective. As human events recede in time, we gain perspective. Thus, we are able to generalize about trends, styles, forms, and techniques of music in past eras. But we are too close to the music of the 20th century to gain such perspective. The most we can do is to observe certain phenomena taking place; we cannot with certainty evaluate them in terms of ultimate significance. In the ever-changing scene, a trend which seems significant today may later prove to be of little consequence.

Diversity of Developments. Twentieth-century music confronts us with a bewildering array of developments which, taken together, impose a barrier to attaining a coherent over-all picture. Individualism is a trait more prominent in 20th-century music than ever before; the roster of important composers who have developed distinctive styles and techniques, more or less independently of major trends, is impressive. Modern music cannot be viewed as a parade of co-ordinated revolutionary changes, but rather as a series of numerous seemingly disconnected "explosions." Further, the disparate trends do not present themselves in neat chronological order; instead, they overlap in time and exert varying degrees of influence on the stream of music. While experimentation continues, romanticism is by no means abandoned.

It seems reasonably safe to say that most of the more radical innovations utilized in the first three decades of this century are, in varying degrees, being assimilated by composers, a process which has in the past been evident following every period of innovation.

It will be our purpose in the present chapter to outline the broad trends which, in various ways, mark a departure from the established musical practice of the 19th century.

Broad Stylistic Trends

Certain broad trends in musical style have developed in the 20th century. Some are derived from or run parallel to developments in painting; some are a continuation of earlier stylistic concepts in music; still others are musical developments which belong distinctly to the 20th century. It should be kept in mind, in any case, that no one trend represents all the music literature of the 20th century; not all compositions fit neatly into one or another of these classifications; most are the result of several influences.

Neoromanticism. The term *neoromanticism* applies to the continuance of German romantic traditions. Post-Wagnerian style continued well into the 20th century. It is characterized not only by a somewhat heavy emotionalism, enormous orchestras, and great symphonic lengths, but also by advances in harmonic idiom and orchestration. Representative composers are Mahler, Bruckner, Richard Strauss (*Ein Heldenleben, Tod und Verklärung*), and Sibelius.

Impressionism. In the last decades of the 19th century, a group of French painters developed a new style which came to be called *impressionism*. The leaders (Monet, Manet, Degas, Renoir, and Pissaro) employed techniques which produced veiled, "atmospheric" impressions of light and color rather than sharply defined contours. Claude Debussy (1862–1918), closely associated with the group, carried the movement into the field of music, partly as a reaction against Wagnerian romanticism. Musical impressionism is not devoid of romantic elements, however. It may be described generally as having refinement, delicacy, vagueness, and an over-all "luminous fog" atmosphere. The technical aspects of impressionism will be listed under Debussy (page 193). Debussy's *Voiles, Reflets dans l'Eau,* and the symphonic suite *La Mer,* and Ravel's *Jeux d'Eau* are a few examples of impressionism. In addition to Debussy and Ravel, some of the composers who employed impressionist styles in various ways are Roussel in France, Delius in England, Albeniz in Spain, Respighi in Italy, Scriabin in Russia, and Griffes in the United States.

Expressionism. The term *expressionism,* like "impressionism," was borrowed from painting. In general, it was intended to mean the expression of the inner self, especially the subconscious, as opposed to impressionism as an interpretation of external things. Expressionism in art, which gave rise to abstraction (e.g., Mondrian, Picasso, Kandinsky, Klee, Brancusi, etc.) and surrealism (Dali), found its parallel in music from about 1910 to 1925 in the radical works of such composers as Schoenberg (e.g., *Pierrot Lunaire,* 1912), Webern, and Berg (e.g., *Violin Concerto*). Expressionistic music is characteristically subjective, dissonant, and atonal (see page 186), although these traits are by no means confined to the expressionistic category.

Neoclassicism. The new classicism of the 20th century represents a return to ideals of the 18th century while retaining modern techniques of harmony, tonality, melody, etc. Ferruccio Busoni (1866–1924) can be counted the foremost pioneer in this movement, which, beginning in the early 1920's, permeates the present scene more than any other broad trend. Neoclassicism is largely antiromantic and predominantly objective. It strives for simplicity and clarity of material, form, texture, and medium. An important attribute of neoclassicism is the revival of interest in contrapuntal technique. Neoclassicism had its first champions among "Les Six" in France. Two composers stand out as leaders in this movement: Paul Hindemith (counterpoint and forms), and Igor Stravinsky (in his middle period). Examples of neoclassicism are Hindemith's *Fourth String Quartet, Ludus Tonalis* (for piano), and Stravinsky's *Octet* and *L'Histoire du Soldat.*

Gebrauchsmusik. A movement which began in 1923 at the chamber music festivals held in Donaueschingen, Germany, came to be referred to as *Gebrauchsmusik,* and it gained considerable momentum in the 1930's. The term, which has been translated as "utility music" or "functional music," describes compositions written for special purposes or particuar occasions. The movement, under the principal leadership of Paul Hindemith, aimed at bridging the gap between composer and audience by making music more directly acceptable by means of simplification of materials. Hence, Gebrauchsmusik is allied to neoclassicism. It also aimed at lessening technical difficulties so that amateur performers could participate in music making. Examples of Gebrauchsmusik are Hindemith's *Plöner Musiktag* (1932), *Wir bauen eine Stadt* (1931), and *Trauermusik* ("Funeral Music"), written on the occasion of the death of King George V in 1936.

American Jazz. Although distinctly a popular art, American dance-band style, generally referred to as jazz, has had such a widespread influence upon serious or nonpopular music that it may be counted among the broad tendencies of modernism. Further, in view of its self-contained importance as a phenomenon of the 20th-century United States, it will be well to consider its development, aside from its implications with serious art music.

THE DEVELOPMENT OF JAZZ. Popular music in the United States has passed through several stages of evolution in its comparatively brief history. These broad currents of style often overlap and influence one another so that the chronology is not always clear.

a. *Ragtime.* Popular music known as *ragtime,* probably derived from minstrel shows, makes its appearance somewhere in the late 19th century. It is essentially a pianistic art characterized by prominence of syncopation in various patterns, conventional harmony (I, IV, and V), and regular phraseology. Ragtime bands originated in New Orleans a little before the turn of the century. They consisted mainly of small groups of Negro musicians who improvised upon ragtime tunes.

b. *Blues.* A style type of popular music known as *blues* influenced both ragtime and later jazz. W. C. Handy's "Memphis Blues" (1909) and his famous "St. Louis Blues" (1914) are early examples of this style. Blues style is unquestionably of Negro origin, though several contemporary "classical" composers have also used it. The subject matter deals with an atmosphere of self-pity, a lost or absent lover, etc. Blues style consists of the following features: (1) predominant use of twelve-measure periods instead of the more conventional eight and sixteen, (2) preponderant use of major keys, (3) emphasis upon plagal or subdominant harmonies, (4) use of the lowered third and seventh degrees in the melody and harmony, (5) wavering above or below true pitch, and (6) progressions of dominant seventh chords, known as "barbershop harmony," a style now considered obsolete.

c. *Jazz.* The elements of the style known as jazz began to make their appearance around 1910, derived from ragtime and blues. Jazz became a distinct style in the 1920's with the beginning of "name" bands (Whiteman, Ted Lewis, Guy Lombardo, etc.). In general, jazz is essentially an orchestral art in terms of arrangement (commercial arrangements called "sweet" or "straight" jazz) or improvisation (called "hot jazz"). The arranger or the performer then becomes more important than the composer, the original melody and harmony becoming secondary in importance to its treatment. Other characteristics of jazz in general are: (1) a more suave, more melodic, and more vocal melody than that of ragtime, (2) a sustained melody over a throbbing accompaniment, (3) superimposition of complex rhythmic patterns, (4) more major than minor tonalities, (5) use of added tones in harmony (particularly the added sixth and/or second degrees in the final tonic), (6) parallelism or seventh and ninth chords, (7) instrumentation: little use of strings, prominence of percussion, woodwinds (particularly saxophone and clarinet), and brass (trumpets and trombones with or without mutes), and special instruments such as the banjo (used in the 1920's, later replaced by the guitar), vibra-harp, etc. Special mention should be made of a pianistic development which began in the middle 1930's, called *boogie-woogie*. This consists of a strongly rhythmic ostinato figure carried in the bass over which the right hand carries variations in diverse figures. The terms *swing* (Benny Goodman, c. 1935), *bebop* (c. 1950–), and *progressive jazz* are later styles of improvisational jazz. The latter aspires to a more sophisticated and less blatant style; many outstanding jazz composers have been influenced by classical music and are producing a kind of modern chamber music.

INFLUENCE OF JAZZ. The indigenous popular styles outlined above have had widespread influence on serious music, not only among composers in the United States but also on those abroad. This influence is manifest in (1) instrumentation and orchestration, especially the use of brass and woodwind instruments (including the saxophone), (2) chords and chord progressions, (3) rhythmic devices, especially syncopated patterns, and (4) use of blues techniques, particularly in harmony and melody. Concert jazz in larger forms got its first strong impetus from George Gershwin's *Rhapsody in Blue* (1924). Notable examples of jazz (in various styles) employed in serious composition are Carpenter's *Concertino* (1915), *Krazy Kat* (ballet, 1922), and *Skyscrapers* (ballet, 1926); Stravinsky's *L'Histoire du Soldat* (1918) and *Ragtime* (for eleven instruments, 1918); Milhaud's *Le Boeuf sur le Toit* (ballet, 1920), *Rag-Caprices* (for piano, 1922), and *La Création du Monde* (ballet, 1923); Gruenberg's *The Daniel Jazz* (for solo voice and small ensemble, 1924); Gershwin's *Concerto in F* (for piano and orchestra, 1925); Honegger's *Concertino* (for piano and orchestra, 1925); Copland's *Music for the Theatre* (1925) and *Concerto* (for piano and orchestra, 1926); Křenek's opera, *Jonny Spielt Auf* (1926); Ravel's *Sonata for Violin and Piano* (1927, second movement entitled "Blues"); Gould's *Chorale and Fugue in Jazz* (1936); Stravinsky's *Ebony Concerto* (written for Woody Herman's Band, 1946); and Liebermann's *Concerto for Jazz Band and Symphony Orchestra* (1954). Recently, there has been a renewed drive towards a fusion of jazz and "classical" elements, with composers from both groups taking part: Charles Mingus, George Russell, Jimmy Giuffre, John Lewis, Bill Russo, Dave Brubeck, Harold Shapero, and Gunther Schuller.

Musical Media

The 20th century has seen some significant changes in the relative importance of various existing musical media and the development of new types of sound generation. Of great significance to 20th-century music is the rise of new musical outlets: high-fidelity transmission of sound (radio, phonograph, tape recording, stereophonic sound). These outlets have made music accessible to a vast audience and have contributed substantially to the current widespread interest in music.

Conventional Media. Although important contributions to various vocal media have been made in the 20th century, interest in instrumental music still dominates the field.

SYMPHONIC MUSIC. The 20th century has witnessed an expansion of municipal symphony orchestras, notably in the United States. Although no essentially new instruments have been added to the orchestral palette, the technique of orchestration has advanced and is characterized generally by greater brilliance, more use of individual instrumental colors, and more transparent textures. Symphonic forms developed in the 19th century continue to be used, though with greater freedom. There is less interest in symphonic program music. Music from modern ballet constitutes a considerable portion of the literature. A new idea in symphonic music made its appearance in the 20th century: compositions for narrator and orchestra (e.g., Copland's *Lincoln Portrait*, Thomson's *Testament of Freedom*, Prokofiev's *Peter and the Wolf*, Schoenberg's *Survivor from Warsaw*, Rogers' *Leaves from the Tale of Pinocchio*).

Incidental music written for the movie sound track has not thus far contributed substantially to orchestral literature. A few successful examples are Copland's *Our Town*, Thomson's *The Plow that Broke the Plains* and *Louisiana Story*, Prokofiev's *Lieutenant Kije* and *Alexander Nevsky*, and Vaughan Williams' *Antarctic Symphony*.

BAND. Until the 20th century, there was a dearth of good music written for large wind ensembles, the repertoire consisting mainly of arrangements of symphonic works. Recently, however, the concert band (or symphonic wind ensemble), as distinct from the military band, marching band, etc., has begun to attract composers, and a number of serious compositions have been written for this medium. Among a growing number of substantial compositions for band may be mentioned Hindemith's *Symphony in B Flat;* Milhaud's *Suite Française* and *West Point Suite;* Holst's *Moorside Suite* (for brass band) and two other suites for band; Vaughan Williams' *Folksong Suite* and *Toccata Marziale;* Barber's *Commando March;* Bennett's *Suite of Old American Dances;* Hanson's *Chorale and Alleluia;* Mennin's *Canzona;* Reed's *Festa Mexicana;* Persichetti's *Divertimento for Band;* Piston's *Tunbridge Fair;* Schuman's *George Washington Bridge;* and Virgil Thomson's *A Solemn Music.*

CHAMBER MUSIC. There has been a notable revival of interest in chamber music in the 20th century. This is an aspect of neoclassicism: a return to simplification and clarity of means as well as to media more compatible with classical ideals of objectivity and absolute music. Further, chamber music is a medium well-suited to contrapuntal writing, another facet of neoclassicism.

Although the string quartet remains a favorite instrumental combination, a great number of chamber music compositions have also been written for various other ensembles, notably for small wind ensembles. A popular combination of instruments at present is the quintet for flute, clarinet, oboe, bassoon, and horn (e.g., Milhaud's *La Cheminée du Roi René, Madrigal,* and *Pastoral;* Ibert's *Trois Pièces Brèves;* and Florent Schmitt's *Chants Elisés*).

The chamber orchestra, too, is experiencing a popularity not seen since the days of the 18th-century divertimento. Compositions for string orchestra (Vaughan Williams' *Fantasy on a Theme of Thomas Tallis,* Stravinsky's *Appolon Musagète,* Barber's *Adagio for Strings,* Diamond's *Rounds for String Orchestra*) and for string orchestra in combination with several solo instruments (Bartók's *Music for Strings, Percussion and Celesta;* Copland's *Quiet City* for trumpet, English horn, and strings; Kennan's *Night Soliloquy* for flute and strings) are not uncommon. Mention should be made here of a revival of 17-century wind music, such as the brass ensembles of Gabrieli and the tower sonatas of Pezel.

Among the numerous prominent 20th-century composers who have contributed substantially to modern chamber music literature may be mentioned Béla Bartók, Paul Hindemith, Arnold Schoenberg, Walter Piston, Quincy Porter, Darius Milhaud, Hector Villa-Lobos, William Schuman, David Diamond, William Bergsma, Leon Kirchner, Elliott Carter, Gunther Schuller, Roger Sessions, Serge Prokofiev, Leos Janáček, Zoltán Kodály, and Dmitri Shostakovich.

PIANO MUSIC. Piano music does not hold as prominent a place as it did in the 19th century. Nevertheless, much significant modern piano music has been added to the literature. Mention should be made of the piano music (sonatas, preludes, etc.) by Scriabin early in the century. The piano music of Debussy (mostly impressionistic preludes with descriptive titles), Ravel, and Satie recalls the excellence of French keyboard music from the days of Couperin and Rameau. Some modern collections of piano pieces are Bartók's *Mikrokosmos*, Milhaud's *Saudades do Brazil* and *The Household Muse*, and Shostakovich's *Preludes and Fugues*. The piano plays an important role in modern concerto literature, in orchestral ensembles, and in chamber ensembles.

CHORAL MUSIC. Although there is renewed interest in the performance of Renaissance and Baroque choral music, composition in this medium does not hold the prominent place that is held by instrumental ensemble music. Nevertheless, a number of 20th-century choral works have received recognition, e.g., Stravinsky's *Symphony of Psalms, Mass*, and *Threni*, Honegger's *King David*, Walton's *Belshazzar's Feast*, Orff's *Carmina Burana*, Moore's *Moby Dick*, Piston's *Carnival Song* (for male chorus and brass choir), Still's *Song of a City*, Hanson's *Lament for Beowulf*, and Thompson's *The Peaceable Kingdom*. In particular, British and American composers have greatly contributed to the literature of short choral works, both sacred and secular.

SOLO SONG. Neither the output nor the popularity of the solo song is as great as in the Romantic period. In general, vocal music has not been affected by the more radical innovations of the 20th century in melodic, harmonic, tonal, and rhythmic techniques. The few noteworthy song cycles of the 20th century include Debussy's *Chansons Bilitis*, Hindemith's *Marienleben*, Carpenter's *Gitanjali*, Barber's *Knoxville* (with orchestra) and *Hermit Songs*. The combination of solo voice with chamber music has had considerable vogue (e.g., Vaughan Williams' *On Wenlock Edge* for tenor, piano, and string quartet; Britten's *Serenade* for tenor, horn, and strings; Toch's *Chinese Flute* for soprano and chamber orchestra; and Barber's *Dover Beach* for baritone and string quartet).

OPERA. Despite significant contributions to the field of opera literature in the 20th century, performance leans heavily on 19th-century repertory.

Serious Opera. Outstanding among modern operas are Debussy's *Pelléas et Mélisande* (impressionistic opera), Britten's *Peter Grimes* and *Billy Budd*, Berg's *Wozzeck* and *Lulu* (atonal operas), Menotti's *The Medium, The Consul, Amahl and the Night Visitors* (composed for television), and *The Saint of Bleecker Street;* Stravinsky's *The Rake's Progress*, Křenek's *Jonny Spielt Auf* (jazz opera) and *The Bell Tower*, Orff's *Die Kluge*, Barber's *Vanessa*, Thomson's *Four Saints in Three Acts* (text by Gertrude Stein), Moore's *The Devil and Daniel Webster*, and Glanville-Hicks' *The Transposed Heads*.

Operetta. Operettas and musical comedies in a light vein have enjoyed a vogue. The following composers are representative: Victor Herbert (1859–1924), Reginald de Koven (1859–1920), Rudolf Friml (1879–   ), Sigmund Romberg (1887–1951), Jerome Kern (1885–1945), Cole Porter (1893–1964), Irving Berlin (1888–   ), Richard Rogers (1902–   ), Frederick Loewe (1904–   ), Leonard Bernstein (1918–   ), Frank Loesser (1910–   ), and others.

Comic Opera. The 20th century has also seen the rise of comic operas of a more sophisticated nature: Wolf-Ferrari (1876–1948), *The Secret of Suzanne;* Stravinsky, *Mavra;* Menotti, *Amelia Goes to the Ball, The Old Maid and the Thief,* and *The Telephone;* Bernstein, *Candide;* Ravel, *L'Heure Espagnole,* and Hindemith, *Hin und Zurück.*

Folk Opera. A trend in opera in America is the folk opera or "grass-roots opera," based on regional legends and tunes. Successful examples of this type are Kurt Weill's *Down in the Valley*, Gershwin's *Porgy and Bess,* and Lukas Foss's *The Jumping Frog of Cala-veras County.*

Opera Workshop. A significant movement in the United States is the opera workshop in American colleges and universities where young singers learn repertory and techniques and where new operas often have their first performance.

BALLET. The ballet, considered here as a separate dramatic form apart from its place in opera, enjoys a place it has not held since the court ballets in the time of Louis XIV. The components of ballet are choreography (the invention and design of dancing), staging, cos-tuming, scenery, and orchestral music, but singing and the spoken word are excluded. Although the revival of the ballet as a distinct and separate form had taken place in the 19th century and reached pre-eminence with the ballets of Tschaikowsky (*Swan Lake, Sleep-ing Beauty,* and *The Nutcracker*) in the last quarter of the 19th cen-tury, modern ballet begins with the creations of Diaghileff and Fo-kine and the music of Stravinsky: *Firebird* (1910), *Petrouchka* (1912), and *Le Sacre du Printemps* (*The Rite of Spring,* 1913). Fol-lowing the lead of Russian choreographers, dancers, and composers, ballet continues to flourish in England and the United States. The list of important ballet music (presented in symphonic concert form as well as in complete ballet form) is long and impressive, including such works as Stravinsky's *L'Histoire du Soldat* (with three dancers, narrator, and small orchestra on stage), *Pulcinella, Jeu de Cartes, Les Noces,* and *Apollon Musagètes,* Ravel's *Daphnis et Chloë,* Falla's *The Three-Cornered Hat,* Poulenc's *Les Biches,* Hindemith's *St. Francis* (from which the orchestral work *Nobilissima Visione* is well known), Roussel's *Bacchus et Ariane,* Milhaud's *Le Boeuf sur le Toit* (comic ballet), and Shostakovich's *The Golden Age.* Ameri-can composers have contributed substantially with such works as Copland's *Appalachian Spring, Billy the Kid,* and *Rodeo,* Thom-son's *Filling Station,* Piston's *Incredible Flutist,* Carpenter's *Sky-scrapers,* and Schuman's *Judith* and *Undertow.*

Innovations in Musical Media. New developments in musical me-dia may be considered under three headings: (1) new combinations of already existing instruments, (2) unusual uses of conventional in-struments, and (3) experiments with new tone generators.

NEW INSTRUMENTAL COMBINATIONS. In the search for novel musical sounds, some composers have been using new combinations of conventional instruments. A few notable examples are Daniel Pinkham's *Concerto for Celesta and Harpsichord Soli;* Schoenberg's *Serenade,* Op. 24, for baritone voice, clarinet, bass clarinet, mandolin, guitar, violin, viola, and cello; Villa-Lobos' *Bachianas Brasileiras No. 1* for eight cellos; Bartók's *Music for Strings, Percussion, and Celesta;* and Chavez' *Toccata for Percussion.*

UNUSUAL USES OF CONVENTIONAL INSTRUMENTS. There has been some experimentation with effects produced by employing the extreme registers of instruments (e.g., the opening bassoon solo in very high register in Stravinsky's *Rite of Spring*). Exploiting special tone effects on string instruments (combinations of pizzicato, sul ponticello, col legno, glissando, harmonics, etc.) are found in such works as Bartók's String Quartets (Nos. 3, 4, 5). Henry Cowell produces exotic sounds by plucking the strings of a grand piano and by glissandi along the length of the wrapped strings (e.g., *Banshee*). Alan Hovhaness also has written some interesting piano music using a mandolin plectrum and tympani sticks on the piano strings while simultaneously using the keyboard in a conventional manner (*Pastorale, Orbit No. 2, Jhala,* etc.). John Cage experimented with new sounds from the piano by attaching to the strings such articles as screws, wooden wedges, cellophane, bobby pins, etc. (e.g., *Sonatas for Prepared Piano*).

NEW TONE GENERATORS. Developments in physical and electronic acoustics have opened the way for numerous experiments in musical tone production. Creations in this category represent the most avant-garde developments in music today. The new sounds, added to new rhythmic, harmonic, melodic, and tonal concepts (to be discussed in the next chapter), make the music extremely difficult to evaluate in terms of normal musico-aesthetic standards.

New tone generators have recently been invented. Harry Partch (1901–   ) employs "bamboo marimba," "cloud chamber bowls," "surrogate kithara," "bass marimba," etc. André Jolivet (1905–   ) has written music for the "ondes martinot."

Electronic oscillators and distortion of tone through tape recorder by means of harmonic filters, alteration of speed, playing the tape backwards, etc. have created a new world of sounds. The movement in France is called *musique concrète;* in the United States it is referred to as tape-recorder music or sometimes as "tapesichord" music. The principal names associated with this development are Pierre Boulez, Pierre Schaeffer, and Pierre Henry in France, Karlheinz Stockhausen in Germany, and Otto Luening, Vladimir Ussachevsky, and Edgard Varèse in the United States.

CHAPTER XXIX

Specific Aspects of Style

IT is important to keep in mind that no single 20th-century innovation—neither the broad trends considered in the preceding chapter,
nor the specific features of style to be discussed in this chapter—
represents all modern music, which is a blend of many influences.

Tonality. One of the most significant aspects of modern music
concerns new concepts of tonality. At no time in the history of music
have these concepts changed so radically as in the 20th century.

CHROMATICISM AND MODULATION. By the middle of the 19th century, three practices had become established in a more liberal musical language and contributed to an increasingly flexible concept of
tonality: (1) the use of more remotely related key centers within a
single composition, (2) the use of chromatic harmony which tends
to unsettle the feeling of a fixed key, and (3) the use of prolonged
modulations during which the key center and tonal direction are
temporarily obscured. Examples of these practices can be found in
the music of Chopin (e.g., *Prelude in E Minor,* Op. 28, No. 4),
Reger, Franck, Wagner, Liszt, and others.

DISPLACED TONALITY. A further extension of 19th-century tonal
evolution resulted in the 20th-century practice known as *displaced
tonality* or *multitonality*. These terms mean that several remotely
related keys (sometimes a half step apart, such as D Major and E-flat
Major) are introduced consecutively with abrupt modulations or else
without any modulation at all (e.g., Bartók's "Through the Keys,"
No. 104 in *Mikrokosmos*).

NEOMODALITY. The church modes (see page 8) replaced by major
and minor scale systems in the course of the 17th century, were re-

introduced for new effects. Neomodal melody and harmony, however, are not purely modal in the pre-Baroque sense; they extract the atmosphere of antiquity and tonal vagueness while retaining other features of modern style. Some examples of neomodality are Debussy's *Cathédrale Engloutie,* Vaughan Williams' *Fantasy on a Theme of Thomas Tallis,* Bartók's *Mikrokosmos* (e.g., Nos. 32, 34, 37, 48, 55, 71), Ravel's *Pavane pour une Enfante Défunte,* Satie's *Gymnopédie,* and Hovhaness' *Arevakal.*

NEW SCALE SYSTEMS. Composers further departed from conventional scale systems by using such scales as the pentatonic (Bartók's *Mikrokosmos,* Nos. 61, 78), the whole-tone scale (Debussy's *Voiles,* Rebikov's *Les Demons s'Amusent*), pseudo-Oriental scales (Rimsky-Korsakov, Roussel), gypsy and other exotic scales (e.g., Godowsky's *Nocturnal Tangier,* McPhee's *Tabuh-Tabuhan,* Bartók's *Bulgarian Rhythm* and *From the Island of Bali*). Other unusual scale systems are represented in Bartók's *Mikrokosmos:* No. 10 based on a D scale with a key signature of one flat (a♭), No. 25 based on a B scale with a key signature of one sharp (c♯), etc. All such departures from conventional scale systems affect tonality.

MICROTONALITY. Division of the octave into more than twelve tones is called *microtonality.* So far, experiments based on this division have had little general acceptance. Microtonal music excludes the use of most conventional instruments, requires a new system of notation, and is so remote from the traditional Western concept of melody that it is apt to sound "out of tune" to our ears. Names of composers associated with this development include Alois Hába, Juan Carrillo, Ivan Vyshnegradsky, Hans Barth, and Harry Partch.

POLYTONALITY. The use of two or more keys simultaneously is called *polytonality,* an innovation which reached its zenith in the 1920's and has since been assimilated in broader techniques. Compositions in which two or more keys are equally and consistently maintained throughout are rare; usually, at one time or another one of the tonal centers dominates, and the different keys often tend to merge. When several keys are more or less equally prominent, the result is that key feeling for a particular tonal center is generally negated. A good example of *bitonal music* (i.e., only two keys) is the Fourth of Milhaud's *Cinq Symphonies,* which has a first movement opening in C major and E♭ minor, followed by a passage in A major against B♭ major, and so on. The Third of these short symphonies opens with the keys of E major (clarinet), D major (bassoon), and shortly after, violins and violas entering in E♭. Other examples of polytonality are in Bartók's *Mikrokosmos* (e.g., Nos. 70, 99, 105, 106). The principal composers who exploited polytonality are Milhaud, Honegger, Bartók, and Casella.

ATONALITY. The ultimate development in modern tonal concepts is *atonality,* which means the complete negation of any tonality. Although many 20th-century composers have written atonal or near-atonal music without a "system," the principal technique is the twelve-tone system (also called *serial technique* and *dodecaphonic music*) devised by Arnold Schoenberg in the 1920's. The system is explained in the discussion of Schoenberg's music (see page 199).

Although atonal music has perhaps not dominated the music of the 20th century, it has nevertheless exerted a tremendous influence, and today it still has a number of enthusiastic advocates. Composers most closely associated with Schoenberg (1874–1951) were Alban Berg (1885–1935), Anton Webern (1883–1945), and Ernst Křenek (1900–   ). Among composers recently engaged in writing atonal music in serial technique (though not in all cases exclusively so) are: Pierre Boulez in France, Karlheinz Stockhausen and Boris Blacher in Germany, Humphrey Searle, Matyas Seiber, and Roberto Gerhard in England, Luigi Dallapiccola, Luigi Nono, Bruno Maderna, and Riccardo Nielson in Italy, Hanns Jelinek in Vienna, Rolf Liebermann in Switzerland, Fartein Valen in Norway; in the United States, various applications of serial technique are to be found in the works of Wallingford Riegger, Stefan Wolpe, Ben Weber, Adolf Weiss, Lou Harrison, Kurt List, Erich Itor Kahn, George Perle, Milton Babbitt, Ross Lee Finney, and Gunther Schuller. It is an interesting point that two anti-atonal composers, Stravinsky and Hindemith, have recently employed serial techniques, and that Schoenberg himself returned to tonality in his last years.

PANDIATONICISM. The term *pandiatonicism,* introduced by Nicholas Slonimsky in *Music Since 1900,* refers to music which is a reaction against the extreme chromaticism of the late 19th century and against the "pan-chromaticism" of the atonalists. Pandiatonic music minimizes the use of accidentals and has a "C-major appearance." Although pandiatonic music is not necessarily atonal, neither is it solidly tonal, and it employs modern harmonic dissonance, rhythm, counterpoint, and chord spacing. Examples of pandiatonic music are Satie's "Embryons desséchés" (*Dried Embryos*), Poulenc's *Suite* (1920), Stravinsky's *Piano Concerto* (1924) and *Serenade* (1925).

Harmony. Harmonic concepts, like those of tonality, were expanded and modified in the 19th century, leading to concepts of harmony and innovations so radical that the harmonic materials of a 20th-century composition are likely to defy analysis from the standpoint of conventional systems. New harmonic ideas may be considered under four headings: (1) chord construction, (2) chord progression, (3) mixed chords, and (4) treatment of dissonance.

CHORD CONSTRUCTION. Until the 20th century, chord construction was exclusively tertiary; that is, chords built by superimposition of thirds (triads consist of two thirds, seventh chords consist of three thirds, etc.). Chord construction in the 20th century is generally more complex.

ADDITIONAL THIRDS. Chords of greater complexity and dissonance result from further addition of thirds: eleventh chords and thirteenth chords.

NEW INTERVALS. Chords constructed with intervals other than thirds have been used in the 20th century. Quartal harmony (chords built in fourths) and quintal harmony (chords built in fifths) are not uncommon. Also, more dissonant chords have in some instances been constructed with intervals of sevenths.

TONE CLUSTERS. In the 1920's, a radical experiment known as *tone clusters* had a brief following. Tone clusters (in notation, having the appearance of a bunch of grapes) are masses of adjacent notes, played on the piano with the fist, flat of the hand, or the entire forearm, producing massive sonorities and percussive effects rather than harmonic color in the chordal sense. The principal advocates of tone clusters were Leo Ornstein, Charles Ives, and Henry Cowell ("Advertisement" and "Tides of Manaunaun").

HETEROGENEOUS INTERVALS. A great deal of modern harmony abandons any set system of chord construction by a given interval and employs instead combinations of heterogeneous intervals.

ADDED TONES. Toward sharper dissonance, composers have used the device of adding tones to otherwise conventional structures (e.g., C–E–G–C♯–F).

MIXED CHORDS. The use of two different chords sounding simultaneously is referred to as *polyharmony* (e.g., C–E–G sounding against G♯–B–D♯). This is a 20th-century extension of the much older double and triple appoggiaturas often occurring in cadences (e.g., C–E–G combined with B–D–F in which the latter chord resolves to the former). Examples of mixed chords or polyharmony are to be found in Stravinsky's famous "Petrouchka chord" (a C-major triad against an F♯-major triad) and in one of Bartók's Esquisses (1908) an A♭-major triad against an E-minor triad. Mixed chords are the normal result of polytonality, but they are not strictly confined to polytonal music.

CHORD PROGRESSION. It is possible for a composer to employ only conventional chord structures, even those limited to triads, and still produce a modern harmonic result by means of unconventional root progressions. As with chord structures, chord progressions are today so diversified and so far removed from orthodox "textbook harmony" that no common practice may be said to exist. A few "modernisms" may be noted here (although some were in use before the 20th century): chords borrowed from the parallel mode (e.g., the chord A♭–C–E♭ in the key of C major), progressions involving chords whose roots are foreign to the key (e.g., the chord F♯–A–C–E♭ in the key of C major) without necessarily effecting a modulation, progressions of chord-root movement by half step or whole step, progressions derived from modal and other unusual scale systems, and parallelism in which intervals, triads, seventh chords, etc. move in parallel motion (e.g., in Debussy's *Images* and *Cathédrale Engloutie*). Two or more independent lines, each consisting of parallel chord progression instead of single melodic lines, are called "chord streams."

TREATMENT OF DISSONANCE. The history of harmony is an almost continuous evolution toward freer and more extensive use of dissonance. Music in the 20th century characteristically employs much more sharply dissonant combinations of tones, employs them more extensively, and has virtually abandoned the former principles of preparation and resolution. Modern dissonance is the result of new concepts of chord structure and chord progression as well as being a derivative of polytonality, atonality, and modern "linear" counterpoint, where the movement of independent lines produces harmonic clashes.

Melody. Although melodic concepts have generally undergone less change than other musical elements, some extremes in melodic style are to be noted.

PROGRESSION. To a considerable extent, 20th-century melodic progression is characteristically disjunct (use of wide skips), angular (skips in opposite directions), and dissonant (progression by dissonant intervals). These traits are particularly evident in twelve-tone music.

FRAGMENTATION. Another departure from conventional melodic concepts is the style known as *melodic fragmentation* or *pointillism*. These terms describe melodic material consisting of one or a few consecutive tones in a group; these tones may be assigned consecutively to different instruments in an ensemble. Extremely disjunct melody produces the effect of fragmentation. Fragmentation is a notable characteristic of Webern's music.

RELATIVE PROMINENCE. In the search for new effects in harmonic and instrumental color and new sonorities, 20th-century composers have frequently subordinated the melodic element. Instances where the melodic element is dominated by other elements or even completely disappears are encountered in such works as Debussy's "Voiles," Ravel's "Jeux d'Eau," Stravinsky's *Rite of Spring,* Honegger's *Pacific 231,* and Chavez' *Toccata for Percussion.* Suppression of the melodic element, however, is only one aspect of 20th-century composition. The other extreme is modern contrapuntal music in which the melodic element is supreme.

Rhythm and Meter. Innovations in rhythm and meter are significant in the 20th century. In general, modern rhythm has greater complexity, a greater variety of patterns, and more elasticity.

NEW METRIC SCHEMES. In an attempt to get away from the rigidity of conventional time signatures, 20th-century composers have devised new metric schemes. Time signatures such as $\frac{5}{8}, \frac{7}{8}, \frac{10}{8}$, etc. are not uncommon. By using accents and irregular note grouping within the measure, complex metric schemes are achieved. For example, in $\frac{8}{8}$ meter, one might employ groupings such as $3 + 3 + 2$, $3 + 2 + 3$, or $2 + 3 + 3$. Examples of modern metric schemes are to be found in Bartók's *Mikrokosmos* (e.g., Nos. 82, 113, 151, 152, 153), Piston's *Passacaglia* for piano, and in the movement entitled "Dance" in Copland's *Music for the Theatre.*

NONMETRIC MUSIC. Some composers have omitted the bar line entirely in experimental attempts to achieve the nonmetric flexibility of plainsong (e.g., Ives's *Concord Sonata*). This device is virtually limited to solo performance because music scored without bar lines is impractical for ensemble performance.

MULTIMETRIC MUSIC. The term *multimetric* describes music in which there are frequent changes in consecutive measures. This device produces complex and rhythmically interesting effects. Examples are to be found in Stravinsky's *Petrouchka, The Rite of Spring,* and *L'Histoire du Soldat,* Bernstein's *Jeremiah Symphony,* and Bartók's *Mikrokosmos,* Nos. 42, 43.

POLYMETRIC MUSIC. When two or more different time signatures are employed simultaneously, the scheme is called *polymetric.* Examples are Ravel's *Piano Trio,* second movement ($\frac{3}{4}$ against $\frac{4}{2}$) and Stravinsky's *Petrouchka* ($\frac{5}{8}$ against $\frac{2}{4}$ and $\frac{7}{8}$ against $\frac{3}{4}$).

DISPLACED BAR LINE. Within conventional time signatures, the bar line may in effect be displaced by accenting (e.g., every third beat in $\frac{4}{4}$ time), by note-grouping across the bar line, by prolonged syncopation, by tying across the bar line, and by melodic and/or rhythmic patterns not conforming to the indicated metric scheme. An example of the latter device is Britten's *Passacaglia* from *Peter Grimes* which has a recurrent eleven-beat rhythmic-melodic pattern in $\frac{4}{4}$ time, or the principal theme of Strauss' *Till Eulenspiegel* which is a seven-beat pattern in $\frac{6}{8}$ time. Other examples of displaced bar line are Bartók's "Ostinato" (from the *Mikrokosmos*), Copland's *Music for the Theatre,* Stravinsky's *Rite of Spring* ("Dance of the Adolescents") and *L'Histoire du Soldat.*

Texture and Sonority. The distinctive quality of 20th-century music is in part attributable to two related properties of music: texture and sonority.

TEXTURE. In music, the word texture means the disposition of melodic materials according to such procedures as monophonic (melody without accompaniment), homophonic (single melody with subordinate nonmelodic accompaniment), and polyphonic (simultaneous combination of two or more melodic lines). As opposed to the prevailing homophonic textures of the classical and romantic periods, contrapuntal (polyphonic) textures play an important and characteristic role in contemporary music, especially in connection with the neoclassical movement.

SONORITY. In contrast to the massive, rich sounds of 19th-century music, 20th-century sonority is characteristically light, transparent, and clear. Such sonorities are produced by relatively few tones or voices sounding simultaneously, wider spacing of tones, use of higher registers, and clarity of timbre (as opposed to mixed instrumental colors). Examples of such 20th-century sonority are Hindemith's *Canonic Sonata for Two Flutes,* Stravinsky's *L'Histoire du Soldat,* Ibert's *Trois Pièces Brève,* Webern's *Concerto for Nine Instruments.*

Form. It is difficult to generalize about 20th-century practice in respect to musical form. Because of new tonal, harmonic, rhythmic, and melodic materials, formal outlines are sometimes complex and obscured. On the other hand, neoclassical simplification of materials, especially in regard to texture and sonority, tend to clarify formal structure. Certainly, composers have sought to avoid banalities and obvious use of conventional structural plans, but it can hardly be said that new musical forms have been created in the 20th century. Composers have reached back to revive older structures such as the fugue, suite, passacaglia, etc., as well as continuing to employ freely modified sonata form.

CHAPTER XXX

Twentieth-Century Composers

THE principal features of 20th-century music to the present having been outlined in the two preceding chapters, we will now consider the more important composers who have made substantial contributions to the musical literature of this century. Each composer (listed according to country) represents a contribution to the musical scene, whether he is traditional, conservative, progressive or avant-garde. Taken together, these composers represent every aspect of musical style in western music of the 20th century.

France

General Considerations. The most significant departures from 19th-century techniques and style were first introduced by French composers. In France, even before the turn of the century, innovations appeared in harmony, tonality, sonority, orchestration, etc. (e.g., Satie's *Le Fils d'Étoiles* (1891), *Sarabandes* (1887), *Gymnopédie* (1888), Debussy's *Prélude à L'Après-midi d'un Faun* (1894), and Dukas' *L'Apprenti Sorcier* (1897). France has continued to hold its position among the leading nations in modern music.

Traditionalists. Prominent French composers, whose creative lives belong partly to the 20th century but who stylistically belong more to the 19th century, are Camille Saint-Säens (1835–1921), Vincent d'Indy (1851–1931), Gustave Charpentier (1860–1956), Joseph Guy-Ropartz (1864–1955), Paul Dukas (1865–1935), Charles Koechlin (1867–1951), Florent Schmitt (1870–1958), Henri Rabaud (1873–1949), Jean Roger-Ducasse (1873–1954), and Henri Duparc (1848–1933).

Debussy and Impressionism. Claude Debussy (1862–1918), who identified himself with the impressionistic movement in French art, produced a highly original style which held a prominent place in the music of the first two decades of the 20th century. His innovations became the tools of impressionist technique in music.

STYLE. Impressionism in music is characterized by a combination of the following devices: (1) the use of neomodality, (2) open fifths and octaves, (3) parallelism and other innovations in chord progression, (4) the whole-tone scale, (5) extensive use of ninth chords, (6) general vagueness of form, (7) free rhythm and less prominence of bar-line regularity, (8) flowing melodic lines, (9) Spanish effects, and (10) wide spacing and the use of the extreme registers of the piano.

WORKS. Debussy is noted primarily for his piano music (suites, "Images," préludes and études), mostly with descriptive titles, orchestral works (such as the tone poems and suites *La Mer, Nocturnes, Iberia,* and *Prélude à L'Après-midi d'un Faun*), an impressionistic opera *Pelléas et Mélisande, La Damoiselle élue,* for women's voices and orchestra, one string quartet, and several sonatas and rhapsodies.

Maurice Ravel. Maurice Ravel (1875–1937) combined impressionistic techniques with distinctly individual traits. His music reflects neoclassical simplification of materials and form, and he occasionally made use of French baroque forms.

STYLE. Although Ravel used most of Debussy's impressionistic devices in his early works, he gradually developed his own musical language. Ravel's music generally has (1) greater clarity of form, (2) less use of the whole-tone scale, (3) more use of eleventh-chord harmony than Debussy's, (4) brilliant and colorful orchestration, and (5) an extensive use of Spanish rhythms, harmony, and melody.

WORKS. Ravel wrote principally for orchestra and for solo piano. His best-known works are *Gaspards de la Nuit, Jeux d'Eau, Tombeau de Couperin,* and *Sonatine* (all works for solo piano), *Ma Mère L'Oye* originally for two pianos; later orchestrated by Ravel), *Rhapsodie Espagnole, Boléro, La Valse,* and the ballet *Daphnis et Cloë* (among the works for orchestra), and some chamber music.

Albert Roussel. Albert Roussel (1869–1937), an older contemporary of Ravel's, was, on the whole, more progressive harmonically and tonally.

STYLE. Generally antiromantic and anti-impressionistic, Roussel's music is comparatively dissonant and tonally advanced, with counterpoint importantly displayed in his style. A marked Oriental flavor, apparent in his music, may perhaps be traced to his visits to the Far East while he was in the navy.

WORKS. Roussel's principal works include *Padmâvati* (an Oriental opera-ballet), *The Spider's Feast* (a ballet-pantomime), *Évocations* (tryptich for soli, mixed chorus, and orchestra), a ballet *Bacchus et Ariane,* four symphonies, and a considerable amount of chamber music.

Erik Satie. Erik Satie (1866–1925), who was among the first to use such devices as neomodality, quartal harmony, parallelism, polytonality, etc., is today noted primarily for his stand against impressionism, for his musical satire, and for his affiliation with "Les Six." He wrote piano music with humorous titles ("The American Cashbox," "Three Pieces in the Form of a Pear," "Unpleasant Glances," etc.), ballet music (*Relâche, Mercure, Parade*), and a "drame symphonique" entitled *Socrate*.

"Les Six." A group of six French composers came into prominence in the 1920's as champions of modern French music opposed to impressionism. They are Milhaud, Honegger, Poulenc, Auric, Durey, and Tailleferre. Although not himself a member of the group, Erik Satie was the leader, and Jean Cocteau, playwright and critic, was the literary spokesman.

Darius Milhaud. Darius Milhaud (1892–   ) is the best-known and most prolific composer of "Les Six," and unquestionably one of the most prominent composers of the 20th century.

STYLE. In the 1920's Milhaud was a leading exponent of polytonality. His music reveals various influences: (1) American jazz (*Creation of the World*), (2) Brazilian dances (*Saudades do Brazil*), and (3) the folk music of his native Provence (*Suite Provençale*). His music displays a great diversity of styles ranging from conservative to ultra-progressive.

WORKS. Milhaud has written music in almost every conceivable category: symphonies, concertos, chamber music, ballets, operas, "minute-operas," music for symphonic band, piano music, and songs. Among his best-known works are *Saudades do Brazil* (suite for piano), *La Cheminée du Roi René* (wind quintet), *Le Boeuf sur le Toit* (ballet), *Suite Française, Suite Provençale,* and *Protée.*

Arthur Honegger. Although Swiss by birth, Arthur Honegger (1892–1955) was a member of "Les Six." His style is strongly dissonant (sometimes polytonal), with strong rhythms, and a predominantly contrapuntal texture. Among his most important works are the oratorios *Le Roi David* and *Jeanne d'Arc au Bucher,* five symphonies, the tone poems *Pacific 231* and *Rugby,* Christmas and Easter cantatas, the opera *Antigone,* and a number of ballets.

Francis Poulenc. The music of Francis Poulenc (1899–1963), the only other prominent member of "Les Six," is generally more conservative harmonically than that of Milhaud or Honegger. His principal achievements are in the fields of ballet, chamber music, and songs.

Louis Durey. The music of Louis Durey (1888–   ) has not received the acclaim it deserves. Although he is not prolific, his music, especially in the field of vocal chamber music, is charming if not profound. *Dix Choeurs de Métiers* (1959), for madrigal choir and chamber ensemble, is among his most recent works.

Jacques Ibert. Jacques Ibert (1890–1962) is a moderately conservative composer who writes competently in all media and displays a typically Gallic skill in the virtuosity of his writing, which is ephemeral, acidly witty, and has light, contrapuntal textures. He is perhaps best known for his symphonic suite *Escales.* In addition, he has a quantity of fine chamber music to his credit, as well as concertos for seldom used solo instruments, such as flute and also saxophone.

Other Composers of the Modern French School. The long list of contemporary French composers shows a diversity of stylistic efforts. The principal composers include: Olivier Messiaen (1908–   ), André Jolivet (1905–   ), Daniel Lesur (1908–   ), Jean Langlais (1907–   ), Yves Baudrier (1906–   ), Jean Françaix (1912–   ), and Pierre Boulez (1925–   ), an atonalist. Mention has already been made of French innovations in musical media and *musique concrète* (see "New Tone Generators," page 182).

Switzerland

General Considerations. Although Swiss composers do not show strongly nationalist trends in music, Switzerland can boast an almost continuous line of gifted composers from Notker and Tuotilo in the 9th century through to the present time. Switzerland is the birthplace of such 20th-century composers as: Honegger, Ernest Bloch, Ernst Lévy (the latter two resident in the United States), Othmar Schoeck (1886–1957), Hermann Suter (1870–1926), Konrad Beck (1901–   ), Albert Moeschinger (1897–   ), Willi Burkhard (1900–1955), and Heinrich Sutermeister (1911–   ).

Frank Martin. Perhaps the most prominent among contemporary Swiss musicians is the composer-pianist Frank Martin (1890–   ). He has composed ballets, incidental music for plays, masses, oratorios, symphonic works, and chamber works, among which may be mentioned the delightful *Petit Symphonie Concertante* for harp, harpsichord, piano, and strings (1945).

Rolf Liebermann. Rolf Liebermann (1910–   ) is mainly known in this country for his sensational *Concerto for Jazz Band and Symphony Orchestra* (1954). His style is eclectic; although he occasionally employs twelve-tone technique, he is not primarily an atonalist. In Europe, Liebermann's reputation rests largely on his symphonic works, operas, and cantatas.

Russia

General Considerations. Because of strongly nationalistic trends and the pronounced individual traits of its composers, Russia was one of the first countries to break away from the domination of 19-century German romanticism. Since the regime of the U.S.S.R. insists that the music of its composers must have direct and ideological appeal to the Russian people, musical conservatism is prevalent, and relatively few musical innovations of the 20th century can be attributed to Russian composers. Russians have repeatedly demonstrated excellence in the field of modern ballet.

Modest Moussorgsky. Although he was a romantic Russian nationalist who contributed no radical innovations, Modest Moussorgsky (1839–1881) is generally credited with having initiated the impulse in Russia which led to 20th-century modernism.

Nikolai Rimsky-Korsakov. Nikolai Rimsky-Korsakov (1844–1908), like Moussorgsky, represents the romantic threshold of modernism. His style is based on nationalism and exoticism (*Scheherazade, Sadko,* etc.), and he made notable advances in orchestration. As the teacher of Ippolitov-Ivanov, Glière, Glazunov, Stravinsky, and others, Rimsky-Korsakov exerted an important influence on early 20th-century Russian styles.

Alexander Scriabin. Alexander Scriabin (1872–1915), though predominantly romantic, came closer than Moussorgsky or Rimsky-Korsakov to modernism. Scriabin's quasi-impressionistic music, and more particularly his innovation of the "mystic chord" (built in 4ths: C–F$\sharp$–B$\flat$–E–A–D) represent distinct departures. He wrote piano music and the tone poems *Poem of Ecstasy* and *Prometheus: a Poem of Fire.*

Igor Stravinsky. To many people, the name of Igor Stravinsky (1882–   ) is synonymous with modern music. His impact on 20th-century music is uncontested. Although Russian by birth and training, his residence in Switzerland, France and the United States makes him a figure more cosmopolitan than national.

STYLE. Although technically versatile and stylistically unpredictable, Stravinsky's music retains certain persistent traits. Among these may be mentioned: (1) brilliant orchestration and novel orchestral effects (e.g., the percussive use of the piano in *Petrouchka*), (2) strongly percussive and irregular rhythmic patterns, (3) polymetric and multimetric schemes, (4) ostinato, (5) little emphasis on melodic and thematic development, (6) dissonant and often polytonal harmony, (7) diversity of textures, and (8) a trend towards transparent sonorities. Stravinsky has employed various tonal schemes ranging from the completely tonal to the atonal; recently, he has been using twelve-tone techniques.

WORKS. Stravinsky has written music in every form and medium. He is perhaps best known for his ballet music: *Firebird, Petrouchka, The Rite of Spring, The Wedding, The Soldier's Tale, Pulcinella, Apollon Musagètes, The Fairy's Kiss, The Card Game, Orpheus,* and *Agon.* Other works, representative of various periods and styles, are the operas *The Nightingale* (later a ballet), *Mavra,* and *The Rake's Progress,* and the opera-oratorio *Oedipus Rex;* the symphonic works *Fireworks, Symphony in E♭, Symphony of Psalms* for chorus and orchestra, *Capriccio* for piano and orchestra, and *Symphony in Three Movements;* numerous chamber works, including *Octet* for wind instruments, *Dumbarton Oaks Concerto,* and *Ebony Concerto;* a *Mass* for boys' voices and ten instruments, and *Threni* (1958, an atonal work for solo voices, chorus, and orchestra).

Serge Prokofiev. The music of Serge Prokofiev (1891–1953), has been popularly acclaimed both inside and outside his country. Prokofiev's style is an admixture of: (1) modern harmonic dissonance, (2) multitonal and occasionally bitonal writing, (3) both lyric and angular melody, (4) straightforward rhythm and meter, and (5) general clarity of form. To some extent, his style leans toward the neo-classical (e.g., the *Classical Symphony*). Among his more important works are the operas *Love for Three Oranges* and *War and Peace,* the symphonic fairy tale with narrator *Peter and the Wolf,* seven symphonies, ballets, nine piano sonatas, concertos for both violin and piano, movie music (*Lieutenant Kije*), and chamber music.

Dmitri Shostakovich. Probably the best-known and most highly regarded composer of contemporary Russian music is Dmitri Shostakovich (1906–   ). Although he employs modern harmonic and tonal procedures, his music is only moderately dissonant and rarely approaches atonality; he is conservative in rhythmic and metric techniques. Shostakovich has composed more than ten symphonies, some operas such as *The Nose* and *Lady Macbeth,* a ballet (*The Golden Age*), and much piano and chamber music.

Aram Khatchaturian. Born in Armenia (1903) and trained in Moscow, Aram Khatchaturian may be termed a musical propagandist. His studies of Armenian folk music have strongly influenced his style. His works include ballets (*Gayne*), concertos for violin, piano, and cello, and chamber music.

Other 20th-Century Russian Composers. There is an impressive list of Russian composers whose musical output belongs mostly or entirely to the 20th century but whose musical styles place them in the conservative or traditional categories. The most important of these are Ippolitov-Ivanov (1859–1935), best known for his symphonic suite *Caucasian Sketches* (1894), Alexander Grechaninov (1864–1956), Alexander Glazounov (1865–1936), Vladimir Rebikov (1866–1920), Sergei Vasilenko (1872–1956), Gregory Krein (1880–), Nicolai Miaskovsky (1881–1950) who is a prolific symphonist with 25 symphonies to his credit, Reinhold Glière (1875–1956), best known for his *Red Poppy* ballet suite, Alexander Krein (1883–), Mikhail Gnessin (1883–1957), Yuri Shaporin (1889–), an opera composer (*The Decembrists,* 1953), Leo Knipper (1898–), Alexander Tcherepnin (1899–), composer-pianist now resident in the United States, Alexander Mossolov (1900–), Michael Starokadomsky (1901–), Vissarion Shebalin (1902–), Dmitri Kabalevski (1904–), Ivan Dzerzhinsky (1909–), Tikhon Khrennikov (1913–), Julian Krein (1913–), Alexei Haieff (1914–).

Austria

General Considerations. Modern music of Austria may be properly said to begin with the post-romantic works of Bruckner (1824–1896) and Mahler (1860–1911). But what is probably the most radical single trend in 20th-century music originated in the works of Arnold Schoenberg and his disciples.

Arnold Schoenberg The music of Arnold Schoenberg (1874–1951) falls into three periods: (1) the post-romantic period from 1897 to 1908 influenced by Wagner, Strauss, and Mahler (*Transfigured Night, Guerre-Lieder*), (2) the transitional-expressionist period from 1909 to about 1920 in which he was moving toward atonality and a new system of composition (*Three Piano Pieces,* Op. 11, *Pierrot Lunaire,* and (3) the tone-row period from about 1921, beginning with *Serenade,* Op. 24. Although the music of Schoenberg has never enjoyed widespread popularity, his ideas and technique have had a tremendous influence on 20th-century composition. His system of atonality has a following throughout the musical world.

THE TWELVE-TONE SYSTEM. The *twelve-tone system* (also called *dodecaphonic* and *serial technique*) is a means of arriving at atonality. Its basic premise is that all twelve tones of the octave have tonal equality (i.e., no tendency toward a tonic). A twelve-tone composition is based on a melodic series consisting of the twelve tones into which an octave is divided. This series, called a *tone row,* is so constructed that it avoids any suggestion of conventional chords or tonal relationships. The tones of a tone row (which in itself is not a theme in the ordinary sense, but more akin to a scale basis) do not have to stay within the limits of one octave. No tone may be repeated in a given voice until all twelve tones have been sounded. The tone row is subject to infinite rhythmic changes, and subsequent statements of the series may be melodically altered in a number of ways: (1) by transposing the entire row to any pitch level, (2) by transposing any tone of the series up or down one or more octaves, (3) by inversion, (4) by retrograde statement (the entire row played backwards), (5) by retrograde by 2, 3, 4, or 6 (e.g., retrograde by 2 would mean playing the original tone row in the order 2 1 4 3 6 5, etc.), and (6) by combining the above devices. A single composition may employ two different tone rows (*Hauptstimme* and *Nebenstimme*). The tones of a row may also be employed in dissonant chordal groups as well as in serial order.

STYLE. Although the styles of dodecaphonic composers differ considerably, there is, nevertheless, a pervading sameness about atonal compositions. In addition to its atonality, Schoenberg's music (and that of other dodecaphonic composers) is characterized by (1) extreme disjunction, angularity, and dissonance of melodic line, (2) extreme harmonic dissonance, and (3) formal complexity and obscurity. Schoenberg additionally initiated a vocal style called *Sprechstimme* or *Sprechgesang* which consists of half-spoken, half-sung texts (e.g., *Pierrot Lunaire, Survivor from Warsaw*).

WORKS. In addition to the compositions already mentioned, the following works are representative: *Book of the Hanging Gardens, Erwartung,* four string quartets, a *Quintet* for wind instruments, *Four Pieces* (Op. 27) and *Canon* (Op. 28) for mixed chorus, *Serenade* for instrumental septet and baritone voice, *Variations for Orchestra, Violin Concerto, Piano Concerto,* and *Variations for Band.*

Alban Berg. Alban Berg (1885–1935) was Schoenberg's foremost disciple. While using the formal construction of his teacher, Berg employed the tone row more freely. His style appears to be less harsh, more romantically subjective, and more lyric. His principal works are *Wozzeck* and *Lulu* (atonal and expressionistic operas),

Lyric Suite for string quartet, and the *Violin Concerto,* subtitled "To the Memory of an Angel."

Anton Webern. The third of the great Viennese atonalists was Anton Webern (1883–1945). His music, unlike that of Berg's, has a classical rather than romantic emphasis; it is tightly constructed, with rhythmic patterns of a complex nature, lean and sparse textures, and brilliant instrumentation. Webern was the first important exponent of so-called *pointillist* or fragmentary techniques in music and, as such, had particular influence on the more avant-garde composers of the present day. Webern was not a prolific composer (his complete works, generally brief because of condensation, are recorded on four 12-inch discs). Among these may be mentioned the *Concerto for Nine Instruments, Quartet* for violin, clarinet, tenor saxophone, and piano, *Symphony, Piano Variations,* songs and chamber music.

Ernst Křenek. Perhaps the most important living composer of the Vienese school of atonalists is Ernst Křenek (1900–). Born and trained in Vienna, Křenek has lived in the United States since 1937. (He became an American citizen in 1945.) He achieved his first fame with the spectacular jazz opera, *Jonny Spielt Auf* in 1927; the opera *Charles V* was his first twelve-tone work. He has composed *The Santa Fe Time Table, The Ballad of the Railroads, What Price Confidence,* piano music, symphonies, concertos, chamber music, and songs. In addition, Křenek is an eminent musicologist with a number of scholarly works to his credit.

Egon Wellesz. A composer and musicologist, resident in England since 1932, Egon Wellesz (1885–) studied with Schoenberg and Adler in Vienna, but eventually abandoned the twelve-tone system. His music is little known outside of England; however, his reputation for scholarly research in Byzantine music is well established.

Josef Hauer. Josef Hauer (1883–1959) developed a twelve-tone system of his own, based on tone groups called *Tropen* which are determined by a theory of overtone agreement. All his music (operas, cantatas, chamber, orchestral, and piano music) is based on this system.

Franz Schreker. Franz Schreker (1878–1934) was an Austrian conductor and composer of operas, noted for musical eroticism and an overripe romantic style.

Ernst Toch. Though born in Vienna, Ernst Toch (1887–1964) spent most of his creative life abroad before immigrating to the United States in 1934. His style has a certain delicacy and clarity, though his music is harmonically dissonant. Toch has written much piano and chamber music, operas, and music for motion pictures and for radio plays. Among his principal works are *The Chinese Flute* for soprano and chamber orchestra, *Big Ben Variations, Hyperion, A Dramatic Prelude* for orchestra, and *Notturno*. He is the author of *The Shaping Forces in Music*.

Gottfried von Einem. With the première of his ballet *Prinzessin Turandot* in 1944, Gottfried von Einem (1918–   ) emerged as one of the most challenging composers in modern Austria. He has since achieved international recognition for his music which is principally in symphonic media: suites, symphonies, concertos, etc.

Germany

General Considerations. Despite preoccupation with military aggression in the first half of the 20th century and the resulting decline in musical creativity, Germany has produced some important modern composers.

Richard Strauss. At the turn of the century, Richard Strauss (1864–1949) was the most powerful musical force in Germany. Stylistically, his music belongs to the late 19th and early 20th centuries. During the last thirty years of his life, his musical productivity was negligible.

STYLE. His style may be broadly classified as post-Wagnerian and neoromantic because of his use of enormous orchestras and massive though brilliant and colorful orchestration, and because of the heavy emotional content of his music. His harmonic and melodic style is progressive, although not extreme in relation to other early 20th-century styles.

WORKS. Strauss' orchestral works consist chiefly of symphonic poems (see works listed on page 161). He wrote operas (*Salome, Elektra, Der Rosenkavalier*) and a great number of Lieder.

Paul Hindemith. In the role of teacher, author, and composer, Paul Hindemith (1895–1963) has exerted a strong influence on 20th-century music. He is a prolific and versatile composer.

STYLE. Hindemith's music is (1) predominantly contrapuntal in a neobaroque style, (2) often harmonically dissonant as a result of linear independence, (3) often melodically disjunct, (4) basically tonal but frequently tonally obscure, (5) neoclassical in its texture and economy of material, (6) masterful in instrumental idiom and orchestration, and (7) generally conservative in rhythmic and metric elements.

WORKS. Hindemith's output includes practically every medium: operas (*Cardillac, Neues vom Tage*), symphonies (*Mathis der Maler* from an earlier opera, *Symphony in E♭, Symphony in B♭* for band), concertos, chamber music, sonatas for various wind instruments, ballet music (*Nobilissima Visione*), choral music (*Apparebit Repentina Dies*), a song cycle *Das Marienleben,* and a number of works in the Gebrauchsmusik category (*Plöner Musiktag, Trauermusik,* etc.). *Ludus Tonalis,* a collection of fugues and interludes for piano, demonstrates Hindemith's contrapuntal skill and versatility. He is the author of textbooks on theory and composition and of *The Composer's World.*

Kurt Weill. Kurt Weill (1900–1950) is known chiefly as a composer of operatic works in a moderately progressive style. He lived in the United States from 1933. His principal works are *Three-Penny Opera* (based on *The Beggar's Opera* by Gay and Pepusch), *The Seven Deadly Sins* (a ballet in song), *The Rise and Fall of the City of Mahagonny, The Eternal Road, Street Scene,* and the folk opera *Down in the Valley.*

Carl Orff. The fame of Carl Orff (1895–) reached the United States in 1952 with the performance of his *Carmina Burana* (composed in 1935–36). He is essentially a composer of stage works. His style is a complete negation of Wagnerianism; it is spare, dry, and rhythmically vigorous. Ostinato is a characteristic device in his music. Principal works include *Carmina Burana, Catulli Carmina, Trionfo di Afrodite, Antigone,* and the folk-tale opera *Die Kluge.*

Werner Egk. A painter of recognized talent and a composer of operas, ballets, and music for radio, Werner Egk (1901–) is a contemporary German composer with an affinity for French culture and subjects (*French Suite* after Rameau, *Chanson et Romance*). Like Orff, he represents a return to directness and simplicity. His music is basically diatonic and tonal, and it avoids the abstract (no sonatas, string quartets, or symphonies). Among a number of significant works are *Die Zaubergeige, Irish Legend,* and *The Examiner.*

Boris Blacher. Another composer of modern Germany is Boris Blacher (1903–   ). He employs a rhythmic system which he calls "variable metres," a sort of rhythmic tone row. Thinness of texture characterizes his style. Blacher has written ballet music, operas, orchestral works, chamber music, some songs, and film and theatre music. Representative works are *Variations on a Theme of Paganini, Study in Pianissimo* (commissioned by the Louisville Orchestra in 1954) and the oratorio *Der Gross Inquisitor.*

Karl Hartmann. Karl Amadeus Hartmann (1905–   ) is essentially a symphonic composer. Although a pupil of Webern at one time, his music is not atonal or dodecaphonic. He employs a chromatic and sharply dissonant material and generally rich textures. His music leans toward romanticism.

Wolfgang Fortner. Wolfgang Fortner (1907–   ) is influential as a conductor, teacher, and composer. Since about 1945 he has employed a freely adapted serial technique. His music is dry and spare, but has a notable lyric quality. Fortner has composed a quantity of church music, operas, ballets, symphonies, concertos, and some works for small instrumental ensembles.

Other 20th-Century German Composers. A number of younger German composers have come into prominence since the war. Among these are Hans Werner Henze (1926–   ), Karl Heinz Stockhausen (1928–   ) who works in serial technique and electronic mediums, Philipp Jarnach, Karl Hoeller, Giselher Klebe, Bernd Zimmermann, Herman Heiss, Nepomuk David, and Heimo Erbse.

England

General Considerations. England's high position among musical nations declined after the Elizabethan era, and, except for the solitary peak of Henry Purcell at the end of the 17th century, she produced no top ranking composers for nearly three centuries. England was dominated by Italian music in the 18th century, and by German romanticism in the 19th century. Musical nationalism was late in developing.

The 20th century has seen a significant rise in England's musical position, attributable to three factors: (1) liberation from the dominance of German romanticism, (2) awakening of interest in her musical heritage, and (3) absorption of 20th-century technical and stylistic developments on the Continent. Without relinquishing her well known affinity for choral excellence, England has risen steadily in the symphonic and operatic fields. The technical and artistic excellence of modern British composers is unquestionable, though there are few avant-garde composers, and the musical scene generally tends to be conservative.

Traditionalists. The following 20th-century British composers are creative artists of recognized stature, though they are scarcely a part of the modern current: Alexander Mackenzie (1847–1935), Hubert Parry (1848–1944), Frederick Cowen (1852–1935), Charles Stanford (1852–1924), Edward Elgar (1857–1934), Ethel Smyth (1858–1944), Edward German (1862–1936), Joseph Holbrooke (1878–1958), Lord Berners (1883–1950), Benjamin Dale (1885–1945), Herbert Howells (1892–   ), Ernest Moeran (1894–1950), and Gordon Jacobs (1895–   ). Added to this list is the name of Arthur Benjamin (1893–1960), Australian-born composer and pianist.

Modern Conservatives. Composers in this group have employed modern techniques in varying degrees, and have developed individual styles influenced by national factors. They are Frederick Delius (1862–1934), Granville Bantok (1868–1946), John Ireland (1879–1962), Cyril Scott (1879–   ), Frank Bridge (1879–1941), Arnold Bax (1883–1953), Arthur Bliss (1891–   ), Peter Warlock (1894–1930), Eugene Goosens (1893–1962), Gerald Finzi (1901–1956), and Constant Lambert (1905–1951).

Gustav Holst. Although his popularity has waned in recent years, Gustav Holst (1874–1934) was an important figure in the English modern renaissance. He was an antiromantic. He is best known today for his symphonic suite *The Planets* (1914–16) which is representative of his mature style. Modern techniques he employed are (1) elasticity of rhythm, (2) multimetric schemes, (3) unusual time signatures, (4) pedal point and ostinato, (5) occasional bitonality, and (6) prominence of the fourth in melodic and chordal construction.

Ralph Vaughan Williams. Probably the most important English composer of the first half of the 20th century was Ralph Vaughan Williams (1872–1958). His music, not devoid of romantic traits, reveals a wide diversity of styles and techniques. Modern devices to be found in his music are: (1) parallelism (especially of 6-4 chords), (2) whole-tone scales (in *The Wasps*), (3) modality (*Fantasy on a Theme of Thomas Tallis*), and (4) other unusual chord progressions. Though often dissonant, Vaughan Williams' music is consistently tonal. He made considerable use of English folk tunes and styles. He excelled equally in symphonic and choral media. Principal works include nine symphonies, operas (*Hugh the Drover* and *Riders to the Sea*), oratorios and other choral works, chamber music and songs (*On Wenlock Edge*, a song cycle for tenor, piano, and string quartet).

Alan Bush. Alan Bush (1900–   ) developed a serial method which he does not employ atonally. His music has rhythmic vigor, melodic disjunction, clear contrapuntal texture, and harmonic dissonance. His vocal works often display his Marxist ideology (e.g., the *Piano Concerto,* 1937, which uses a male chorus in the finale). His style has been described generally as epic and dramatic.

Edmund Rubbra. Edmund Rubbra (1901–   ) shows influences of Holst (with whom he studied) and Vaughan Williams. His polyphonic style is mainly derived from Tudor composers. Although he occasionally uses chord streams, his harmonic, melodic, and rhythmic techniques tend to be conservative. Rubbra has written masses, motets, madrigals, and symphonies.

William Walton. Among the many prominent English composers born in the first decade of the 20th century, William Walton (1902–   ) is probably the most celebrated. Though his works are not radical, he has assimilated modern techniques in an individual manner. Walton is neoclassical in his use of polyphony and clarity of textures; his harmony is pungent without following a system; his melodic invention, especially in a characteristic lyric style, is remarkable; and his orchestration is often brilliant. Not the least of his qualities is a rhythmic vitality, often in a multimetric framework.

Among Walton's most important works are *Façade* (chamber orchestra with recited poems by Edith Sitwell), *Portsmouth Point, Sinfonia Concertante, Viola Concerto*, the oratorio *Belshazzar's Feast*, the opera *Troilus and Cressida*, and distinguished scores for the films *Henry V* and *Romeo and Juliet*.

Lennox Berkeley. Lennox Berkeley (1903–   ) has been described as a miniaturist. A pupil of Nadia Boulanger, Berkeley's music has a flavor that is more French than English. Quiet delicacy, clarity, and simplicity are apparent in his harmony, counterpoint, and instrumentation. His principal works include *Divertimento, Nocturne, Stabat Mater, Crux Fidelis*, and some successful music for chamber ensembles and piano.

Alan Rawsthorne. Alan Rawsthorne (1905–   ) is almost exclusively an instrumental composer. Notable traits of his style are harmonic dissonance from use of chromatic cross relations, recurrence of melodic patterns, and formal structure based on baroque-like extension of thematic material rather than on sectional treatment. He is a master of the variation form. He has composed some modern idiomatic piano music (*Bagatelles, The Creel*), concertos, symphonies, and chamber music.

Michael Tippett. Displaying equal competence in vocal and instrumental media, the music of Michael Tippett (1905–   ), particularly in his use of counterpoint, is derivative from 16th- and 17th-century English music in which fields he is a scholar. Tippett's use of cross rhythms and transferred accents is reminiscent of Stravinsky and Bartók. His vocal melodic line is characteristically ornate. Harmonically he is conservative. Among his important works are the oratorio *A Child of Our Time*, a song cycle *The Heart's Assurance*, an opera *The Midsummer Marriage, Fantasia Concertante* for strings, other orchestral works, and some chamber and piano music.

Benjamin Britten. The fame of Benjamin Britten (1913–   ) rests principally on his reputation as one of the foremost composers of opera in the 20th century, although he has written many successful instrumental works as well.

STYLE. Melody plays an important role in all of Britten's music. His melodic lines are modern without being extreme. Britten makes skillful use of counterpoint but it does not dominate his style. His harmony is essentially diatonic but often sharply dissonant; his music is basically tonal; his textures are characteristically light and transparent; his orchestration is bright and colorful. Britten is a master of sectional forms and variations.

WORKS. Britten's principal operas are *Peter Grimes, The Rape of Lucretia, Albert Herring, Let's Make an Opera* (which makes unique and ingenious use of audience participation), *Billy Budd, The Turn of the Screw,* and *Gloriana.* Other significant works are *Serenade* for tenor, horn, and strings, *Young Person's Guide to the Orchestra* (a clever set of variations and a fugue on a theme from Purcell), *Sinfonia da Requiem, Spring Symphony* (a cantata), *Hymn to St. Cecilia* (an a-cappella choral work), and songs (*The Holy Sonnets of John Donne* and *Les Illuminations*).

Other 20th-Century English Composers. A number of British composers who have come to the fore since the Second World War are: Arnold Cooke (1906–   ) and Stanley Bate (1913–   ), both students of Hindemith; Bernard Naylor (1907–   ), a choral composer; Richard Arnell (1917–   ), Peter Racine Fricker (1920–   ), Malcolm Arnold (1921–   ), and Ian Hamilton (1922–   ), the last three being promising instrumental composers; and Humphrey Searle (1915–   ), the leading dodecaphonist in Britain today. Three women have had some standing in England, although their music is virtually unknown abroad: Priaulx Rainier (1903–   ), Elizabeth Lutzens (1906–   ), a tone-row composer, and Elizabeth Maconchy (1907–   ).

Hungary

General Considerations. Hungarian nationalism properly began with Ferenc Erkel (1810–1893). The 20th century has so far produced few composers, and only one musical giant, Béla Bartók. Odön Mihalovich (1842–1929) wrote operas in Wagnerian style. Ernst Dohnanyi (1879–1960) belongs to 19th-century traditions. Younger Hungarian composers are Paul Kadosa (1903–   ) and Tibor Serly (1900–   ) who was a pupil of Bartók.

Béla Bartók. One of the truly great figures of 20th-century music is Béla Bartók (1881–1945). Not only a foremost composer, teacher, and pianist, he was also a noted scholar who collected and edited folk music. He created no new systems nor founded any school, but his music represents almost every aspect of modern techniques.

STYLE. Although progressive in style, a romantic strain runs through his music. French impressionism made some impact on his early music (e.g., *Bluebeard's Castle,* 1911). Hungarian folk elements also permeate his music. Details of his style are: (1) short melodic structures, (2) little conventional lyricism, and (3) dissonant harmony, often extremely so. Although he avoided complete atonality and serial technique, his music is often tonally obscure. He occasionally employed polytonality. He used new scale systems in addition to those found in Hungarian folk music. With equal effectiveness, Bartók employed contrapuntal and homophonic textures, often in the same composition. New sonorities and new instrumental effects abound in his music (e.g., *String Quartets* Nos. 3, 4, and 5). Rhythmic vitality, sometimes approaching Stravinsky's percussive dynamism, is an essential feature of his style. Among the distinctive features of his music are economy of thematic material and his technique of extension and variation. Structurally, Bartók's music is both subtle and complex.

WORKS. One of Bartók's greatest masterpieces is *Music for Strings, Percussion, and Celesta* (1936). His six string quartets represent a panorama of his stylistic development from 1908 to 1939. He wrote three piano concertos, a violin concerto, and *Concerto for Orchestra.* A remarkable 20th-century collection of piano music is the *Mikrokosmos,* a collection of 153 graded pieces in six volumes which represent almost every kind of 20th-century device in rhythm, meter, tonality, scale systems, chord structures, progressions, etc.

Zoltán Kodály. Zoltán Kodály (1882–1967), collaborating with Bartók, made a specialty of collecting folk songs. His music is more national and individual than modern. He is best known for the nationalist comic opera *Háry János,* his *Psalmus Hungaricus, Missa Brevis,* and *Dances from Galanta,* and a *Te Deum.* He has composed concertos, sonatas, and quartets.

Italy

General Considerations. The musical scene in Italy during the first two decades of the 20th century was dominated by the tradition of verismo opera (Puccini, Leoncavallo, Mascagni). There was a general neglect of instrumental music, even of Italy's 17th- and 18th-century heritage, until the poet d'Annunzio prepared the way to a revival of interest. A few daring composers strove to break with the operatic tradition by employing 20th-century idioms in instrumental media. By the middle of the 20th century there was a notable interest in atonal serial techniques.

Traditionalists. A number of composers continued to write music in the 19th-century style. Giovanni Sgambati (1841–1914), Giuseppe Martucci (1856–1909), and Leone Sinigaglia (1868–1944) wrote symphonic works of a somewhat Brahmsian nature. Composers who continued in the Puccini tradition are Franco Alfano (1876–1954), Ermanno Wolf-Ferrari (1876–1948), and Riccardo Zandonai (1883–1944).

Ferruccio Busoni. One of the pioneers of modern Italian music was Ferruccio Busoni (1866–1924), a pianist, composer, editor, critic, teacher, and author. In composition, he was somewhat of an eclectic, but he adopted new harmonic and tonal concepts and was generally a neoclassicist. His principal contributions were in piano music, but he also wrote symphonic works, operas, and some chamber music.

Alfredo Casella. Alfredo Casella (1883–1947) is generally considered the "prime mover" of the antiromantic and anti-verismo movements in Italy. Although his music was little understood or appreciated in Italy, he effected the restoration of instrumental and contrapuntal music to the Italian scene. He also experimented with atonality, polytonality, and new harmonic dissonances, but eventually returned to a diatonic, tonal basis, and to the simplification of forms and content.

Francesco Malipiero. Francesco Malipiero (1882–   ) worked with Casella toward a modern Italian music. A musicologist, he edited the works of Monteverdi, Vivaldi, and others. In his compositions romantic symphonism was replaced by older Italian models based on linear design. He composed numerous operas, choral works, and symphonic and chamber music. A recent work is *Fantasie di Ogni Giorno* (1954) commissioned by the Louisville Orchestra.

Ottorino Respighi. For many years, the principal figure in modern Italian instrumental music was Ottorino Respighi (1879–1936). His music helped to establish the trend towards an instrumental renaissance, but his style is more romantic than modern, a mixture of Straussian and impressionistic techniques. Resphigi is best known for two symphonic poems, *The Fountains of Rome,* and *The Pines of Rome,* and for his *Concerto Gregoriano.*

Ildebrando Pizzetti. The leader in modern Italian opera is Ildebrando Pizzetti (1880–   ). His music is completely subservient to the drama. Among his important works are *Lo Straniero, Fra Gherardo, Orseolo,* and *L'Oro* and *Fedra.*

Giorgio Ghedini. Giorgio Ghedini (1892–   ) belongs to the generation born in the last decade of the 19th century. His music employs radical dissonance and a neoclassical texture derived from the concerto grosso style of Vivaldi.

Vittorio Rieti. Vittorio Rieti (1898–   ), who moved to the United States in 1940 and became an American citizen in 1944, is also a neoclassicist and generally conservative. He has composed successful ballet music, chamber music, and orchestral works. Typical of his style are the *Partita for Harpsichord, Flute, Oboe, and String Quartet* and *Introduzione e Gioco delle Ore.*

Mario Castelnuovo-Tedesco. Another conservative, Mario Castelnuovo-Tedesco (1895–   ) is partly neoromantic and partly neoclassical. His music is markedly lyrical and, he claims, influenced in this respect by the works of Schubert. In particular, he has contributed greatly to 20th-century guitar literature in works such as the *Concerto* for guitar and orchestra and the *Quintet* for guitar and string quartet.

Antonio Veretti. Antonio Veretti (1900–   ), director of the Pesaro Conservatory since 1950, is a composer of operas, film music, oratorios, and a number of orchestral works.

Goffredo Petrassi. One of the most important contemporary Italian composers is Goffredo Petrassi (1904–   ). His versatile technique employs most modern devices of tonality: (1) displaced tonality (*Partita*), (2) fusion of modal, tonal, polytonal and atonal writing (*Coro di Morti*), and (3) free use of tone-row technique in the cantata *Noche Oscura.* His style is usually dissonant and contrapuntal, and has a characteristic rhythmic drive. *Psalm IX* is an important choral work, and *Quinto Concerto* is a recent symphonic piece.

Luigi Dallapiccola. The leader of Italian dodecaphonic music is Luigi Dallapiccola (1904–   ). He is predominantly a vocal composer who uses serial technique; however, his music, instead of becoming angular due to the characteristics of the twelve-tone system, forces the system to yield to his own Italianate lyricism. Some of his important works are *Divertimento, Cinque Frammenti di Saffo* (voice and chamber orchestra, using different series with tonal accompaniment), *Sex Carmina Alcaei* (a tone row in a series of canons), the opera *Il Prigioniero (The Prisoner), Quaderno Musicale di Annalibera* (a strictly serial work), *Goethe Lieder* for voice and three clarinets, and *Variations for Orchestra*.

Riccardo Nielson. Riccardo Nielson (1908–   ), not to be confused with the Danish composers Carl and Ludolf Nielsen, was a neoclassicist until approximately 1942 and an atonalist thereafter. His style has a basic simplicity and an absence of extreme dissonance. He has composed operas (*L'Incubo* and *Il Guidice*), a radio drama (*La Via di Colombo*), two choral rhapsodies, piano sonatas, and string music.

Mario Peragallo. Mario Peragallo (1910–   ) makes free use of dodecaphonic material. His important works to date are the opera *La Gita in Campagna, Violin Concerto, Double String Quartet, Fantasy for Piano, Fantasy for Orchestra,* and an a-cappella work, *De Profundis.*

Roman Vlad. Born in Rumania in 1919, but living in Rome since 1939, and as a naturalized citizen since 1951, Roman Vlad employs a mixture of tonal and serial atonal materials. Among his important works are *De Profundis,* the ballet *La Dama delle Camelie, Symphony* (1948), *Divertimento,* and the opera *La Storia di una Mamma.*

Other 20th-Century Italian Composers. The following composers, mainly using dodecaphonic techniques, are currently active: Bruno Bettinelli (1913–   ), Riccardo Malipiero (1914–   ), Guido Turchi (1916–   ), who is influenced more by Bartók than by Schoenberg, Valentino Bucchi (1916–   ), Bruno Maderna (1920–   ) and Camillo Togni (1922–   ) who are both dodecaphonic extremists, Luigi Nono (1924–   ) a pointillistic composer, and Franco Donatoni (1927–   ).

Spain

General Considerations. Spanish music of the 20th century is highly permeated with national folk elements, especially with those of Spanish dances. There is little ultramodern music; most of it is basically romantic, sometimes quasi-impressionistic. As in Italy, there has been a notable awakening of interest in Spanish music of the past; leaders in this movement were the musicologists Felipe Pedrell (1841–1922), who made important studies of Spanish folk music and also edited the music of Victoria, Morales, Milan, and others, and Kurt Schindler (1882–1935), who compiled an invaluable anthology of Spanish folk music.

Albeniz and Granados. Isaac Albeniz (1860–1909) and Enrique Granados (1867–1916), whose lives extended into the 20th century, belong stylistically to 19th-century romanticism.

Manuel de Falla. The most prominent name among Spanish composers in the first half of the 20th century is Manuel de Falla (1876–1946). His romantic style includes some mild modernisms of rhythmic complexity, moderate tonal obscurity and harmonic dissonance, and colorful orchestration. His principal works are the opera *La Vida Breve*, the ballets *El Sombrero de Tres Picos* and *El Amor Brujo*, and *Nights in the Gardens of Spain* for piano and orchestra.

Joaquin Turina. Like Falla, Joaquin Turina (1882–1949) was strongly influenced by his studies in Paris. Although his style is also prominently Andalusian, it is more academic than Falla's. He wrote a quantity of Spanish-style piano music and orchestral works, among which may be mentioned *Danzas Fantasticas*, *Scene Andalouse*, and *Canto a Sevilla* for voice and orchestra.

Carlos Surinach. Probably the most important Spanish composer in the contemporary scene is Carlos Surinach (1915–   ), who has won international acclaim as conductor as well as for his compositions. He settled in New York in 1951. Among his important works are *Sinfonietta Flamenca*, *Ritmo Jondo* (ballet), *Feria Magica*, and *Fandango*.

Other 20th-Century Spanish Composers. Roberto Gerhard (1896–   ), living in England since 1939, was a student of Schoenberg in Vienna; Oscar Espla (1886–   ) is both theorist and composer;

Jaime Pahissa (1880–   ), Rodolfo Halffter (1900–   ) and his brother Ernesto (1905–   ), and Julian Bantista (1901–   ) are less well known Spanish composers of the present.

Czechoslovakia

General Considerations. Czech music of the 20th century, although it has absorbed some modern trends, is dominated more by strong nationalistic folk influence. In the early part of the century, the domination of German romanticism was also apparent.

Romantic Nationalists. Czech nationalism began in the 19th century with Bedřich Smetana (1824–1884) and continued into the 20th century with Zdeněk Fibich (1850–1900), Antonin Dvořák (1841–1904), and Joseph Foerster (1859–1951), all of whom remained stylistically affiliated with German romanticism.

Josef Suk. A pupil of Dvořák, Josef Suk (1874–1935) represents a continuation of the national-romantic tradition, but with more rhythmic elasticity and chromatic harmony. His melodic style is generally lyric and there is a national rhapsodic element in his music. His structural technique encompasses thematic metamorphosis rather than sectional or sonata forms. His principal works are the symphonic poems *Prague* and *A-growing,* and *Epilogue* for baritone and bass solo, chorus, and orchestra.

Vítězslav Novák. The romantic music of Vítězslav Novák (1870–1949), mostly consisting of piano music, songs, and operas with patriotic themes, was influenced by Moravian and Slovak styles, notably in his arrangement of folk songs with accompaniment of derived counterpoint.

Otakar Ostrčil. Otakar Ostrčil (1879–1935) was a composer-conductor who adopted new techniques while at the same time retaining a strong romantic national flavor. He was interested in Indian mysticism (e.g., the opera *Kinala's Eyes*). Other operas are *The Bud, Jack's Kingdom, The Legend of St. Zita.*

Leoš Janáček. The most important of 20th-century Czech composers is Leoš Janáček (1854–1928). In his research and theoretical writings on Czech folk song, he is the Czech counterpart of Bartók and Kodály in Hungarian music, and, like Bartók, he absorbed the folk element in his compositions. This is manifested in his song cycle *The Diary of One Who Disappeared,* as well as in other compositions. Intensity increased by repetition is another trait which is found in his *Sinfonietta* and *Concertino* for seven instruments. His works also include the operas *Káta Kabanova, The Vixen, The Makropulos Case,* and, most importantly, *Jenufa* and his last opera, *From a Death-House.* His *Glagolitic Mass* is an excellent choral work.

Alois Haba. Alois Haba (1893–) was mentioned as one of the proponents of microtonality. His microtonic systems were derived from inflection of Moravian folk music. His music tends toward athematic or nonrepetitive thematic organization. He has written piano music, folk-song arrangements for women's voices, and the opera *Mother.*

Bohuslav Martinů. The music of Bohuslav Martinů (1890–1959) is today the most frequently performed and internationally recognized of all works by modern Czech composers. Long a resident of France and the United States, Martinů fused cosmopolitan with national elements. His style is progressively modern. He was a prolific composer of large-scale works for symphony, opera, ballet, as well as vocal and chamber music.

Other 20th-Century Czech Composers. The following contemporary composers are less well known outside their country: Otakar Jeremiáš (1892–), Emil Axman (1887–1950), Ladislav Vycpálek (1882–), Pavel Bořkovec (1894–), Emil Burian (1904–), Jaroslav Ježek (1906–1942), Isa Krejči (1904–), Miloslav Kabeláč (1908–), Vaclav Dobiáš (1909–), Kelement Slaviký (1910–), Jan Kapr (1914–), Jan Hanuš (1915–), Jiři Pauer (1919–), Stěpán Lucký (1919–), Alexander Moyzes (1906–), Eugen Suchoň (1908–), Ján Cikker (1911–), Simon Jurovský (1912–), Ján Zimmer, and Karel Husa (1921–), who was appointed to a post at Cornell University in 1954.

Scandinavian Countries

Denmark. Perhaps because of her proximity to the European continent, Denmark has assimilated modern developments more quickly than have other northern countries. In Danish music the foremost name in the first half of the 20th-century is that of Carl Nielsen

(1865–1931), a composer of symphonies and chamber music who had a strong influence on other Danish composers. Knud-Aage Riisager (1897–   ), who was influenced by French neoclassical tendencies (Roussel), is another prominent figure in modern Danish composition. In addition to these composers, the most significant names in Danish music today are Jørgen Bentzon (1897–1951), Finn Høffding (1899–   ), Vagn Holmboe (1909–   ), and Niels Viggo Bentzon (1919–   ).

Norway. Norwegian music is still dominated by Edvard Grieg (1843–1907) and therefore by a nationalistic and somewhat conservative style. Compositions are largely modeled on folk tunes, both harmonically and melodically. Among the more progressive contemporary composers in Norway are Bjarne Brustad (1895–   ), Harold Saeverud (1897–   ), Klaus Egge (1906–   ), and Fartein Valen (1887–1952).

Sweden. The outstanding composers in Sweden today are Hilding Rosenberg (1892–   ), Gösta Nystroem (1890–   ), Moses Pergament (1893–   ), Dag Wiren (1905–   ), Lars-Erik Larsson (1908–   ), and, among the younger men, Karl-Birger Blomdahl (1916–   ), Sven-Erik Bäck (1919–   ), and Ingvar Lidholm (1921–   ).

Finland. Twentieth-century Finnish music seems, until now, to have been dominated almost wholly by that of the late Jan Sibelius (1865–1957), whose music, though reflecting a spirit both individual and national, is nevertheless conservatively romantic in the 19th-century tradition. Other Finnish composers of about the same generation are Armas Jaernefelt (1869–1958) and Selim Palmgren (1878–1951). Younger composers include Vaino Raitio (1891–1945), Uuno Klami (1900–   ), Nils-Erik Ringbom (1907–   ), Nils-Erik Fougstedt (1910–   ), Erik Bergman (1911–   ), Einar Englund (1916–   ), and Tauno Pylkkänen (1918–   ).

Other European Countries

Holland. The dominant figure in 20th-century Dutch music is Willem Pijper (1884–1947), whose music reflects the Netherlands tradition of contrapuntal excellence plus modern harmonic and tonal procedures. Other composers of the modern Dutch school are Hen-

drik Andriessen (1892–   ), Guillaume Landre (1905–   ), Leon
Ortheil (1905–   ), Bertus van Lier (1906–   ), and Henk Badings
(1907–   ).

Belgium. Twentieth-century developments have met with relatively little response in Belgium. Among the composers who have
been active in this century may be mentioned Pierre Benoit (1834–
1901), Jan Blockx (1851–1912), Edgar Tinel (1854–1912), Joseph
Jongen (1873–1953), Marcel Poot (1901–   ), and Paul de Malein-
greau (1902–   ) an organist and neoclassicist.

Greece. One composer stands above all others in contemporary
Greek music: Nikos Skalkottas (1904–1949). A pupil of Schoenberg
(1927–1931), his music is predominantly dodecaphonic. He was a
prolific composer who wrote mostly large-scale works: symphonies,
concertos, etc. About one-third of his total output was chamber
music. Other Greek composers are George Lambelet (1875–   ),
a composer of songs; Manuel Kalomiris (1883–1962), Mario Varvo-
glis (1885–   ), Petro Petridis (1891–   ), and George Pondiris
(1892–   ).

South and Central America

The culture of Latin America is a mixture of native Indian, Negro,
and European elements (predominantly Spanish and Portuguese).
These racial elements are prominent in the folk songs, dances, and
composed music of the countries. The 20th century has witnessed a
significant rise of musical activity in most of the Latin American
countries, the most important being Argentina, Brazil and Mexico.

Argentina. An abundance of folk-song material, mostly of Gaucho
origin, provides a rich source of native material used by Argentine
composers, many of whom have had European training.

ALBERTO WILLIAMS (1862–1952), a pianist, conductor, poet, and
composer, dominated Argentine music in the first half of the century. He was primarily a symphonic composer (9 symphonies, a
number of symphonic poems and suites). He used descriptive titles
and native subjects, and his technique derived from French impressionism.

JUAN CASTRO (1895–   ), versatile and prolific, has been active
and influential as a conductor and organizer, as well as a composer.

His style is modern, neoclassical, sometimes nearly atonal, harmonically dissonant, and texturally clear. Among his important and representative works are the symphonic poems *A Una Madre*, *La Chellah*, the suites *Suite Breve*, *Three Symphonic Pieces*, and *Sinfonia*, *Sinfonia Argentina*, the ballet *Mekhano*, and piano pieces *Toccata* and *Danza Guerrera*.

JUAN CARLOS PAZ (1897–   ) was the founder, in 1936, of the association called *Conciertos de la Nueva Musica* (Concerts of New Music). His style includes a number of modern trends: neoclassical polyphony, jazz (*Jazz Movements*), polytonality, atonality, and, since about 1935, dodecaphonic techniques (*Composiciones en los 12 Tonos, Passacaglia,* etc.). He avoids the use of native or regional elements in his music. Other representative compositions are *Canto de Navidad, Julian the Emperor, Polytonal Variations,* and *Movimiento Sinfonico*. Paz has also composed a quantity of piano music and chamber music.

ALBERTO GINASTERA (1916–   ) is the outstanding contemporary Argentine composer. His style can best be described as economical and concentrated. He uses native material as a thematic basis for his music, which is written mostly in conventional forms but with dissonant and pungent harmonies within a basically tonal framework. Among a large number of successful works may be mentioned his ballet *Panambi* based on an Indian legend, *Concierto Argentino* for piano and orchestra, a ballet for flute and string quartet entitled *Impressiones de la Puna, Cantos del Tucuman* for soprano, flute, violin, harp, and two drums, *Tres Piezas* for piano, a song in tango rhythm *Canción al Arbol del Olvido,* and *Pampeana No. 3* for symphony orchestra.

OTHER CONTEMPORARY ARGENTINE COMPOSERS. The following Argentine composers have made substantial contributions to 20th-century music: Arturo Berutti (1862–1938), Julian Aguirre (1868–1924), Carlos Buchardo (1881–   ), Ernesto Drangosch (1882–1925), Manuel Carillo (1883–   ), Felipe Boero (1884–   ), Floro Ugarte (1884–   ), Gilardo Gilardi (1889–   ), Enrique Casella (1891–   ), José Castro (1892–   ) who is the brother of Juan and is one of the founders of the *Gruppo Renovación* devoted to the promotion of national contemporary music, Jacobo Ficher (born in Russia in

1896, now a naturalized Argentine citizen), Honorio Siccardi (1897–), Luis Gianneo (1897–), Carlos Suffern (1905–), Roberto Morillo (1911–), Carlos Guastavino (1914–).

Brazil. The largest of the South American countries, Brazil has a wealth of vivacious and brilliant folk music derived from primitive Indian, Negro, and Portuguese sources. Twentieth-century Brazilian composers have made extensive and effective use of this material, especially of songs and dances such as the *modinha, toada, batuque, coco, congada, jongo,* and *samba,* to name just a few. A special type is the *chôro,* originally a kind of music improvised freely and contrapuntally by a group of players and usually based on Brazilian folk material. Brazil has made great progress in its musical organizations and education.

HEITOR VILLA-LOBOS (1881–1959) is the most prominent and internationally famous composer in all South America. His primary concern in composition was the infusion of native material into his music. Although basically conservative, his music has a high degree of individuality and diversity. He has written in virtually all forms and for some unusual instrumental combinations. Among his large output may be mentioned a series of works for various media, vocal and instrumental, called *Chôros.* Other works are *Descobrimento do Brazil, Amazonas, Dansas Africanas, Bachianas Brasileiras* (a number of instrumental pieces which apply Bachian counterpoint to Brazilian melody), 5 piano concertos, 11 symphonies, 12 string quartets, other chamber music, songs, and piano music including two sets entitled *Francette et Pia* and *A Prole do Bebe.*

FRANCISCO MIGNONE (1897–) is primarily a composer of instrumental music. He has used native materials, especially the rhythms of Brazilian Negro dances. Some of the works based on native material are *Fantasia Brasileira* for piano and orchestra, *Batucaje* (a dance for orchestra and native instruments), *Sinfonia de Trabalho,* and *Festa das Ingrejas.* Mignone has composed a considerable quantity of piano and chamber music, and he has had some success as a composer of popular Brazilian songs and dances.

CAMARGO GUARNIERI (1907–) is a Brazilian modernist who follows the trend of nationalism through creating Brazilian-styled melody in a neoclassical contrapuntal setting. After Villa-Lobos, he is the best known Brazilian composer outside his country. His works include the symphonic poem *Curuca,* a number of orchestral dances (*Perereca, Ponteios, Toadas, Dansa Brasileira, Dansa Selvagem,* etc.), a comic opera *Pedro Malazarte,* concertos for piano, violin, cello, piano music, songs, and chamber music.

OTHER CONTEMPORARY BRAZILIAN COMPOSERS. Other important composers of 20th-century Brazilian music are Joao Gomes de Araujo (1846–1942), Alberto Nepumuceno (1864–1920), Francisco Braga (1868–   ), Barrozo Netto (1881–1941), Francisco Casabona (1894–   ), Brasilio Itibere (1896–   ), Oscar Fernandez (1897–   ) who is founder and director of the Conservatorio Brasileiro de Musica in Rio de Janeiro, José Siqueira (1907–   ), Eleazar de Carvalho (1912–   ), and Claudio Santoro (1919–   ).

Mexico. A vigorous nationalist movement in 20th-century Mexico has resulted in a fusion of Spanish and Indian elements, both in popular and composed art music. Mexico claims an impressive number of competent musical organizations, scholars, educators, and composers.

MANUEL PONCE (1886–1948), famous the world over for his song "Estrellita," was the first Mexican composer to exploit native materials. Having studied with Dukas in France, he has absorbed modern French techniques of harmony and orchestration. Among his works may be mentioned *Chapultepec, Ferial, Concierto del Sur* for guitar and orchestra, and a *Violin Concerto.*

CARLOS CHAVEZ (1899–   ) is Mexico's foremost musician, an organizer, educator, conductor, and composer. His style is both modern and national in a distinctly original way. His best-known works are the ballet *H. P.* (Horsepower), *Sinfonia India, Sinfonia Antigona, Sinfonia Romantica, Toccata for Percussion.* In orchestral works, Chavez has employed native instruments as well as native melodic material. He has composed a number of piano works, and a choral work *El Sol* based on an original Mexican *corrido* (a type of Mexican folk ballad).

SILVESTRE REVUELTAS (1899–1940) was a violinist and conductor who did not begin to compose seriously until he was 31 years old. His style was a mixture of indigenous elements (rhythm and melody), conservatively modern harmony, and occasional romantic lyricism. Formally, his music follows a free structural plan. His most important works are *Cuauhnahuac, Homenaje a Federico Garcia Lorca,* and *Sensemaya.* He wrote the music for a number of films.

DANIEL AYALA (1908–   ) is a Mayan Indian, native of Yucatan, who studied with Revueltas. His compositions use Mayan modes and rhythms in modern settings. In 1934 he formed the *Grupo de los Cuatro* (Group of the Four) with Moncayo, Contreras, and Galindo. Among his works, all based on Mayan folklore, are *Uchben X'Coholte* (symphonic poem), *U Kayil Chaac* for soprano and chamber orchestra in the Mayan language, *Tribu* for orchestra including native instruments, *El Hombre Maya, Los Pescadores Seris, Los Danzantes Yaquis,* and a number of works for voice and various chamber groups.

SALVADOR CONTRERAS (1912–   ) studied violin with Revueltas and composition with Chavez. He is one of the Grupo de los Cuatro. He is a neoclassicist who employs modern counterpoint, harmony, and rhythms, and at the same time maintains a strongly national flavor in his works, chief among which are *Tres Poemas* for soprano and chamber orchestra, *Musica para Orquesta Sinfonica, Corridos* for orchestra and chorus, and *Obertura en Tiempo de Danza* which utilizes multimetric schemes.

OTHER CONTEMPORARY MEXICAN COMPOSERS. Julian Carillo (1875–   ) is noted for his development of a microtonal system called *Sonido 13* which calls for octave subdivision into quarter tones, eighth tones, and sixteenth tones (*Preludio a Cristobal Colon* for soprano, flute, violin, and guitar). Other 20th-century Mexican composers are José Rolon (1883–   ), Candelario Huizar (1888–   ), Miguel Jimenez (1910–   ), Blas Galindo (1910–   ), and Pablo Moncayo (1912–1958).

Bolivia. The leading composer of Bolivia is José Velasco Maidana (1899–   ) whose ballet *Amerindia* is based on Bolivian folklore. Other composers are Eduardo Caba (1890–   ), Antonio Bravo (1885–   ), Simeon Roncal (1872–   ), and Teofilo Vargas (1868–   ).

Chile. Humberto Allende (1885–   ) is one of Chile's foremost composers, a pioneer of modern music, and a nationalist whose *Second Symphony* (*La Voz de las Calles*) and *La Despedida* for soloists and orchestra make use of native materials. Domingo Santa Cruz Wilson (1899–   ) is a contrapuntal composer whose *Canta de los Rios de Chile* is his major work. Other Chilean composers are Prospero Prado (1881–   ), Armando Carvajal (1893–   ), Pablo Garrido (1905–   ), Carlos Isamitt (1885–   ), Alfonso Llona (1912–   ), and Jorge Blondel (1905–   ).

Colombia. The leading Colombian composer is Guillermo Uribe-Holguin (1880–   ) whose style is a mixture of impressionism, modern dissonance, and native rhythms and melody.

Cuba. The most prominent names in Cuban music are Alajandro Caturla (1906–1940), Ernesto Lecuona (1896–1963) known for his popular orchestral work *Andalusia,* Amadeo Roldan (1900–1939), and Eduardo Fuentes (1874–1944).

Peru. Although many Peruvian composers have been trained abroad, they have made use of native Incan materials. Principal composers are Daniel Robles (1871–1942) who is noted primarily for his extensive collections of native music, Luis Pacheco de Cespedes (1893–   ), Andre Sas (1900–   ), and Teodoro Valcarcel (1900–1942). Another group of notable contemporary composers includes Roberto Valdes (1900–   ), Raoul de Verneuil (1901–   ), Carlos Sanchez Malaga (1904–   ), Alfonso de Silva (1903–1937), and Ulises Lanao (1913–   ).

Venezuela. Principal composers in Venezuela are Vicente Emilio Sojo (1887–   ), Juan Bautista Plaza (1898–   ), Juan Lecuna (1898–   ), Maria Luisa Escobar (1903–   ), and Moises Moleiro (1905–   ).

Canada

General Considerations. Canadian music is a mixture of French, English, and American influences. There are a number of prominent Canadian-born composers of modern music.

Colin McPhee. Colin McPhee (1901–1964) graduated in 1921 from the Peabody Conservatory in Baltimore, went to France for further study, and returned to live in the United States in 1926. He is noted for his interest in Balinese music, extracting material which he has used in his compositions (*Tabuh-Tabuhan, Bali,* and *Balinese Ceremonial Music* for two pianos).

Gerald Strang. Born in Alberta (1908), Gerald Strang received his education in California. He is a progressive modern composer who is fond of elaborate contrapuntal devices (e.g., *Mirrorrorrim* for piano). His compositions are mostly in chamber music media.

Henry Brant. Born in Montreal, Henry Brant (1913–   ) studied at McGill University School of Music, Juilliard School of Music, and with Goldmark, Copland, Antheil, and Riegger. He is an avowed experimentalist in media (*Sonata Sacra* for hardware and piano) and in styles both past and present. His *Symphony in B Flat* and *Saxophone Concerto* make use of jazz materials. Brant is currently using antiphonal and polyphonic techniques, and "polyphony of tempos" as well as various unusual combinations of instruments. His representative works include *Antiphony Origins, Stresses, Millennium 1, Millennium 2* and *Galaxy.*

Other 20th-Century Canadian Composers. Among a growing number of competent Canadian composers may be mentioned Ernest MacMillan, Healey Willan, Claude Champagne, Hector Gratton, Alexander Brott, Jean Coulthard, Maurice Dela, Robert Fleming, Graham George, Roger Matton, Oscar Morawetz, Jean Papineau-Couture, Godfrey Ridout, Harry Somers, and Jean Vallerand. Four leading twelve-tone composers are: John Weinzweig, Barbara Pentland, Pierre Mercure, and Otto Joachim.

The United States

General Considerations. The United States has become, in the 20th century, one of the leading musical nations of the world. It has risen to the fore in all areas of musical activity: (1) education (schools, colleges, conservatories, etc.), (2) performance (concert artists, opera, symphony orchestras, etc.), (3) publication (scores, books, magazines), (4) acoustical science and engineering (instruments, sound reproduction, etc.), (5) musicology, and (6) composition.

NATIONALISM. There is no single indigenous American style, no trend toward a specific American music such as is found in certain European countries and in Latin America. American music is a complexity of heterogeneous styles. There are several reasons for this lack of a unified national style.

a. *Scarcity of Native Folk Music.* Because the country is young and because it is a nation of heterogeneous peoples, the United States has relatively little folk music of its own. The indigenous element is in part supplied by (1) composed songs of a folk nature such as the Stephen Foster melodies, (2) cowboy songs and other regional ballads, (3) American Indian music, and (4) Afro-American folk music. Jazz, which stems from Afro-American origins is a distinctly indigenous element, but it is only one of many factors in American music.

b. *European Influence*. Strong traditions of European music have worked against an indigenous American style. The influx of European musicians, conductors, composers, and teachers in the 19th and 20th centuries is partly responsible. Also, until recently there was a prevalent notion that musicians and composers had to be trained in Europe in order to acquire sound musicianship. The products of excellent music schools and conservatories in the United States have now almost completely abolished this misconception.

c. *Eclecticism*. Until recently, American composers tended to follow various musical innovations originating in Europe: impressionism, expressionism, etc.

d. *Individualism*. Individualism is a strong national trait which continues to play a major role in American culture, and it tends to work against the development of a uniform American style.

American Composers. The following list of American composers, arranged chronologically according to year of birth, is neither complete nor final. Further, it should be kept in mind that in the cases of living composers, evaluation of styles and musical contributions should be considered tentative, for these are constantly changing.

TRADITIONALISTS. The following composers made significant contributions to music, but are identified with 19th-century romantic styles and techniques based on European tradition: Dudley Buck (1839–1909), John Knowles Paine (1839–1906), Arthur Foote (1853–1937), Horatio Parker (1853–1919), George Chadwick (1854–1931), Edgar Stillman Kelley (1857–1944), Charles Loeffler (1861–1935), Edward MacDowell (1861–1908), Mrs. Henry Beach (1867–1944), Henry Gilbert (1868–1928), Frederick Converse (1871–1940), Henry Hadley (1871–1937), who founded the National Association for American Composers and Conductors, Arthur Farwell (1872–1952), who founded the Wa-Wan Press (1901–1912) for the publication of American compositions, Edward Burlingame Hill (1872–1960), and Daniel Gregory Mason (1873–1953).

CHARLES IVES (1874–1954). The head of a successful insurance firm, Ives composed as an avocation, but became one of the most phenomenal composers of 20th-century music. He learned music originally from his father and later studied with Horatio Parker at Yale University. Unhampered by conventional techniques, Ives experimented with devices such as polytonality, microtonality, polyharmony, polyrhythm, multimetric and nonmetric writing, unusual instrumental combinations, etc. long before they were introduced by European composers. He also composed music in more conventional styles. Ives wrote a large number of songs, orchestral works, chamber music, choral music, and piano pieces, all of which possess a strikingly fresh individuality.

JOHN ALDEN CARPENTER (1876–1951). Carpenter, like Ives, was a businessman by profession. He was among the first to use ragtime and jazz styles in classical compositions. He is best known for his orchestral suite *Adventures in a Perambulator,* his ballet music *Krazy Kat* and *Skyscrapers,* and the song cycle *Gitanjali.*

CARL RUGGLES (1876–   ). The music of Carl Ruggles is uncompromisingly contrapuntal and dissonant. He employed a ten-tone serial technique. Among his best known works are *Men and Mountains* for chamber orchestra, *The Sunken Bell* (an opera), *Portals* for strings, *Angels, Evocations* (piano), and *Organum for Orchestra.*

ERNEST SCHELLING (1876–1939). Schelling is noted primarily for his orchestral work *Victory Ball* (1923). He was also a noted pianist and conductor.

DAVID STANLEY SMITH (1877–1949). A pupil of Horatio Parker at Yale and later Dean of the School of Music at Yale, Smith composed chamber music and choral and orchestral works in an academic, conventional style.

ERNEST BLOCH (1880–1959). Although born in Switzerland and trained in Germany, Bloch was resident in the United States from 1916. Jewish elements permeate much of his music which in style and form is free, rhapsodic, and conservatively modern. Among his important works are *Trois Poèms Juifs* (symphonic poem), *Schelomo* for cello and orchestra, *Meditation Hebraïque* and *From Jewish Life* for cello and piano, *Baal Shem* for violin and piano, *Israel* (a symphony with voices), the operas *Jezebel* and *Macbeth*, *Scherzo Fantastique* for piano and orchestra, *America*, an epic rhapsody for orchestra which quotes a number of American tunes, and four string quartets.

CHARLES T. GRIFFES (1884–1920). Griffes' style is impressionistic and pseudo-Oriental. He has written songs, piano pieces, and orchestral works, among which may be mentioned *Poem for Flute and Orchestra*, *The Pleasure Dome of Kubla Khan*, and *The White Peacock* (from the piano suite entitled *Roman Sketches*, later orchestrated as a symphonic poem).

LOUIS GRUENBERG (1884–   ). Jazz plays a dominant role in the music of Louis Gruenberg, as indicated in the following titles: *Jazz Suite*, *Daniel Jazz* (a chamber work for tenor and 8 instruments) *Jazzberries*, *Polychromatics*, *Jazz Masks*, *Six Jazz Epigrams*, and *Three Jazz Dances*. His opera, *Emperor Jones* (based on the play by Eugene O'Neill) and his *Violin Concerto* also contain prominent jazz elements.

WALLINGFORD RIEGGER (1885–1961). Riegger is the most important American composer of twelve-tone music. Modern rhythms and contrapuntal textures are prominent in his music. He has worked principally in orchestral media, but has contributed substantial chamber and vocal works as well. Among his major orchestral pieces are *Dichotomy*, *Dance Rhythms*, *Festival Overture*, *Passacaglia and Fugue*, *Variations for Piano and Orchestra*, *Quintuple Jazz*, *Overture for Orchestra*, and the *Fourth Symphony*.

DEEMS TAYLOR (1885–1966). Conservative, romantic, and a somewhat Wagnerian style are characteristics of Taylor's operas: *The King's Henchman*, *Peter Ibbetson* and *Ramuntcho*. Other works are *Through the Looking Glass* for orchestra, and the cantatas *The Chambered Nautilus* and *The Highwayman*.

EDGARD VARÈSE (1885–1965). Varèse, born in France, was an avowed experimentalist in musical media, including tape-recorder music, harmony, and rhythms. His music is highly dissonant, uses sensational sonorities, complex rhythms, and shows little regard for structural clarity. Major works include *Arcana, Metal, Espace, Intégrales, Offrandes, Hyperprism, Ionisation, Density 21.5, Octandre,* and *Equatorial,* the latter written for baritone voice, organ, trumpets, trombones, percussion, and theremin.

JOHN BECKER (1886–1961). Becker was an experimentalist who used dissonant harmony within a renaissance-type of polyphony. He was a prolific composer of symphonies, concertos, choral works, and chamber music.

RICHARD DONOVAN (1891–   ). A teacher of theory at Yale University since 1928 and an organist and choral conductor of reputation, Donovan has composed in numerous media and in a freshly individual and direct manner. Most of his music has clear sonorities and contrapuntal textures. *New England Chronicle, Suite for String Orchestra and Oboe, Symphony in D, Quartet for Woodwinds,* and *Mass* for unison voices and organ are among his significant compositions.

ADOLPH WEISS (1891–   ). A student of Schoenberg, Weiss is one of the American dodecaphonists. *American Life* is an atonal jazz work for orchestra. He has composed a quantity of music for orchestra and chamber ensembles.

FERDE GROFÉ (1892–   ). Grofé, a skillful orchestrator, is best known for popular orchestral suites descriptive of American scenes (*Grand Canyon Suite, Mississippi Suite,* etc.) and for his orchestration of Gershwin compositions, such as *Rhapsody in Blue.*

DOUGLAS MOORE (1893–   ). In addition to being a teacher (Columbia University) and author (*From Madrigal to Modern Music*), Moore has made a distinct contribution to American opera with his *The Devil and Daniel Webster, Giants in the Earth,* and *The Ballad of Baby Doe.* Two other stage works are *The Headless Horseman* and *The Emperor's Clothes.* Moore utilizes other American subjects to advantage in his *Moby Dick* for orchestra and chorus, and *Farm Journal* and *The Pageant of P. T. Barnum* for orchestra.

PAUL PISK (1893–   ). A musicologist, teacher, and composer, Pisk has gained considerable recognition with such compositions as *Passacaglia for Orchestra, Music for String Orchestra, Suite on American Folksongs,* a cantata entitled *The Storm,* and a *Brass Quartet.*

BERNARD ROGERS (1893–   ). A pupil of Bloch, Farwell, and Boulanger, a teacher at the Eastman School of Music since 1929 and the author of a textbook on orchestration, Rogers is a composer with a pictorial slant and a conservatively modern technique. Among significant works are *The Passion, Soliloquy* for flute and strings, *Five Fairy Tales, Two American Frescoes,* and the charming *Leaves from the Tale of Pinocchio* for narrator and chamber orchestra.

WALTER PISTON (1894–   ). Piston, in addition to being one of the foremost American composers of contemporary music was a distinguished teacher of composition at Harvard University from 1926 to his retirement in 1960 and an author of valuable treatises on harmony, counterpoint, and orchestration. He has been the recipient of numerous honors, awards, and commissions for his work in these various fields. He is a craftsman in the neoclassical tradition and has also absorbed 20th-century techniques making them a part of his own highly individual style. Especially notable characteristics are contrapuntal mastery, ingenious melodic invention, skillful formal organization of materials, brilliant orchestration, and vital rhythmic structures. A certain romantic lyricism in his work is tempered by modern dissonance. Dry wit and humor are evident in his music. He has a long list of substantial compositions to his credit: symphonies, miscellaneous symphonic works, concertos, chamber music, choral music (*Carnival Song* for men's chorus and brass instruments), and ballet (*The Incredible Flutist*).

DANE RUDHYAR (1895–   ). In addition to being a mystic, painter, writer, and student of Oriental philosophy, Rudhyar is an atonalist composer. Orchestral works include *The Surge of Fire, To the Real, Ouranos, Hero Chants* and *Paean to the Great Thunder* (a symphonic poem with recitation).

LEO SOWERBY (1895–   ). A musical spokesman for midwestern regionalism in American music, Sowerby is best known for his symphonic poem *Prairie* and for his organ works in modern style.

WILLIAM GRANT STILL (1895–   ). Still is the foremost Negro composer in the United States. His works on Afro-American themes include *Darker America, From the Black Belt, Africa, Afro-American Symphony, Song of a New Race* (his *Second Symphony*), and his most impressive work *And They Lynched Him on a Tree* for contralto, chorus, orchestra, and narrator.

› HOWARD HANSON (1896–   ). As head of the Eastman School of Music, Hanson is one of the foremost educators of the country. Through his various important activities he has done much to promote American music. As a composer, he is a traditionalist whose music, more romantic than modern, includes successful symphonic works, choral music (*Lament for Beowulf, Hymn for the Pioneers, Cherubic Hymn*), opera (*Merry Mount*), and chamber music.

ROGER SESSIONS (1896–   ). The music of Sessions may be described as progressively modern, complex, and intensely serious, and it contains a number of stylistic influences which he has absorbed to make a distinctive style of his own. Sessions, who teaches at Princeton University, is not a prolific composer. His orchestral suite *The Black Maskers* is perhaps his best known composition. Other works are *Idyll of Theocritus* for soprano and orchestra, the opera *Trial of Lucullus,* string quartets, symphonies, and music in various media (piano, organ, voice, chorus).

VIRGIL THOMSON (1896–   ). Thomson is one of many American composers who studied with Boulanger in Paris. For years he was a music critic on the *New York Herald Tribune.* Thomson's music reflects some influence of "Les Six," a tendency toward simplicity and directness. He employs a diversity of modern tonal and harmonic devices. Among major works are the operas *Four Saints in Three Acts* and *Mother of Us All* (on texts by Gertrude Stein), the ballet *Filling Station,* a large number of short piano compositions called *Portraits* written over a period of years, *Symphony on a Hymn Tune,* and the film scores for *Louisiana Story* and *The Plough that Broke the Plains.* He is also the author of a number of books on musical subjects.

HENRY COWELL (1897–   ). The most prolific and stylistically diverse of contemporary composers, Cowell is one of the most prominent composers in America. He has also been active as teacher, author, and promoter of contemporary music. His style and technique stem from a number of sources. Cowell's early fame was achieved through his experimentalism in tone clusters and novel effects with the piano. He has long shown an affinity for Asiatic systems which lend diversity and a certain exotic quality to his music. He has frequently employed early American hymns and "fuguing tunes" in distinctly modern settings. Characteristic folk-song and dance elements stem from his childhood familiarity with Irish jigs and reels (his father was Irish), Tennessee mountain music (his mother came from that state), American country dances (he lived on farms in Kansas and Oklahoma), and Chinese and Japanese tunes he learned in early childhood in San Francisco. His music ranges from conservative to extremely progressive. He was founder of New Music Editions in 1927, and president of the American Composers Alliance for many years. Cowell has composed 13 symphonies to date and music both instrumental and vocal in almost every conceivable medium, including works which employ native Oriental instruments. A few compositions representative of various aspects of Cowell's music may be listed here: *Mela and Fair* (a mixture of East Indian and American materials), *The Seven Rituals of Music* (*Symphony No. 11*), *Hymn and Fuguing Tune No. 10, Tales of Our Countryside* (use of tone clusters and Irish folk elements), *Toccanta* for soprano, flute, cello, and piano.

QUINCY PORTER (1897–1966). Long associated with Yale University, Porter was a composer and violinist whose interest was principally in the field of chamber music, especially in the composition of string quartets. His *Concerto Concertante for Two Pianos and Orchestra* was commissioned by the Louisville Orchestra in 1953.

HERBERT ELWELL (1898–   ). For years a music critic, for the *Cleveland Plain Dealer,* Elwell is best known for his orchestral suite from the ballet *The Happy Hypocrite.*

ERNST BACON (1898–   ). Bacon has cultivated American folk music through his operas *A Tree on the Plains* and *A Drumlin Legend* and his orchestral suites *Ford's Theatre* and *From These States.*

GEORGE GERSHWIN (1898–1937). Famous for many "hit tunes" and Broadway musical shows, Gershwin successfully applied jazz idiom to composition in large forms (*Rhapsody in Blue, Piano Concerto in F,* and *American in Paris*). His *Porgy and Bess* is one of the great folk operas of the century.

ROY HARRIS (1898–   ). Harris is another of several top-flight American composers who studied with Nadia Boulanger in Paris.

His rugged individualism is somewhat akin to that of Walt Whitman and Carl Sandburg, and there is an atmosphere of the American West in his music. He has made considerable use of American tunes (e.g., the overture *When Johnny Comes Marching Home* and *Folk Song Symphony* for chorus and orchestra). Perhaps his finest works are his *Third Symphony* and *Seventh Symphony*, each written in a single movement.

HARRISON KERR (1899–   ). Dean of the College of Fine Arts of the University of Oklahoma since 1949, Kerr is a twelve-tone composer in a rather freely tonal manner. His most characteristic devices are prominent use of fourths, dissonant counterpoint, and multimetric schemes. He has also been active as editor and promoter of American music.

RANDALL THOMPSON (1899–   ). Thompson has taught composition at several American universities. He is known chiefly for his a-cappella-choral work *Peaceable Kingdom*. He has composed other choral music, a few symphonic works, and much chamber music, all in a somewhat conservative neoclassical style.

GEORGE ANTHEIL (1900–1959). Long associated with Hollywood film music, Antheil also produced a number of serious works in progressively modern vein, the most famous of which was *Ballet Mécanique* for ten pianos and assorted "noise makers" including an airplane propeller. His avant-garde ideas earned him the nickname "bad boy of music." Later compositions were less experimental in character, though not conservative.

AARON COPLAND (1900–   ). A pupil of Goldmark and Boulanger, Copland combines with his distinctly personal style ingredients of American folklore and borrowed nationalism which he calls "tourist music" (e.g., *El Salón México*). In the 1920's he employed jazz techniques (*Music for the Theatre, Concerto for Piano and Orchestra*). Outstanding among his works dealing with American subjects are the ballets *Appalachian Spring, Billy the Kid,* and *Rodeo*. Generally, Copland's style tends toward simplicity, textural clarity, and at times a certain austerity.

OTTO LUENING (1900–   ). Luening is a prominent experimentalist in the media of electronics and tape-recorder music (*Fantasy in Space, Low Speed, Dynamophonic Suite,* etc.). As a teacher, he has exerted a considerable influence on younger composers. In less experimental media, Luening has composed a large quantity of songs and chamber music.

HARRY PARTCH (1901–   ). For more than thirty years, Partch has been experimenting with new musical instruments which he has invented. His music is microtonal and atonal, and he is especially interested in creating music to accompany modern dance.

STEFAN WOLPE (1902–   ). Wolpe is a European-born exponent of twelve-tone music which he has adapted to his own specialized harmonic-contrapuntal technique; he calls this "spatial organizations" (*Studies on Basic Rows*). Representative works include *Toccata for Piano, Encouragements* for piano, and *Quartet* for trumpet, saxophone, piano, and drums.

NIKOLAI LOPATNIKOFF (1903–   ). Russian-born and resident in the United States since 1939, Lopatnikoff has received considerable acclaim and numerous awards. He is a subjective modern composer, mainly of orchestral works and piano music.

MARC BLITZSTEIN (1905–1964). Blitzstein is best known for his two "social" operas, *The Cradle Will Rock* and *No for an Answer*. In these works he demonstrated a particular feeling for theatre and an absorption of modern techniques. Symphonic works are *The Airborne Symphony* and *Freedom Morning*.

PAUL CRESTON (1906–   ). A self-taught composer, Creston generally avoids descriptive or programmatic approaches in his compositions. He combines musical abstraction with a subjective quality. Important representative works are *Threnody* (tone poem), *Three Mysteries, Three Chorales from Tagore,* and a considerable amount of chamber music.

ROSS LEE FINNEY (1906–   ). Finney began as a traditionalist in style and has shown great interest in American folk tunes. In the latter category may be mentioned the cantata *Pilgrim Psalms* and the orchestral works entitled *Variations, Fugue and Rondo* (after William Billings). Recently he has shown a marked trend toward tone-row chromaticism, and he has written several important works using serial technique.

NORMAND LOCKWOOD (1906–   ). Chamber music and choral works are Lockwood's principal media. He is noted more for his use of American folk materials than for any special modern techniques. A major composition is the oratorio *Children of God*.

BURRILL PHILLIPS (1907–   ). Phillips is a conservative composer who is known chiefly for his orchestral work *Selections from McGuffey's Reader*.

MIKLOS ROZSA (1907–   ). Hungarian-born Rozsa has a well established reputation as a composer of film scores and as a teacher. Apart from his movie music, he has composed symphonic and chamber works which avoid programmatic and descriptive associations.

ELLIOTT CARTER (1908–   ). A pupil of Piston at Harvard University and Boulanger in Paris, Carter has lately achieved much deserved recognition as a composer of serious and expressive music. He has absorbed modern techniques to create his own highly individual style. He has written successful orchestral and chamber music, and he excels as well in the choral medium. Among the latter may be mentioned *Heart Not So Heavy As Mine, The Defense of Corinth, The Harmony of Morning,* and *Emblems*. A recent orchestral work is *Variations for Orchestra*. Carter has also written two string quartets and other chamber music.

HALSEY STEVENS (1908–   ). A teacher, critic, composer, and the author of a scholarly book on Béla Bartók, Stevens is a figure of growing importance in American music. He has composed noteworthy works in all media. A compact three-movement symphony entitled *Triskelion* is representative of his style.

RAY GREEN (1909–   ). Green is one of several composers who have effectively utilized American hymnody and fuguing tunes in a progressive modern style (e.g., *Sunday Sing Symphony, Festival Fugues*).

HERBERT HAUFRECHT (1909–   ). Haufrecht has attempted to integrate folk music and jazz in compositions such as *Square Set* for strings and *Woodland Serenade*. He has also contributed substantially to the field of children's music (*Ferdinand the Bull* for narrator and orchestra, *Robin Hood, The Little Red Hen,* etc.).

LEON KIRCHNER (1909–   ). Schoenberg, Sessions, and Bloch were Kirchner's teachers in composition. His music is dissonant, structurally free, and rhapsodic. Folk elements, reminiscent of Bartók, are to be heard in his music.

PAUL NORDOFF (1909–   ). The music of Paul Nordoff, some of which has been widely performed, includes ballets for Martha Graham (*Every Soul Is a Circus, Salem Shore*), orchestral works (*Prelude and Three Fugues*), chamber music and choral music (*Secular Mass*), and *Lost Summer* for soprano and orchestra.

ELIE SIEGMEISTER (1909–   ). Without confining himself to any one region, Siegmeister has used American folk music widely (*Ozark Set, Prairie Legend, Western Suite, Sunday in Brooklyn,* etc.). His diverse musical interests include music for Broadway musicals and television shows, teaching, editing (*Treasury of American Song,* with Downes), writing (*Music Lover's Handbook*), conducting, and the organizational promotion of American music.

HOWARD SWANSON (1909–   ). Born in Atlanta, and a student of Elwell and Boulanger, Swanson achieved fame first through his songs. Representative works in the instrumental field are *Short Symphony, Night Music* for woodwinds, horn, and strings, and *Soundpiece* for brass quintet.

SAMUEL BARBER (1910–   ). One of the most widely performed American composers of his generation, Barber has progressed from a neoromantic style (*Adagio for Strings* and *Symphony in One Movement*) to more complex and dissonant works (*Second Essay for Orchestra* and *Medea Suite*). Among his other works are *Knoxville: Summer of 1915* for soprano and orchestra, *Hermit Songs, Capricorn Concerto, Vanessa,* and *Antony and Cleopatra* (1966).

PAUL BOWLES (1910–   ). Eclecticism is the principal characteristic of Bowles' music which combines a number of diverse trends (neoclassicism, jazz, neoprimitivism, tone clusters, etc.). Among a large number of works may be mentioned *Scènes d'Anabase* for tenor, oboe and piano, *Facsimile* (ballet), and the opera *The Wind Remains.*

BERNHARD HEIDEN (1910–   ). Born in Germany where he was a student of Hindemith, Heiden came to the United States in 1935, and is currently teaching in Bloomington, Indiana. He has been active as a composer, teacher, and pianist. In a modern contrapuntal style, he has written works principally for orchestra and some chamber music for various combinations, including a quintet for horn and strings.

WILLIAM SCHUMAN (1910–   ). Formerly director of the Juilliard School of Music, Schuman is a musician of many interests, principally, those of composer and administrator. He studied with Roy Harris. He writes music in a progressively modern style tonally and harmonically. His *New England Triptych* uses William Billings themes. *Undertow* and *Judith* are modern ballets. *Credendum* is a three-movement symphonic piece.

ALAN HOVHANESS (1911–   ). Hovhaness is one of the most unusual and original composers on the contemporary scene. He has capitalized on his Armenian heritage and his scholarly interest in the musical cultures of the Near East. In addition to these stylistic attributes, Hovhaness employs simple textures, Medieval and Renaissance devices, unusual media, including exotic instruments and novel effects with piano strings, and a strange but appealing exoticism achieved through repetitive rhythms and melodic figures. Representative works are *Mysterious Mountain, Arevakal, Armenian Rhapsody, Khaldis* (concerto for piano, 4 trumpets, and percussion), *Jhala* (for piano), *Concerto No. 7* for orchestra, and a *Quartet* for flute, oboe, cello, and harpsichord.

ROBERT MCBRIDE (1911–   ). Born in Arizona, McBride is an advocate of "practical" music which has an immediate audience appeal. His music bears such titles as *Pumpkin Eater's Little Fugue, I Feel So Left Out* and *Life Is so Beautiful* for student orchestra, *Workout for Chamber Orchestra, Bop Sophisticate,* etc. It is obvious from these titles that American dance styles have a prominent place in his music.

GIAN-CARLO MENOTTI (1911–   ). An exceptional gift for the musical theatre has made Menotti the leading composer of opera in America. He was born in Milan where he absorbed the tradition of Italian opera. He came to the United States in 1938 and studied at the Curtis Institute of Music. His harmony and tonality are, in varying degrees, stylistically 20th-century without diminishing the effect of melodic invention and a dramatic sense. Menotti writes his own librettos. His operas include the comic operas *Amelia Goes to the Ball, The Old Maid and the Thief* (commissioned by N. B. C. for radio performance), and *The Telephone* (a one-act opera buffa), the tragic operas *The Medium* and *The Consul,* and the first television opera *Amahl and the Night Visitors*. More recent operas are *The Saint of Bleecker Street* and *Maria Golovin*. He has also written the libretto to Barber's opera *Vanessa*.

WAYNE BARLOW (1912–　). A graduate of the Eastman School of Music and a member of that school's faculty since 1937, Barlow is best known for his rhapsody entitled *The Winter's Past* for oboe and strings, based on Carolina folk tunes.

ARTHUR BERGER (1912–　). Berger was a pupil of Piston, Boulanger, and Milhaud. His music reflects a close attention to details, a strong sense of rhythm, and a fondness for melodic disjunction. His principal media are chamber and orchestral music. In the latter medium, *Polyphony* is a representative work.

JOHN CAGE (1912–　). Cage is an experimentalist who has achieved some fame with his compositions for "prepared piano" (see page 182) and for percussion ensembles.

DON GILLIS (1912–　). Like Grofé and Gould, Gillis has exploited quasi-popular elements in American music, such as minstrel tunes, jazz, spirituals, etc. with clever orchestrations and often with a humorous touch (e.g. *Symphony 5½*). Representative works for orchestra are *An American Symphony, Prairie Poem, The Alamo,* and *Saga of a Prairie School* (*Symphony No. 7*).

PEGGY GLANVILLE-HICKS (1912–　). Australia-born, trained in Melbourne and London (Vaughan Williams, Jacob, Morris), Peggy Glanville-Hicks has lived in New York since 1939. She is the leading woman composer in America today. Her style has recently become less severe but no less original and varied. Her works include music for chamber orchestra (*Etruscan Concerto* for piano and chamber orchestra, *Three Gymnopédie,* etc.), songs, and an opera *The Transposed Heads*.

HUGO WEISGALL (1912–　). Born in Czechoslovakia, Weisgall came to the United States in 1920. He is a composer of modern-style stage works, both comic and serious operas (e.g., *Six Characters in Search of an Author, The Stronger, The Tenor*), and has also written some large-scale works for orchestra and chorus.

NORMAN DELLO JOIO (1913–　). Dello Joio, born in New York City, studied with Wagenaar and Hindemith. He is a neoclassicist with a keen interest in Gregorian material. Among his compositions may be listed *Mass of the Angels, Ricercari* and *Sinfonietta* for piano and orchestra, *The Mystic Trumpeter* for mixed chorus, solo voices and French horn or piano, the symphonic suite *Air Power,* and *Variations, Chaconne and Finale* for orchestra.

MORTON GOULD (1913–   ). Gould is known for many cleverly orchestrated arrangements of popular music as well as for his original compositions in a quasi-popular style, including *Chorale and Fugue in Jazz, Cowboy Rhapsody, Interplay for Piano and Orchestra,* etc.

GARDNER READ (1913–   ). Having studied with composers of widely different styles both in America (Hanson, Rogers, and Copland) and abroad (Sibelius and Pizzetti), Read has cultivated many different styles without being dominated by any one. He is the author of *Thesaurus of Orchestral Devices.*

OTHER AMERICAN COMPOSERS. In addition to the composers listed above, there are many born since 1910 who have reached musical stature since 1950. Among these may be mentioned Everett Helm (1913–   ), Kurt List (1913–   ), Kent Kennan (1913–   ), Norman Cazden (1914–   ), Irving Fine (1914–1962), Roger Goeb (1914–   ), Gail Kubik (1914–   ), Charles Mills (1914–   ), David Diamond (1915–   ), Homer Keller (1915–   ), Robert Palmer (1915–   ), George Perle (1915–   ), Vincent Persichetti (1915–   ), Milton Babbitt (1916–   ), Ellis Kohs (1916–   ), Ben Weber (1916–   ), Lou Harrison (1917–   ), Ulysses Kay (1917–   ), Robert Ward (1917–   ), Leonard Bernstein (1918–   ), Frank Wigglesworth (1918–   ), Jacob Avshalomov (1919–1965), Harold Shapero (1920–   ), William Bergsma (1921–   ), Halim El-Dabh (1921–   , an Egyptian living in the United States since 1950), Andrew Imbrie (1921–   ), Lukas Foss (1922–   ), Chou Wen-Chung (born in China in 1923, living in the United States since 1946), Peter Mennin (1923–   ), Daniel Pinkham (1923–   ), Lester Trimble (1923–   ), Ezra Laderman (1924–   ), Robert Starer (1923–   ), Gunther Schuller (1925–   ), Seymour Shifrin (1926–   ), and Russell Smith (1927–   ).

Glossary

A Cappella. Sung without accompaniment; i.e., chorus without instrumental support.

Accent. Emphasis or stress placed upon a tone.

Air. A melody.

Antiphonal. One choir answered by another choir.

Aria. A song, usually employed in connection with a dramatic work such as opera or oratorio.

Arpeggio. An ascending or descending series of tones of a chord, played consecutively.

Atonality. Absence of key feeling.

Authentic Cadence. The dominant chord followed by the tonic.

Authentic Mode. Any church mode in which the range of the melody lies between the final and the octave above.

Bar Line. Vertical line through the staff to indicate metric divisions of a composition.

Bass. The low register of instrumental or vocal music.

Beat. A measured pulse. E.g., in 4/4 time there are four beats to a measure.

Bitonality. The use of two different keys simultaneously.

Brass. Wind instruments in which the tone is produced by lip vibration.

Broken Chord. The tones of a chord played consecutively.

Cadence. The chord progression or melodic progression used to terminate a phrase or a section of a composition.

Canon. A contrapuntal form in which two or more parts in succession take up the same melody.

Cantabile. In a singing style.

Cantus Firmus. A borrowed melody used as the basis of a polyphonic composition.

Chamber Music. Music for a small group of solo instruments, intended for performance in a small room rather than a large auditorium.

Chanson, French word for "song."

CHANT. Liturgical melody, nonmetric, and monodic. E.g., plainsong.

CHOIR. A group of singers, usually associated with liturgical performance; or an instrumental group in the orchestra (e.g., brass choir, woodwind choir, etc.).

CHORALE. Protestant hymn tune.

CHORALE PRELUDE. A contrapuntal composition for organ based upon the chorale melody.

CHORD. A group of simultaneously sounding tones.

CHORUS. A body of singers; also a composition or part of a composition written for vocal ensemble.

CHROMATIC. Tones foreign to the key. A scale proceeding by semitones.

COLORATION. Melismatic ornamentation applied to melody such as plainsong.

COLORATURA. Rapid scales, figures, ornaments, usually applied to an operatic aria.

CONSONANCE. Combinations of tones in harmony that produce agreeable repose.

CONTRAPUNTAL. In the style of counterpoint; i.e., several individual melodies combined.

CONTRARY MOTION. Two melodies moving in opposite pitch directions; one melody ascends while the other descends.

COUNTERPOINT. The combination of two or more melodies; almost synonymous with polyphony.

CRESCENDO. Gradual increase of loudness.

DECLAMATION. Questions involving setting of music to text: proper accenting of syllables, pronunciation, stress on important words, etc.

DIATONIC. The use of the natural tones of the scale, excluding chromatic or altered tones.

DIMINUENDO. Gradual decrease of loudness.

DISSONANCE. Combinations of tones in harmony that produce unrest and require resolution; i.e., consonance following dissonance.

DOMINANT. The fifth tone of the scale, or the chord built on that tone.

DOTTED RHYTHM. Rhythm produced by recurrent use of a dot following a note which adds half its value to the note.

DOUBLE BAR. Two vertical lines drawn through the staff to indicate the end of a principal section in the composition or the final close.

DOUBLE FUGUE. A fugue with two distinct subjects, each usually presented in a separate exposition.

DOUBLE STOPPING. Bowing on two strings of the violin simultaneously, producing a harmonic interval.

DUPLE METER. Two strong beats to the measure.

DYNAMICS. The aspect of music related to loudness and softness.

EIGHTH NOTE. One eighth the time value of a whole note.

ELEVENTH CHORD. A chord of six different tones, five superimposed thirds.

EMBELLISHMENT. Melodic ornamentation consisting of trills, grace notes, mordents, etc.

ENSEMBLE. Any group of singers and/or instrumentalists.

FIGURATION. Recurrent melodic pattern.

FIGURED BASS. The use of numerals below a bass melody to indicate harmony.

FLAT. A symbol meaning to lower the tone in front of which it appears.

FLORID. Highly ornamented melodic line.

FORM. The structure of a musical composition.

FORTE. Loud.

FUGAL. In the style of a fugue; i.e., making use of contrapuntal imitation.

FUGHETTA. A short fugue or fugal section in a composition.

GLISSANDO. The execution of rapid scales by sliding the finger along the keyboard or violin string.

HALF NOTE. Half the time value of a whole note.

HARMONY. The practices of chord construction and chord progression.

HOMOPHONIC. A predominating melody with subordinate accompaniment.

HYMN. A religious song in verse and stanza form.

IMITATION. The use of a theme or melodic fragment consecutively in different parts of a polyphonic composition.

INSTRUMENTATION. The problems of instruments and instrumental combinations employed in ensemble music.

INTERVAL (HARMONIC). The pitch difference between two simultaneously sounding tones, referred to as 2nds, 3rds, 4ths, etc.

INTERVAL (MELODIC). The pitch difference between two consecutive tones, referred to as 2nds, 3rds, 4ths, etc.

INVERSION. Melodic inversion means the alternation of a given melody so that each melodic interval of the original melody is represented by the same interval moving in the opposite direction, up instead of down and vice versa.

KEY. The tone around which melodic and harmonic progressions gravitate.

KEYBOARD INSTRUMENT. Any instrument, such as the piano, organ, harpsichord, etc., which is manipulated by means of a series of black and white keys.

LIBRETTO. The text of an opera or oratorio.

LIED, LIEDER *(pl.)*. German word for "song."

LIEDERBUCH. German song book.

LINE. The horizontal or melodic aspect of a composition.

LITURGICAL. Pertaining to the church service.

LYRE. A small, harplike instrument.

LYRIC. Songlike style, opposed to dramatic and coloristic styles.

MAJOR. Based upon a scale that has half steps between the 3rd and 4th degrees and between the 7th and 8th degrees.

MEDIUM, MEDIA *(pl.)*. The instruments and/or voices required for the performance of a given composition.

MELISMA. An ornamental melodic passage, usually vocal, in which case it implies the use of numerous melodic tones to one syllable.

MELODY. A succession of tones of different pitch and usually different duration.

METER. The measuring of music according to a recurrent group of regular pulses.

METRIC. Measured: regular groups of regular pulses.

MINOR. Based upon scales that have a half step between the 2nd and 3rd degrees of the scale.

MODALITY. Use of the church modes.

MODE. The arrangement of half steps and whole steps in scales; hence major mode, minor mode, Dorian mode, etc.

MODULATION. The harmonic process of changing from one key to another.

MONODY, MONODIC. Music which is limited to a single melodic line without accompaniment.

MOTIVE. A group of tones in a melody that have a special rhythmic and/or melodic character.

MOVEMENT. The main sections of a large work (symphony, sonata, concerto, etc.) which are complete compositions in themselves.

MULTITONALITY. Numerous remotely related keys used consecutively in a composition.

MUSICOLOGY. The scholarly study of music, as differentiated from the art of composition, performance, interpretation, etc.

NATURAL. A sign placed before a note indicating cancellation of a sharp or flat.

NINTH CHORD. A chord consisting of 5 tones, 4 superimposed thirds.

NONCHORDAL TONES. Tones sounding with a chord that are not part of that chord.

NONHARMONIC TONES. The same as nonchordal tones.

NOTATION. The graphic representation of music by symbols that indicate pitch and duration of tone.

OCTAVE. An interval of eight degrees; the tones on the staff that have the same letter names are one or more octaves apart.

ORCHESTRATION. The study of effects produced by the combination of various instruments and instrumental resources.

OSTINATO. A short melody repeated over and over, usually in the bass.

OVERTURE. The instrumental form used to precede large dramatic works such as opera and oratorio.

PARALLEL MOTION. Two or more melodic lines moving in the same direction and the same intervals at the same time.

PART. The single melodic line of a polyphonic composition.

PEDAL POINT. A sustained or repeated tone, usually in the bass, which sounds through changing harmonies.

PENTATONIC. A five-tone scale.

PERCUSSION. Instruments, such as drums, gongs, triangles, etc., that are played by being struck.

PHRASE. A small section of a musical composition that is terminated by some form of cadence (harmonic close, melodic close, rhythmic pause).

PIANO. To play or sing quietly or softly.

PICKUP BEAT. The tone of a phrase beginning with an unaccented tone and preceding an accented beat; anacrusis.

PITCH. The degree of highness or lowness of tone. Determined by rate of vibration.

PIZZICATO. A plucked string (as opposed to a bowed string).

PLAGAL CADENCE. The subdominant chord followed by the tonic chord.

PLAGAL MODE. The modes that range a fifth above and a fourth below the final.

PLAINSONG. Ecclesiastical melody, nonmetric, unaccompanied, modal.

POLYPHONY. Music employing two or more parts or melodies.

POLYTONALITY. The use of several different keys simultaneously.

PREPARATION. A dissonant note is prepared when it occurs immediately before as a consonant or chordal tone.

PROGRAM MUSIC. Music that has extramusical associations, is narrative or descriptive.

PSALM. Song based on the biblical Book of Psalms (which includes 150 religious poems).

QUADRUPLE FUGUE. A fugue with four distinct subjects or themes.

QUARTER NOTE. A note having one fourth the value of a whole note.

RANGE. The distance between the highest and the lowest note of a melody, a voice, or an instrument.

REGISTER. The range or a section thereof in a voice, instrument, or melody.

REGISTRATION. The combination of stops used in organ playing.

RELATIVE MAJOR. The major key, a third above the minor having the same key signature.

RESPONSORIAL. Performance of a chant in alternation between solo voice and chorus.

RHYTHM. The patterns of long and short durations of notes, also involving accented and unaccented tones.

ROOT. The tone on which a chord is built (e.g., the tonic is the root of the tonic triad).

SCALE. Any series of adjacent tones arranged in a plan of half steps and whole steps.

SCORE. The vertical alignment of two or more staves in a composition consisting of several parts.

SEQUENCE (PATTERN). The repetition of a melodic pattern at successively higher or lower intervals.

SEQUENCE (PLAINSONG). A type of plainsong in which text is added to the melisma of an alleluia.

SEVENTH CHORDS. A chord consisting of four tones.

SFORZANDO. Term meaning suddenly loud.

SHARP. Symbol meaning to raise the tone in front of which it appears.

SIXTEENTH NOTE. A note having one sixteenth the time value of a whole note.

SONORITY. Richness or fullness of sound.

STAFF. Parallel horizontal lines (normally 5) on which notes are placed to indicate exact pitch.

STRINGED INSTRUMENT. Any instrument (but usually referring to the bowed instruments) which produces musical tone by the vibration of a string from bowing or plucking.

STYLE. The character of music determined by musical elements such as harmony, rhythm, melody, tone color, etc.

SUBDOMINANT. The fourth degree of the scale or the chord built on that degree.

SUBJECT. The theme or melody of a fugue.

SUITE. A group of instrumental compositions; often, but not necessarily, implying a group of instrumental dances.

SYNCOPATION. Accenting weak or unimportant beats or parts of beats in a measure.

TEMPO. The speed at which a composition is performed, indicated by such terms as andante, moderato, largo, etc.

TETRACHORD. A section of a scale consisting of four adjacent tones.

THEME. A melody which is the basis of a composition or part of a composition.

TIE. A curved line connecting otherwise repeated notes.

TONALITY. The gravitation of music around a key or a tonal center.

TONIC. The first tone of a scale or the chord built on that tone.

TRANSCRIPTION. Rewriting a musical composition for another medium.

TREBLE. The high register.

TREMOLO. Rapid reiteration of a note (on a string instrument by drawing the bow back and forth quickly in very short strokes across the string) or rapid alternation between two different notes (fingered tremolo).

TRIAD. A chord consisting of three tones (root, third, fifth).

TRIPLE METER. Three beats to the measure.

TRIPLE STOPPING. Causing three tones to sound simultaneously on a bowed string instrument.

TUNE. A melody.

TUTTI. Played by the entire orchestral ensemble.

UNACCOMPANIED. Melody without instrumental support or subordinate material.

UNISON. Two or more parts singing or playing the same melody at the same time.

UNPREPARED DISSONANCE. *See* Preparation.

VIRTUOSITY. Brilliant display of technical facility.

VOICE. The individual part in a polyphonic composition. (It does not necessarily mean "to be sung.")

WHOLE NOTE. The basic unit of time in music.

WHOLE-TONE SCALE. A scale of six tones all a whole tone or whole step apart.

WIND INSTRUMENT. Any instrument which is played by blowing.

WOODWIND. Wind instruments that produce musical tone by vibration of a reed, except the flute, which has no reed.

Bibliography

General Histories of Music

Dickinson, E., *The Study of the History of Music* (1908).
Einstein, A., *A Short History of Music* (1954).
Ferguson, D., *A History of Musical Thought* (3rd ed., 1959).
Finney, T., *A History of Music* (rev., 1947).
Grout, D., *A History of Western Music* (1960).
Kinsky, G., *The History of Music in Pictures* (1929).
Lang, P., *Music in Western Civilization* (1941).
Leichtentritt, H., *Music, History, and Ideas* (1938).
Moore, D., *From Madrigal to Modern Music* (1942).
Nef, K., *An Outline of the History of Music* (rev., 1957).
New Oxford History of Music (Series).
> Vol. I. *Ancient and Oriental Music.* Ed. by Wellesz, E., 1957.
> Vol. II. *Early Medieval Music up to 1300.* Ed. by Hughes, D., 1954.
> Vol. III. *Ars Nova and the Renaissance, c. 1300–1540.* Ed. by Hughes, D., and G. Abraham, 1960.

Oxford History of Music, The (7 vols., 1901–1929).
Prunières, H., *A New History of Music* (1943).
Sachs, C., *Our Musical Heritage* (2nd ed., 1955).
Scholes, P., *The Listener's History of Music* (3 vols., rev., 1943–1956).

Special Periods and Subjects

Abraham, G., *A Hundred Years of Music* (1964).
Allen, W., *Philosophies of Music History* (1939).
Apel, W., *Gregorian Chant* (1958).
———, *Masters of the Keyboard* (1947).
———, *Notation of Polyphonic Music* (5th ed., 1961).
Barrett, W., *English Glees and Part-Songs* (1886).
Beaumont, W., *Complete Book of Ballets* (1937, 1942).

Bekker, P., *The Changing Opera* (1935).

————, *The Story of the Opera* (1926).

Brisay, A. de, *The Organ and Its Music* (1935).

Brockway, W., and H. Weinstock, *The World of Opera* (1962).

Bukofzer, M., *Music in the Baroque Era* (1947).

————, *Studies in Medieval and Renaissance Music* (1950).

Burney, C., *A General History of Music from the Earliest Ages to the Present Period* [1789] (2 vols., 1955).

Cabrol, A., *The Mass, Its Doctrine and History* (1931).

Cagey, E., *Ballad Opera* (1937).

Carpenter, N., *Music in the Medieval and Renaissance Universities* (1958).

Carse, A., *History of Orchestration* (1925).

Casella, A., *The Evolution of Music through the History of the Perfect Cadence* (1924).

Cobbett, W., *Cyclopedic Survey of Chamber Music* (2nd ed., 3 vols., 1963).

Copland, A., *Our New Music* (1941).

Dale, K., *Nineteenth Century Piano Music* (1954).

Dannreuther, E., *Musical Ornamentation* (2 vols., 1893).

Davison, A. T., *Church Music: Illusion and Reality* (1952).

Dent, E., *Opera* (rev., 1949).

Dickinson, E., *Music in the History of the Western Church* (1902).

Dolmetsch, A., *Interpretation of the Music of the XVIIth and XVIIIth Centuries* (1915).

Donnington, R., *The Instruments of Music* (Barnes & Noble, Inc., 1962).

Douglas, W., *Church Music in History and Practice* (rev., 1962).

Dyson, G., *The New Music* (2nd ed., 1926).

Einstein, A., *Music in the Romantic Era* (1947).

————, *The Italian Madrigal* (3 vols., 1949).

Ewen, D., *New Book of Modern Composers* (rev. ed., 1961).

————, *History of Popular Music* (Barnes & Noble, Inc., 1961).

Fellowes, E., *The English Madrigal Composers* (2nd ed., 1948).

Finck, C., *Songs and Song Writers* (1925).

Forsyth, C., *Music and Nationalism* (1911).

Foster, M., *Anthem and Anthem Composers* (1901).

Glyn, M., *About Elizabethan Virginal Music and Its Composers* (1924).

Grout, D., *A Short History of Opera* (2nd ed., 2 vols., 1965).

Hansen, P., *An Introduction to Twentieth Century Music* (2nd ed., 1967).

Haydon, G., *The Evolution of the Six-Four Chord* (1933).

Heyman, K., *The Relation of Ultramodern to Archaic Music* (1921).

Hill, R., *The Symphony* (1949).

Jeppesen, K., *The Style of Palestrina and the Dissonance* (1927).

Křenek, E., *Studies in Counterpoint* (1940).

Leichtentritt, H., *Musical Form* (1951).

Machlis, J., *Introduction to Contemporary Music* (1961).

Mackinley, M., *Light Opera* (1926).

Mason, D. G., *The Romantic Composers* (1930).

Merritt, A., *Sixteenth Century Polyphony* (1939).

Newman, W., *The Sonata in the Baroque Era* (1959).

Niecks, F., *Programme Music* (1907).

Patterson, A., *The Story of the Oratorio* (1909).

Peltz, M. E., *Introduction to Opera* (2nd ed., Barnes & Noble, Inc., 1962).

Reese, G., *Music in the Middle Ages* (1940).

——, *Music in the Renaissance* (rev., 1959).

Richardson, A., *The Medieval Modes* (1933).

Robeck, N. de, *Music of the Italian Renaissance* (1928).

Rufer, J., *Composition with Twelve Notes* (1954).

Sachs, C., *The History of Musical Instruments* (1940).

——, *The Rise of Music in the Ancient World* (1943).

——, *A World History of the Dance* (1963).

Salzman, Eric, *Twentieth-Century Music: An Introduction* (1967).

Slonimsky, N., *Music since 1900* (3rd ed., 1949).

Streatfeild, R., *The Opera* (1925).

Strunk, O., *Source Readings in Music History* (1950).

Ulrich, H., *Chamber Music* (1948).

——, *Symphonic Music* (1952).

Vaughan Williams, R., *National Music* (1934).

Veinus, A., *The Concerto* (1964).

Verwer, H., *Guide to the Ballet* (Barnes & Noble, Inc., 1963).

Wagner, P., *Introduction to the Gregorian Melodies* (1907).

Waite, W., *The Rhythm of Twelfth-Century Polyphony* (1954).

Wallaschek, R., *Primitive Music* (1893).

Westerby, H., *The History of Pianoforte Music* (1924).

Note. For related articles and further bibliography in periodicals and works in foreign languages, see Willi Apel, *Harvard Dictionary of Music* (1944). For a visual review of the history of instruments, *Musical Instruments,* a selection of 50 prints showing instruments and players as portrayed in art from earliest days, is available for $1.50 from University Prints, Cambridge 38, Massachusetts.

Nationalities

Abraham, G. *Studies in Russian Music* (1935).

Barzun, J., *Music in American Life* (1956).

Calvocoressi, M., and G. Abraham, *Masters of Russian Music* (1936).

Chase, G., *America's Music* (1955).

———, *The Music of Spain* (2nd ed., 1960).

Dent, E., *Music of the Renaissance in Italy* (1934).

Fuller-Maitland, J., *Masters of German Music* (1894).

Hill, E. B., *Modern French Music* (1924).

Howard, J. T., *Our American Music* (4th ed., 1965).

———, *Our Contemporary Composers* (1940).

Idelssohn, A., *Jewish Music in Its Historical Development* (1929).

Kaldy, G., *A History of Hungarian Music* (1903).

Lasserre, P., *The Spirit of French Music* (1917).

Luper, A., *The Music of Brazil* (1943).

Newmarch, R., *The Music of Czechoslovakia* (1942).

Rayson, E., *Polish Music and Chopin Its Laureate* (1916).

Reis, C., *Composers in America* (rev., 1947).

Sabanief, L., *Modern Russian Composers* (1927).

Slonimsky, N., *Music of Latin America* (1945).

Streatfeild, R., *Masters of Italian Music* (1895).

Trend, J., *The Music of Spanish History to 1600* (1926).

Urban, L., *The Music of Bohemia* (1919).

Walker, E., *History of Music in England* (3rd ed., 1952).

Biography

For details of biography, articles in one of the numerous music dictionaries are suggested (Grove, Baker, Oscar Thompson, *et al.*) and comprehensive bibliography under each article.

Record Anthologies

2000 Years of Music. Sachs. 2 12″LP.

History of Music in Sound (10 vols.).

Masterpieces of Music Before 1750 (3 12″ discs).

Score Anthologies

Apel, W., and A. T. Davison, *Historical Anthology of Music* (2 vols., 1947, 1950).

Einstein, A., *Beispielsammlung zur Musikgeschichte,* 4th ed., Teubner, Leipzig (1930).

Parrish, C., *A Treasury of Early Music* (1958).

Parrish, C. and J. F. Ohl, *Masterpieces of Music Before 1750* (1951).

Riemann, H., *Musikgeschichte in Beispielen,* Breitkopf & Härtel, Leipzig (1930).

Schering, A., *Geschichte der Musik in Beispielen,* Breitkopf & Härtel, Leipzig (1931); reprinted, Broude Bros. (1950).

Steinitzer, Max, *Musikgeschichtlicher Atlas,* Ruckmich, Freiburg (1908).

Wolf, J., *Sing- und Spielmusik aus älterer Zeit,* Quelle & Mayer, Leipzig (1931).

Index

A

A Cappella music, in Renaissance, 38, 39; in baroque church, 86; in French baroque church music, 87

A Una Madre, Castro, 218

ABACO, FELICE DALL' (1675–1742), 101

Academic Festival Overture, Brahms, 158

Académie Royale de Musique, 77

Accompanied solo song, 69

Acis and Galatea, Handel, 79, 109

Action in Brass, Cowell, 212

Act-tunes, 70

Adagio for Strings, Barber, 178, 234

ADAM DE LA HALLE, 11

ADAM OF ST. VICTOR, 10

Adam and Eva, Theile, 78

Addison, 67

Adventures in a Perambulator, Carpenter, 225

"Advertisement," Cowell, 187

Aeolian mode, 9

Africa, Still, 228

Afro-American Symphony, Still, 228

Agnus Dei of the Mass, 10

Agon, Stravinsky, 197

A-growing, Suk, 214

AGUIRRE, JULIAN (1868–1924), 218

Aïda, Verdi, 142

Air, 92

Air Power, Dello Joio, 237

Airborne Symphony, The, Blitzstein, 232

Alamo, The, Gillis, 182

ALBENIZ, ISAAC (1860–1909), 213

ALBERT, HEINRICH (1604–1651), 83

Albert Herring, Britten, 208

Alberti bass, 114

Alceste, Gluck, 128

ALDHELM, BISHOP (c. 640–709), 23

Alexander Nevsky, Prokofiev, 177

ALFANO, FRANCO (1876–1954), 210

Algarotti, Count, 127

Alleluia of the Mass, 10

Allemande, 91; in harpsichord music of the 16th century, 57

ALLENDE, HUMBERTO (1885–), 221

Also sprach Zarathustra, R. Strauss, 161

Alto Rhapsody, Brahms, 150

Amahl and the Night Visitors, Menotti, 180, 236

Amazonas, Villa-Lobos, 219

Ambitus, 8

Ambrosian chant, 9

Amelia Goes to the Ball, Menotti, 180, 235

America, American; *see also* United States

America, Bloch, 226

American Cash-Box, The, Satie, 194

American In Paris, An, Gershwin, 230

American Indian music, 224

American Life, Weiss, 227

American Revolution, 113, 167

American Symphony, An, Gillis, 236

Amerindia, Maidana, 221

L'Amfiparnasso, Vecchi, 44

Amor Brujo, El, Falla, 213

An die ferne Geliebte, Beethoven, 140, 151

Anapaest, 12

And They Lynched Him on a Tree, Still, 229

Andalusia, Lecuona, 222

ANDRIESSEN, HENDRIK (1892–), 216

ANERIO, FELICE (c. 1560–1614), 39

Angels, Ruggles, 225

D'ANGLEBERT, HENRI (1635–1691), 93

Anglican Chant, 42

Anglican church music, 39, 40, 42, 88

Angularity of melody, 50; in modern music, 189

Anna Magdalena Bach's Music Notebook, Bach, 108

251